Understanding School Learning:

A New Look at Educational Psychology

Michael J. A. Howe
University of Alberta

Harper & Row, Publishers
New York, Evanston, San Francisco, London

0053848

104254

154.4
HOW

Understanding
School Learning:
A New Look at Educational Psychology

With love to Sylvia

Contents

Preface

Man's striking ability to profit from learning has always been a source of wonder and delight, but only recently have we begun to examine human learning with the systematic methods of inquiry that have been used for centuries in scientific study of the external world. Although psychologists have now obtained a large body of scientific data from experimental research into learning, teachers understandably have been somewhat impatient with the findings brought to their attention: Too often it has seemed that the knowledge obtained has little bearing upon the varieties of school learning that are required in education. However, research now is providing increased understanding of school learning, and this progress will contribute to large practical gains in the quality of learning in schools.

Having a slight aversion to lengthy textbooks, I have attempted to include in a fairly short book the principles of learning and the conceptual framework that a longer text might provide, cutting down on the number of detailed descriptions. The result is less comprehensive and less useful as a source of reference than a longer volume would have been, but this will cause no great hardship.

I am grateful to a large number of people who have directly or indirectly contributed to what is expressed in these pages. My thinking has, I like to think, benefited from numerous conversations that on one occasion or another have involved most of the members of the Educational Psychology Department at the University of Alberta. As sources of stimulation I would especially like to mention Richard Barham, John Biggs, and Gerry Kysela. In addition, I would like to express my appreciation to the students who read earlier drafts of the manuscript as parts of courses in educational psychology and who were kind enough to remark encouragingly.

With never a word of complaint Joan Andrishak cheerfully and skillfully typed out the major part of several versions of the manuscript, often from incoherent tapes or illegible handwriting. My sincere thanks to her.

Finally, I would like to thank my wife and children for coping so well with all the burdens that the writing of books places upon a family.

M.J.A.H.

Understanding
School Learning:
A New Look at Educational Psychology

Chapter 1
Introduction

This book about human learning is written for teachers and others who are interested in helping students learn. The author's belief is that there now is considerable knowledge about human learning, and specifically about the types of learning that contribute to the changes and growth in understanding and awareness that constitute education. Since the 1960s research on school learning has been providing a body of knowledge and insights on learning that has real value for the teacher.

Anyone who has seen the inside of a college or university department of psychology or education knows that scores of books have been written about learning. Do we really want one more? In justifying an affirmative answer, the author would suggest that teachers have not always gained much from reports of research, and that this is true even in the case of some materials specifically designed for teacher education. One likely reason has been a tendency among researchers in the past to assume that all forms of learning are basically very similar, so that most scientific knowledge gained from experiments on learning is, at least indirectly, valid for the classroom. In fact, as we shall make clear in later chapters, much of the learning that happens in classrooms, is, by its highly symbolic, abstract nature, different in important ways from the simpler types of learning that for legitimate scientific reasons have most often received the attention of experimental psychologists engaged in investigations of basic learning processes. Consequently, knowledge of such studies, although potentially invaluable for scientific understanding, cannot alone provide a full understanding of the variables important in school learning.

A second problem in some accounts of research on learning lies in the implicit assumption that the only useful contributions to the understanding of school learning are those produced by psychologists engaged in experimental research. One can search through many of the best and most recent textbooks on educational psychology without finding a single reference to the insights of educational writers and thinkers, such as John Holt or Herbert Kohl. These and other authors who are currently engaged in the educational enterprise have some extremely perceptive and important things to say about learning that have powerful implications for those involved in creating learning environments. A related limitation in some of what has been written for teachers about learning is the very limited attention given to matters that cannot be accommodated within a purely scientific frame of reference. Some of the issues that impinge most directly on learning in schools involve questions of morals, values, and social priorities. These issues are certainly not only the concern of experimental psychologists, but they cannot be ignored, if contributions to the understanding of human learning are to be useful for practicing teachers. Certainly, objectivity, scientific neutrality, and precision are essential in attempts to achieve a basic understanding of learning processes. However, to communicate knowledge about learning in a manner that is valuable to those engaged in teaching also requires thought about questions not answerable on a purely scientific basis, such as "Learning for what end?" and "What is worth learning?" The ways an individual chooses to answer these questions provide influences on learning as central and integral as any which contribute to the education of human beings.

It is largely due to the efforts of those researchers who are highly sensitive to the complex problems of trying to find out about the sophisticated and changing processes of learning that are required in education, that the past few years have seen exciting gains in knowledge and understanding of learning at school. Simon and Newell (1971), discussing the relations between the professions and the basic sciences that should nourish them, point out that it is only within the present century that medicine and engineering can be said to rest solidly on a foundation of scientific knowledge. Research is starting to provide such a foundation for the profession of education, and its impact is becoming increasingly powerful.

Complaints and Remedies in Education

At a superficial level there is considerable agreement both about what is wrong with education today and about what should be done about it. Numerous writers have voiced their dissatisfaction with the learning that is going on in schools. They complain that the children are too often bored, anxious, and frightened, that curricula are dull and irrelevant to the needs of the people in the 1970s. Generally speaking, those who make these claims are not cranks. They do not insist that all education has to be practical or relevant in a narrow, immediate, or purely vocational sense; nor do they believe in a hothouse conception of education in which the goal of learning is to acquire the maximum amount of knowledge in the minimum time. Nor are they dreamers with little idea of what is possible and what is not possible in schools, or of what children can and cannot do. For the most part, the criticisms are articulated by realistic, hardheaded, experienced men and women, who on the basis of contact and experience in the schools, often as teachers, have concluded that much of what now happens in the classroom does not take full advantage of the capacities of the human learner for acquiring through learning those increases of skills, knowledge, awareness, and understanding that constitute real education.

The fact that many of these criticisms have been made before—by Rousseau, James, Dewey, and others—does not make them any the less valid. Indeed, the importance of the arguments becomes more prominent and the validity of the criticisms less escapable with the growing evidence that things can be better and that it is possible to have schools which do provide exciting environments for learning. There is no doubt that schools *have* changed, and for the better. It is in a time like the present, when the growth of knowledge makes the possibility of change apparent, that the demands for improvement become most potent and convincing.

Just as there seems to be considerable agreement among those who are saying what is wrong with learning in schools today, so too there is at least the appearance of agreement among those who would prescribe remedies. Most educators would agree with suggestions that schools must give closer attention to the needs of the individual learner, that teachers must be concerned with creativity, that greater efforts must be made to make what is taught in schools relevant and interesting, that active learning in which the learner has an important participatory role needs to be stressed, and that discovery should be an important element in learning. Many would agree that there needs to be more emphasis on inquiry skills, that initiative and enterprise should receive more encouragement, that schools have been placing too much emphasis on conformity in the classroom, and that students need freedom in the classroom so that they can learn to make decisions for themselves. Also, with the tremendous changes in society, it is essential for children to learn how to learn independently, to learn how to solve problems, and to learn that knowledge and information alone are not all-important.

The list could be continued to give further documentation of the general agreement about what is wrong with education and about what needs to be done. Numerous remedies have been proposed. The language heard at school sounds progressive; there is a lot of talk about individuality, creativity, discovery, and so on. Too often, however, one suspects there is little behind the words. Sometimes it seems that they are being used as slogans, as if to invoke a catchword, such as "creativity," is to alter what is happening in the classroom. Of course, it does not happen. The fashionable terms seem to have become clichés for impressing visitors and convincing oneself that the school environment really is alive, progressive, open to new ideas. One of the most depressing examples of mass-produced education seen by the author was in a so-called experimental project whose leaders used the phrase "individual learner" with impressive frequency. It is as if everyone wants to jump on the bandwagon, but few are willing to do more than utter the phrases that identify it. In short, there does appear to be evidence of agreement about how to remedy what is wrong in today's schools, but rather little is actually being done to improve matters.

The Need to Understand Learning

The various suggestions about how to improve learning seem to convey a lot of good sense. If people appear not to have thought very deeply about them, perhaps one thing that is lacking is a broad conceptual framework on which to base an understanding of learning processes. Such a framework may help educators perceive how some of the current ideas and proposals about school learning relate to one another, contributing to what approaches an integrated understanding of learning in educational contexts. With a better understanding of meaningful learning, it may become harder to misuse concepts, such as creativity, discovery, and the like, as unrelated catchwords and slogans. Gaining a good understanding of the basic processes involved in meaningful human learning certainly leads one to advocate the activities proposed in some of the suggestions. A stress on the importance of, say, the individual's role in learning is more convincing when it is seen to result from an understanding of human learning processes, rather than being simply an offshoot of a current bandwagon. Given a broad understanding of the nature of learning in man, many of the intuitively attractive specific proposals and suggestions that have been made for improving learning in school are seen to have roles in the development of proper environments for human learning.

Thus, an understanding of some of the processes underlying meaningful learning may enable us to look rather objectively at the questions and issues that are presently getting attention in education. At present, controversies, such as the grading versus nongrading issue, the differences between educators in their emphasis on the processes of learning versus acquisition of content, freedom versus control, and ability grouping versus heterogeneous grouping, seem to be debated mainly on the basis of beliefs, attitudes, prejudices, and opinions, rather than on considerations of reason or objective evidence. It is true that some elements of these questions and issues can only be settled for the individual on the basis of personal beliefs and values and cannot be answered by scientific evidence alone. Science cannot provide all the answers. On the other hand, when we do have a clear scientific understanding of classroom learning, quite a few of the issues turn out to be at least partly answerable on the basis of knowledge. The more that is known, the more important and powerful do knowledge and understanding become in making decisions and formulating policies that determine the conditions in which children and adults try to learn. Experimental research is essential for providing this knowledge.

Learning in Schools

The word "learning" sounds deceptively simple; it is short, familiar, and frequently used. In fact, there are many different types and forms of learning, the differences between them being far greater than might be expected. Hence, detailed knowledge about one type of learning might have limited relevance for the understanding of another variety of learning. In particular, not all knowledge about learning can be expected to be of great value to the person who wants to know about the specific types of learning that are encountered in schools. Until fairly recently it was commonly thought that the job of educational psychologists was to take the "basic" knowledge experimental psychologists had acquired concerning learning in rats and other simple organisms and concerning very simple learning in humans, and to apply this to classroom learning. However, psychologists working in educational research have become sensitive to the fact that the differences between children learning in schools and rats learning in mazes are so great that whatever is discovered about the latter is likely to have limited applicability or relevance to the former. There is beginning to be less emphasis on attempts to extrapolate and apply to the classroom the results of simple learning experiments. More emphasis is being placed on experiments that directly explore meaningful human learning, in the attempt to understand the processes involved. In the next few chapters we shall make clear what is meant by "meaningful" learning, but for the present we shall simply state that the adjective "meaningful" will be used to refer to learning that seems to have aspects in common with the various types of learning, generally symbolic and sometimes abstract, that lead to a person becoming educated. We shall resist the temptation to get involved in attempting a definition of the word "educated" at this stage.

The Learner in Learning

However much is known about learning and whatever is discovered in the future, there is a limit on the extent to which teachers can use this understanding in determining the course of learning in a particular student. Humans are not only extremely complex but also very different from each other, and the ways in which an individual feels and behaves are likely to vary considerably from one occasion to another. The human being is, to say the least, an unpredictable animal. We can never exactly predict or control the course of his learning. When the nature of human learning is examined there emerges a second reason against the teacher's having constant precise control over students' learning. Meaningful learning, far from being simply an assimilative, acquisitive process, is most often found to take the form of a positive, generative, outgoing kind of activity, in which the individual learner has an active role in coding, in interpreting, and in processing whatever data is available to him in ways that are very much determined by his individual experience. This matter is discussed in much greater detail in Chapter 3, but for the moment we can point out that however carefully one tries to control or program an individual's learning activities and however much is known about learning processes, one cannot predict with complete accuracy what he will learn. Human learners are not automatons.

Yet knowledge remains invaluable. In later chapters it is suggested that less emphasis should be placed on the efforts of teachers to carefully direct and program children's learning, and more on helping students learn to carry out and control for themselves the types of learning activities that will be valued in their own lives and that will help their continued intellectual growth. As a point of view this is neither original nor unusual, but it becomes more persuasive when it is seen to follow from our knowledge of growth and learning in the individual.

It is worth noting that this book is about learning, and it is not about how to teach. It is certainly possible to write about teaching, although many of the skills required in a good teacher cannot be gained from reading, however well-written the text, but it is not this author's intention to tell anyone how to teach. Yet a good understanding of how learning occurs in children will be extremely valuable to a teacher who makes an effort to integrate and use what he has learned from reading and from experience, although it is not hard to find people who have profited little from either. A teacher's own growth seems to be related to the extent to which he can bring together the sorts of knowledge that can be gained from reading, from thinking, and from personal experience, so that each contributes to what is learned from the other. In addition, certain rather subtle types of perceptiveness and sensitivity to the thinking and feeling of young learners seem to be found in good teachers. Such qualities, which are hard to specify or measure, and which Carl Rogers and others summarize by the simple phrase "being human," are important, and they cannot be gained just by reading.

Aims of the Book

It is intended that this book should be useful and relevant to those who teach in schools. "Relevance" does not necessarily imply an immediate or automatic practical application of knowledge. In some parts of this volume, for example in Chapter 2, information is given which can be applied more or less directly in many classroom situations, with marked positive results. More often, the aim is to provide a broader understanding of human learning processes, which the teacher can use in making intelligent classroom decisions. To be relevant does not require that knowledge be presented as a series of simple rules and prescriptions. Gulfs between practical and theoretical contributions are sometimes more apparent than real, and those who make practical contributions are sometimes charged with being anti-intellectual, narrow, and philistine, whereas scholars who provide theoretical insights are seen as dry, arid, and having little understanding of the realities of life. The absurdity of this state of affairs is made clear by Jerome Bruner's remark that there is nothing so practical as a good theory.

Of course, what is relevant in a written account depends partly on the reader. An author can only write what he thinks will be valuable for the majority of the people who will read what he has to say. Once I recommended to a class John Holt's excellent book *How Children Fail* (1964), an account of what goes on in classrooms, which many readers have found extremely interesting and valuable. Later, one student attacked me quite vehemently, saying that the ideas were familiar to her and that reading the book was a waste of her time. She seemed to regard it as a personal affront that I should suggest she might profit from reading it. The point is that no written account can be valuable for everyone. The cliché about one man's meat certainly applies to published knowledge.

The present volume is not intended to be comprehensive; it by no means tries to cover every area of human learning. There is room for comprehensive textbooks, but this does not attempt to be one. The reasons are largely those of simple preference, but the author has a particular objection to the assumption implicit in some lengthy textbooks that most knowledge about school learning can be presented in a single package. I am not convinced that this is the case and feel that students in any course benefit from exposure to the ideas of at least several authors. Hopefully, no reader of this book will begin and end his reading on school learning with this volume.

Some areas of psychology that often appear in books on learning are excluded from the present one. For example, the reader will find little about the historical development of theories of learning or about animal learning, nor is there very much discussion of the acquisition of simple responses in humans. There is now quite a large body of knowledge about meaningful learning, and it seems wisest to concentrate on this knowledge. It is sometimes claimed that knowledge about simple learning is basic to any understanding of more complex human learning. In some respects this is a compelling argument, and accordingly, some aspects of research on simple learning are introduced, but the emphasis is on research into meaningful learning. If this volume were intended primarily for psychologists, the point of emphasis might be different. Much that is important to researchers in complex learning can be gained from a deep understanding of theory and research based on simple learning and conditioning, but it is doubtful whether descriptions such as the usual textbook paragraphs on Pavlov, typically accompanied by a picture of one of his dogs, do much to further anyone's understanding of learning processes. More frequently, the result is confusion. As the volume is primarily intended to be valuable for teachers, I believe that an emphasis on meaningful learning situations is justified. Even within this area the book does not attempt to be comprehensive. Rather, it tries to explore a limited number of important themes, with the object of forming a clear conceptual framework for understanding the role of learning in education and a solid basis for deeper explorations into particular aspects of human learning.

Hence, the reader will find some of the "traditional" content of books on the psychology of human learning omitted. However, this book will be no less demanding than those based more exclusively on the findings of experimental psychology. The base is broader, since ideas have been drawn not only from experimental research, but also from humanistic psychology, philosophy, and the contributions of others who have thought deeply about learning in schools. It is a sad commentary on the state of affairs in science and education today that one finds oneself impelled to justify an approach to learning that is less exclusively tied to one particular area of study than most. Specialization, not only in knowledge but also in ways of discovering knowledge, has proceeded to such an extent that we perceive single disciplines as filling natural divisions of reality, and attempts to get away from this fragmentation can appear rather odd.

Two related themes are basic to this text. The first is that human behavior is strongly influenced by human needs, and the second is that for most learning to be effective, the learner needs to proceed in a highly active manner, organizing, interpreting, and coding the information that he confronts in ways that are sometimes idiosyncratic and often complex. These themes will be expanded in the early chapters. Chapter 2 looks at ways in which human behavior is controlled and modified by needs. In Chapters 3, 4, and 5 some of the main characteristics of meaningful learning in the human being are examined. Chapter 6 describes how learning and intelligence are related and examines the role of language. In Chapter 7, we return to the discussion of needs in relation to control of human behavior and pose some questions about the importance of who and what does the controlling. Chapters 8, 9, and 11 draw on the contents of the earlier chapters on school learning for application to practical educational issues and problems concerning relevance, the use of questions and inquiry, and the role of programmed instruction and technology. Chapter 10 considers some aspects of simple forms of learning and memory that are important in education. In Chapters 12 and 13 we return to some broader discussion of influential factors in school learning. In particular, in Chapter 12, we examine some matters that concern the role of the teacher, and Chapter 13 considers the problems encountered in conducting experimental research into meaningful human learning.

Chapter 2

The Control and
Modification of Human Behavior

Choices and Decisions

People in the adult world have to make plenty of choices, evaluations, decisions, and these generally require them to use information or knowledge that has been acquired previously. If my car will not start, I have to do something about it; a sensible choice must be made about what sort of action is most likely to solve the problem. Should I take the short route to work, which tends to get fouled up in heavy traffic, or an alternative route, which is longer but less affected by traffic? When I get to the building housing my office I have to decide whether to wait for the elevator or to walk. If I walk up the stairs I may feel tired and irritated when I get to the top; on the other hand, the exercise might be good for my long-term chances of survival.

These are all very humdrum situations compared with those in which we make what seem to be the important decisions of life. The important point is that deciding, judging, choosing, and evaluating happen and are essential for day-to-day living. A person can make effective choices only if he has appropriate and relevant information. Thus, if I know what hour of day it is I am in a position to judge the amount of traffic on the road, and this will help me to decide which route to take to work. It is clear that having information or knowledge is not sufficient alone. One has to be able to *use* it effectively. Just as information is acquired through learning, we also learn various skills and abilities for using it effectively. A person who is able and effective at making decisions is described as being "independent," or "self-reliant," and as having "a mind of his own." A man with initiative is highly regarded in the modern world and favorably compared to a person lacking his qualities, who may be described with disparaging words like "automaton" or "zombie." The attributes of the latter may still be useful in some enclaves of authoritarian and highly structured societies, but in a world where certainties and absolutes are more often dangerous than functional, it is increasingly apparent that the abilities to do what one is told and obey orders are hardly sufficient for the citizens of a good society.

It does seem that schools have often failed to do much to develop independence and initiative in learning, or to provide broad opportunities for making use of the knowledge and skills that have been acquired. Using knowledge requires making judgments, choosing, and making decisions, and all these necessitate what we label with that emotionally laden word, "freedom." The extent to which these qualities—self-control, independence, and the like—are acquired by an individual depends just as much on the availability of appropriate learning experiences as does the acquisition of knowledge. It was stated in Chapter 1 that a common criticism of contemporary school education is that there is too much emphasis on the acquisition of specific knowledge and not enough emphasis on providing opportunities for students to gain the skills, habits, and attitudes that will enable them to learn in situations where there is an absence of the structure and detailed guidance that can be provided by teachers.

The most common argument in favor of putting greater weight on the acquisition of skills that provide independence in learning is that, as the rate of change in society becomes increasingly rapid, the individual must either adapt to differences in his environment or become alienated. The classic example is the man whose job becomes obsolete, but in the future other areas of change may provide equally large problems. It is argued by critics of the schools that education systems today are failing to provide their students with the skills required for learning to adapt to the constant state of change that the students will meet when they leave school. Some thinkers have claimed that the failure of individuals to keep in step with the environmental changes imposed by technological advances constitutes a danger to mankind. As far-fetched as this argument may be, there is sufficient hard truth underlying the fashionable preoccupation with problems of change to justify the suggestion that students who leave school ought to possess qualities that will equip them for continual and varied learning experiences in their subsequent lives.

Modifying Classroom Behavior

The qualities we have described as being necessary for individuals to decide and direct their own learning can be summarized by the term "self-control." An understanding of some of the ways in which human behavior is controlled is required, and hence the remainder of this chapter is concerned with investigating the mechanisms of control. We shall describe some investigations in which attempts are made to modify classroom behavior in a manner that increases the probability of learning in students. These investigations are called studies in "behavior modification." Not all control of behavior is self-control, and examining situations in which human behavior is largely controlled by external factors (for example, when a student's activities are controlled by a teacher, using a reward system) will be useful in demonstrating general principles about the control of behavior, which are equally valid when the actions of a student are largely controlled by external influences, and when the individual is in relatively direct and full control of his own behavior.

As it happens, the research involved in understanding how behavior is controlled and the research that examines more specifically the nature of human learning are closely intertwined. An understanding of each of these aspects of inquiry is both dependent on and contributes to an understanding of the other. Accordingly, after beginning our investigation into the nature of behavioral control in the present chapter, we shall postpone the inquiry until Chapter 7, which follows an examination (in Chapters 3 to 6) of some processes and principles central to human learning.

To commence the investigation of the nature of control we shall examine the findings of some classroom experiments. These studies were designed for a practical purpose: to discover how teachers in elementary schools might achieve the degree of control (in the narrow sense of "classroom control") necessary for effective classroom communication. There will be some discussion here of the research in relation to the practical problems, but it is important to keep in mind that we also have a broader interest in examining these studies, namely to gain an understanding of general principles relating to the control of human behavior.

A number of studies have been carried out to determine the most effective methods for classroom control by teachers. Quite a lot of teachers worry about the problems of classroom management and control, and a teacher who worries about her failure to achieve control or who spends much of her energy in trying to achieve order cannot concentrate on her real job, helping children learn. The classroom of such a teacher is likely to be tense and stressful, whereas learning seems to occur most effectively when the atmosphere is calm and relaxed. Some readers may recoil in horror at the mention of classroom control and discipline in a book about learning. They might argue that such problems are simply symptoms of bad teaching and occur mainly when children are bored and uninterested, in which case the teacher is clearly at fault. There is a good deal of truth in this reasoning, and the descriptions of experiments on classroom control are not intended to provide faultless prescriptions for good teaching. At this stage we are trying to find evidence that will cast some light on how human behavior is controlled, and these experiments happen to be very useful for that purpose.

It would not be wise to underestimate the practical utility of experimental findings about classroom control. If a young teacher who finds that her classroom is in a state of chaos, so that she has little control over what is going on, comes to seek help, the comment that her discipline problems are merely a symptom of the fact that her whole approach to teaching requires changing might be largely correct but not very helpful in the immediate circumstances. On the other hand, if she can be provided with methods or techniques that will help her achieve a calm and relaxed classroom atmosphere in which effective communication is possible, at the very least she will be able to concentrate on teaching and perhaps improve it.

Research Findings

Now for some results. In a study by Becker, Madsen, Arnold, and Thomas (1967), the authors were faced with a situation in an urban elementary school where the classroom behavior of some of the children made learning very difficult for themselves and others. The precise nature of the disruptive behavior differed from one individual to another. One 7-year-old boy was very noisy and fought with others, blurted out, and could not stay in his seat. Another boy, 8 years of age, picked on the girls, hit other boys, bullied children smaller than himself, and got loud and angry when he was reprimanded. The study examined the effects of certain methods and techniques used by the teacher on ten disruptive children. A typical child was Alice, a 7-year-old girl who sulked a lot, sat in her chair moving her hands and legs or sucking her thumb, and usually seemed to ignore her teacher. Before the experiment observers had rated the incidence of her disruptive behavior, defining "disruptive" behaviors as those which interfered with classroom learning, violated rules for permissible behavior established by the teacher, and/or reflected particular behavior a teacher wanted to change. In Alice's case, disruptive behavior had been noticed in about 50 percent of the observations made over periods of 20 minutes a day for five weeks.

For the experimental procedure Alice's teacher was given specific instructions, together with necessary training and support, concerning her reactions to Alice's disruptive behavior. Some of the instructions were common to all the children in the study. For example, the teacher was told to ignore behaviors that interfered with learning or teaching, unless a child was being hurt by another, and to give praise and attention to behaviors that facilitated learning, at the same time telling the child why he was being praised by using such phrases as "I like the way you're working quietly," "That's the way I like to see you work," and "Good job, you're doing fine." There were some special rules for Alice. For example, the teacher was told to praise her for sitting in her chair and concentrating on her own work, for using her hands for things other than sucking, and for attending to directions given by the teacher or to communications from other students. Alice's behavior was observed for a period of eight weeks, during which the teacher carried out these instructions.

During this period the incidence of deviant behavior in the observation periods, as rated by observers, dropped from 50 percent to around 20 percent and stayed at this reduced level. In other words, Alice's disruptive behavior was very considerably reduced. Of course, this is only one instance. It is conceivable that the experiment just happened to coincide with an improvement in Alice's behavior. However, all but one of the ten children studied in this experiment made similar improvements, and it is unlikely that all these changes were due to chance. Originally, disruptive behavior occurred in the ten elementary school children on 62 percent of the occasions on which they were observed. When a teacher followed the instructions specified by the experimenters, the figure dropped to 29 percent. A particular technique which the authors found effective when a child was disruptive was to ignore the misbehavior, but at the same time praise a child who was behaving in a manner compatible with learning.

The results of a second study show what happened when the teachers followed rather similar instructions in a more extreme, even desperate, situation. The school was in a ghetto area of Boston, and the experiment was confined to one classroom, which in terms of noise, chaos, and disorder was by far the worst in the school. In this study the authors, Orme and Purnell (1968), found that behavior was very disruptive among the children, who were from grades 3 and 4. It included tearing up papers, throwing books, singing, yelling, taking the desks apart, and running out of the classroom. Some idea of the gravity of the situation is given by the fact that in a 20-minute period one of the two teachers noted that every child had been struck by another pupil at least once. When the children were fighting, the teacher was only able to restrain two or three pupils at a time, and the others would fight on unrestrained—a nightmarish situation by any standards.

The instructions given to the teachers in this experiment were similar to those used in the previous sudy. At first a child might be praised whenever he was simply sitting with his hand up, since this was at least incompatible with fighting. At a later stage, the teacher would reserve his praise or encouragement for behavior that was more positively appropriate for learning. Deviant or disruptive behavior was simply ignored, except when it seemed likely that physical damage would occur to a child. An additional feature of this experiment was that good behavior could earn points, which could be saved and exchanged for tangible rewards. The children used the points to buy articles, such as candy and balloons, or they could save a large number of points and purchase various experiences judged to be both attractive to the children and educationally valuable, such as a ship-building project and field trips to interesting museums. Thus, in the present study, appropriate behavior earned the children not only the teacher's praise and encouragement but material rewards as well.

The results were just as striking as those of the previous experiment. Before the experimental changes, observers' ratings of the children's behavior, using video tapes produced by a small hidden television camera in the classroom, showed that the children, on average, spent around 40 to 50 percent

of their time in behavior that appeared inappropriate for learning. Under the experimental system, the average incidence of
disruptive behavior dropped to about 20 percent. Various
categories of behavior were observed, and all of those judged
to be appropriate for learning rose, whereas all the inappropriate or disruptive categories decreased. So again, the teachers
were able to influence the behavior of the children in ways
that would appear to help produce the sort of classroom atmosphere in which communication and learning is likely to
occur.

Control and Punishment

What are we to make of these results? One reaction, common among the "Give them an inch and they'll take a mile"
type of teacher, a breed by no means extinct, is that this sort
of thing could not possibly work. Or at least, "It may work for
them, but it certainly wouldn't work with my kids." However,
the fact is that it does work and that it has been shown to
work time and time again. It might appear that ignoring disruptive behavior, and thus "letting them get away with it,"
would lead to all sorts of disorder, but the plain fact, as reliably shown in the results of well-controlled experiments, is that
when ignoring deviant behavior is coupled with the teacher's
giving attention, praise, and encouragement to appropriate
behavior, disruptive forms of behavior decrease, at least in
elementary school children. One might object on the grounds
that it is wrong not to prevent or punish deviant behavior, or
that it is more important to understand such behavior than to
control it. We shall not attempt to deal with these questions
here but simply observe what the results show concerning the
efficiency of teachers' control methods. The results do make
it clear that the teacher's action strongly influence how the
children behave.

All the successful studies we have described avoided the
use of punishment, and at this point a few remarks about
punishment are pertinent. Looking at punishment purely from
the point of view of its effect on behavior, ignoring all moral

and ethical considerations, one can briefly summarize the results of research by saying that punishment, over the long run, is not always very effective in controlling behavior, that it is extremely difficult to predict the results of punishment in a given situation, and that there are various equally unpredictable side effects, some of which have negative effects for education (Bandura, 1969). Punishment certainly may be effective in temporarily suppressing destructive behaviors or in redirecting attention. Its effects are typically immediate; this is probably a reason for the wide use of punishment. If a teacher punishes or threatens a child who is misbehaving in class, the immediate effect will most probably be for the child to desist, and from the teacher's point of view it is clear that his action has been effective. It is sometimes difficult to realize that actions which have the most immediate and visible effects may be ineffective in the long run. If I bark and you run away, it is clear to me that my behavior is affecting yours, but if one tries to influence behavior by encouraging or ignoring various actions, the effects, although more powerful in the long run, are not quite so immediate and striking. A teacher might understandably regard the immediate results of her techniques as the best indications of their effectiveness. However, the evidence leaves no doubt that, in the longer run, usually within a day or two, a strategy of ignoring inappropriate and attending to appropriate behavior has far greater influence on a pupil's behavior than one of attempting to prevent disruptive activities by threats, reprimands, and punishments.

If punishment is inadvisable, how about the value of having clear, unambiguous rules? The answer seems to be that rules are useful in achieving classroom control, but only when they are accompanied by encouragement of appropriate behavior. Madsen, Becker, and Thomas (1968) carried out an experiment in which they required second- and third-grade teachers to systematically vary their own behavior in a number of different ways. First, they observed and measured the incidence of inappropriate behavior when the teachers were using their original methods of control. This provided a base-line measure. In the first experimental condition, the effect of careful specification of rules by the teacher was measured, to test the claim that just telling children what is expected of them influences their behavior. The teachers were told to make five or six clear short rules, to be written in a conspicuous location in the classroom, to review the rules with the class at least four times per day, encouraging the children to recite them, and to keep reminding the class of the rules. Otherwise, the teacher was to maintain his usual behavior.

The measured results of this experimental change were quite simply nil. The frequency of inappropriate behavior was, on average, no higher or lower on the days when the teacher carefully specified the rules than it had been during the previous days. What about the effects of ignoring disruptive behavior? The instruction to ignore such behavior was common to all the studies we have previously described, although it was always combined with emphasis on encouraging appropriate behaviors. It would be interesting to know what are the effects of simply ignoring disruptive behaviors. During the next few days, Madsen and his colleagues examined the effects of this variable. The teacher was told quite simply to ignore inappropriate behavior, and otherwise to act as normally as possible. How did this affect the children? Again there was no change at all, with disruptive behavior remaining at the previous level.

If neither specifying rules alone nor simply ignoring inappropriate behavior has any effect, perhaps the combination of the two procedures would be effective. This possibility was examined over a three-day period in which a teacher was told to combine the careful specification of rules with ignoring inappropriate behavior. This combination did have an effect, but not a desirable one, the children behaving worse than in the previous conditions. The teacher, incidentally, found this phase of the experiment very unpleasant.

The results so far were that neither rules nor ignoring inappropriate behavior had any effect, and that a combination of the two increased the level of disruptive behavior. The fourth experimental condition was to combine rules, ignoring inappropriate behavior and praising appropriate behavior. The instructions for using praise and encouragement were similar to those given in the earlier studies. This extract from the instructions given to teachers provides an insight into how they were encouraged to act:

> *Teachers are inclined to take good behavior for granted and pay attention only when a child acts up or misbehaves. We are now asking you to try something different. This procedure is characterized as "catching the child being good" and making comments designed to reward the child for good behavior. . . . Pay close attention to those children who normally engage in a great deal of misbehavior. Watch carefully and when the child begins to behave appropriately, make a comment such as, "you're doing a fine job." It is very important during the first few days to catch as many good behaviors as possible. Even though a child has just thrown an eraser at the teacher (one minute ago) and is now studying, you should praise this study behavior. . . . We are assuming that your commendation and praise are important to the child. This is generally the case, but sometimes it takes a while for praise to become effective.*
>
> *(Madsen, Becker, and Thomas, 1968, page 145.)*

This combination of procedures did have a strong, beneficial effect on behavior. In one classroom inappropriate behavior occurred, on average, in around 40 percent of the observation periods during the base-line and rules conditions and more often when rules and ignoring inappropriate behavior were combined. With the combination of all three factors, the average incidence of disruptive behavior was around 20 percent. In another classroom disruptive behavior had occurred on around 65 percent of the observation periods on average. With the combination of rules, ignoring, and praise, this figure went sharply down to around 30 percent. In short, this combination had strong beneficial effects, whereas none of the previous conditions led to improved behavior. It is just conceivable that these results occurred not for the apparent reason, but simply because in the course of the experiment the teacher was gaining more practice with dealing with children or was becoming more perceptive. The investigators checked this possibility by providing after the combined condition a further period in which the teacher was instructed to return to the methods of control that were used in the original base-line condition. The level of disruptive behavior reverted to that of the earlier base-line period, so one can be reasonably sure that the previous changes were a result of the experimental conditions. This study, and most other experiments in this area, are open to criticism on methodological grounds. The numbers of subjects in such studies tend to be small, the reliability of the observations is not always high, the teachers were not always successful at following the instructions, and there are ambiguities in interpreting the results. Certainly we cannot regard any one study as entirely conclusive. However, quite a number of findings of similar studies have been published (see, for example, the review by Howe, 1970c) with similar results, indicating that the methods used have consistent effects in elementary school classrooms.

The findings of these studies in behavior modification leave little doubt that the combination of ignoring disruptive pupil behaviors and giving attention in the form of praise and encouragement to behaviors which are conducive to learning is highly effective for classroom management in elementary schools. One practical problem is that it is sometimes impossible to ignore completely deviant pupil behaviors. For example, in the study by Orme and Purnell, some of the fighting could result in children being physically hurt. Also, the other children in the classroom may be distracted by a misbehavior and maintain the behavior by watching and laughing at it. In circumstances such as these, where it is not possible for the teacher to ignore all disruptive activities, the question arises as to the most effective teacher strategy for dealing with the situation. O'Leary and Becker (1968) carried out a study in which they compared the effects of reprimanding disruptive behavior quietly with the effects of reprimanding in a manner audible to the whole class. The results showed disruptive behavior to occur on 53 percent of the observation periods under the latter condition, compared with 39 percent in the condition of quiet reprimands. In combination with attention to constructive pupil activities, quiet reprimands appear to be the best alternative when disruptive behavior cannot be ignored.

Particularly interesting are the results of the one variant of the behavior modification studies. Thomas, Becker, and Armstrong (1968) measured the effects of changes in the pattern of teacher approval and disapproval on an already well-behaved elementary school class of 28 children, mostly from middle-class homes. Observations at the outset of the study showed that the teacher customarily praised and encouraged positive behavior. In this investigation, the experimenters reversed the procedure used in most studies of this sort by requiring the teacher to withdraw the approval and praise that she customarily gave and to increase the frequency of her disapproving of certain of her students' behaviors, by scolding, threatening, and raising her voice. The main effect of this change was to raise the amount of disruptive behavior. In the initial period, with the teacher using her regular, largely positive methods of control, disruptive behavior occurred on about 9 percent of observed occasions. This rose to 25 percent in a condition where the teacher was instructed to give no approval, and in a further condition in which the teacher was told to combine no approval with frequent disapproval, disruptive behaviors increased to 31 percent. The reliability of this effect is shown by the fact that when the teacher resumed the normal methods of control, disruptive behavior returned to the original level.

The main interest of this finding lies in the demonstration of the extent to which the behavior of what is regarded as a "good" class is dependent on the behavior of the teacher. People tend to assume that some children behave well in class and some do not, and that to a large extent, this behavior is independent of what the teacher does. Some classes are regarded as "tougher" than others, and it is commonly thought that one can expect a lot more trouble with problems of control and discipline in urban schools, particularly those in ghettos, than in schools in the more affluent suburbs. Many factors determine how children behave, but the findings just described suggest that differences in teachers' methods of control do contribute substantially to the differences in classroom behavior. One possibility is that when a teacher in a ghetto school is told that his class is likely to be "difficult," she may decide to use a "firm" approach, give frequent punishment and disapproval and little encouragement to appropriate behavior, and concentrate on "not letting them get away with anything." The findings of the study quite clearly show that this type of teacher strategy is precisely the one most likely to lead to disruptive behavior on the part of the children, resulting in a self-fulfilling prophesy. In other words, the teacher's expectancies may influence his own behavior in a manner which leads to the expectancies about the children being confirmed: a classic vicious circle.

Explanation of the findings of these studies of classroom control will be useful both for showing how the results can be extended and applied in practical situations and for demonstrating certain general principles underlying the control of behavior. Using some terminology and concepts associated with the research of B. F. Skinner (1938), it can be said that behavior is "reinforced" when it results in a desirable outcome for the individual. Thus, an organism maintains reinforced behavior, as in the case of a pigeon whose pecking behavior is maintained by rewards in the form of food pellets. Most young children find the attention of adults rewarding (especially in a classroom situation where adults are somewhat scarce), and hence the attention of a teacher acts as an effective reinforcer. Thus a child whose disruptive behavior results in teacher attention is likely to maintain this behavior; it has been reinforced. The fact that the attention comes, for instance, in the form of a reprimand may not be as important to the child as the teacher might expect. Reprimand or not, the child receives highly valued attention.

When the teacher ceases attending to disruptive behavior and instead ignores it, the disruptive behavior is no longer reinforced. Behaviors that are not reinforced tend to diminish in intensity; they are said to "extinguish." Hence, we would expect that disruptive behaviors would decrease when ignored, and this is what happens in the classroom experiments. The effect is increased when constructive behaviors receive attention. This has the effect of developing in the individual an effective sequence whereby constructive behavior is reinforced (by teacher attention) and tends to be maintained. Insofar as constructive behaviors are incompatible with disruptive activities, they are also valuable for diminishing the latter. This can be demonstrated by one of the procedures in the study by Orme and Purnell (1968). The teachers rewarded (reinforced) hand-raising behavior, and this not only increased the frequency of the hand-raising activity but, since it is very difficult to fight when one hand is raised, diminished the frequency of fighting.

A concept useful in research on behavior modification is "shaping" behavior. It is all very well to find that behavior that is emitted will be maintained by reinforcement, but there is a problem when the desired behavior is not being emitted, and therefore reinforcing it is out of the question. In a classroom situation, for instance, a teacher might want to increase attention to learning tasks behavior by reinforcement but observe no such behavior to reinforce. A procedure that has often been found effective in changing behavior is to "shape" new responses by initially rewarding responses that roughly approximate the desired behavior, and then only rewarding successively closer approximations to the behavior that is required. For example, the teacher we have just mentioned might commence by rewarding individuals who sit quietly for short periods and then give rewards following successively longer periods of attention to the task.

In using concepts such as "reinforcement" one tends to place emphasis on what the person who is controlling someone's behavior is doing, rather than on the person whose behavior is controlled. It will be useful now to switch our attention to the latter, and to discuss the role of his needs in controlling behavior.

Needs and Behavior

Most elementary school children when they are in the school need encouragement, praise, and, especially, attention. In most schools there is only one teacher for every twenty or more children, so the supply of adult attention is rather scarce. If the teacher gives such attention when the children are behaving appropriately, and if the children do have a need for such attention, the appropriate behavior results in satisfaction of this need.

Maslow and others make the assumption that human behavior is governed by human needs. In a sense, this is no more than a circular definition of need, but thinking about the statement that human behavior is governed by human needs can help us understand how behavior is controlled. To paraphrase part of the previous discussion, we can say that behavior which results in a human's needs being supplied tends to be repeated. Whatever a person happens to need, whether it be money, food, excitement, understanding, self-esteem, or whatever, can determine his behavior. In this sense, needs depend very much on the individual. If a man has a craving for tobacco, he certainly needs it. A scientist might say that the human body has no basic need for tobacco, but as far as the man is concerned that is irrelevant.

The strategy followed by teachers in most of the studies described in this chapter, in which attention was withheld following disruptive behavior but provided as a consequence of constructive activities, was successful because most young children have quite a strong need for adult attention. Individuals have various needs, and whereas some needs are common to all (for example, the need for food) there are considerable differences between individuals both in their precise needs and their relative strengths. As children learn, their needs alter and become more complex. Teacher attention may supply an important need for young children, but it is unlikely that adolescents or adults have so strong a need for it. Consequently, the procedures we have described would probably have little effect on individuals above elementary school age. Note that the general principle that human behavior is determined by human needs still applies. The behavior of adolescents and adults is certainly controlled by their needs, but those needs are likely to be different and probably more complex than those of young children.

A teacher who is aware of the needs of the children will be able to predict and understand much of what happens in the classroom. This is illustrated by an example of a classroom situation in the author's experience. The evidence is anecdotal, with no objective measures or controls, and it is conceivable that the interpretation is wrong, but it does seem to clarify some of the relationships that exist between the needs of a child and the actions of the teacher, and the results of the teacher's ignorance about such needs.

The Case of Charlie

I was visiting a third-grade classroom in a Massachusetts elementary school. Most of the children were sitting round a table, taking turns reading aloud. The majority seemed to find this reasonably interesting, and each child would read a passage and then sit and attend while the others read in turn. One boy acted very differently from the others. He would frequently get up, run around, and scribble on the board. Often he would squirm around in his chair and shout or make various curious sounds. The teacher had to keep telling him to sit down and be quiet, since his activities were clearly interfering with the classroom activities. When this child was called on to read, he invariably would not know where his place was in the book, and when it was found for him he would read very badly and sometimes stop reading completely for no apparent reason. Even when he was reading aloud, he would at the same time make faces and use a sort of silly shrieking voice. This boy's reading performance in the situation was much inferior to that of the class average, and no one seeing him would have much doubted but that he was a very poor reader for his age and that he was also a severe discipline problem for the teacher. In fact, his problems seemed so severe that one could readily understand the teacher's feeling that she could do very little for him.

It just happened that I had observed this same boy, whose name was Charlie, about 10 minutes prior to the reading session, when he had been sitting at his desk on his own. On that occasion I had been walking around the room, and he looked up at me and asked if he could read to me. I agreed, and he read aloud, and the quality of his reading and his general behavior were just what one would expect in an average child of his age. There was no hint of any reading problem nor of any problems to do with the boy's behavior. In short, it is as if one were seeing two entirely different children; there was absolutely nothing in common between the way Charlie behaved when I first saw him on his own and his behavior with the teacher a few minutes later.

Perhaps the principle that human needs determine human behavior can be used to help explain this situation. The teacher had no idea what she could do to make Charlie's behavior less disruptive, and she merely concentrated on trying to contain his wilder outbursts. To say that the child was emotionally disturbed is probably quite accurate, but it is not very helpful for the teacher who had to try to help him learn, and the striking discrepancy between his behavior in the two situations in which I observed him remains unexplained. It will be more useful to think in terms of Charlie's needs. Let us assume that in both situations Charlie's behavior was directed towards satisfying a need that was important to him. To find out what was important for him we might observe what elements the two different situations had in common.

One possibility is that Charlie was getting a good deal of attention. Certainly his activities were markedly different, but they had in common the result that they were providing the attention of an adult. In the situation where I was with him, he was getting attention by acting in a way which most people would describe as normal. Why did he not act in the same way with the teacher? Perhaps he had found that acting in a normal way, in the face of competition for attention from the other children, did not produce the amount of attention that he needed. The only way he knew to get the amount of teacher attention that he required was by acting in a disruptive, noisy way—in other words, by being a nuisance. Thus, the "disturbed" behavior was, for him, the most effective way (perhaps the only way) that he had for gratifying his essential need. The more the teacher threatened, cajoled, reasoned, or punished him, the more attention Charlie received, and the more disruptive his behavior became, the better, as far as his receiving attention was concerned.

Obviously Charlie was an unusual child, with emotional problems that the teacher alone could not solve. Perhaps, she could do something to improve his classroom behavior. If the teacher can accept the fact that Charlie has a very strong need for attention so that his behavior will be directed towards meeting that need, she might try to modify her own behavior so that Charlie's actions in trying to meet his need are appropriate for learning, rather than disruptive. In other words, the teacher might change her responses to Charlie's behavior so that the most effective manner for him to obtain attention would be to behave in ways that neither interfered with his own learning nor disrupted the classroom. For instance, the teacher might give much more attention in the form of praise and encouragement to behavior on Charlie's part that was consistent with learning and withdraw attention (as far as possible) from Charlie's deviant behavior, the strategy which we have observed to be effective in a number of studies described in this chapter.

In general, in order to predict the effect of a teacher's actions on a child's behavior, one has to understand the child's own needs. Presumably reprimands, threats, and punishment are distasteful for most children. However, in the act of delivering them, the teacher also provides attention, and if the need for attention is stronger than the distaste for reprimands and the like, as it clearly was in the case of Charlie, the disruptive behavior is maintained. Other children in Charlie's class might have found that they could get the amount of attention they needed by behaving in more appropriate ways, avoiding unwanted punishments and reprimands. So the teacher must be aware not only of the needs of children in general, but of the individual needs of particular children. Her actions determine whether children meet their needs by behaviors that are predominantly consistent or inconsistent with learning. Teachers sometimes use the phrase "Oh, he's only trying to get attention," as if such behavior is certainly unjustified, and has no place in the classroom. Whether or not a teacher likes a child's attention-getting behavior, it is important to realize that the need directing that behavior is real enough and that the child's behavior will be directed to meeting it.

We have said that humans have a variety of needs but that the need for attention seems to be particularly strong among young children in school. Other powerful needs can be just as effective in interfering with learning. In a starving man the need for food is likely to be preemptive, and he is not likely to pay much attention to learning unless he thinks that this will produce food for him.

Maslow's Need Hierarchy

There are both similarities and differences in the needs of individuals, and some needs are generally more important than others. Maslow's (1943) need hierarchy illustrates that some basic needs predominate over other needs, various needs coming into prominence as others are filled.

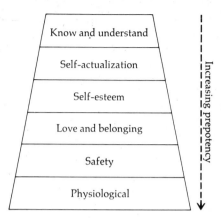

Figure 1. Maslow's hierarchical need system.

Look at Figure 1. The different types of need are arranged in what Maslow calls a hierarchical need system, in which those at the bottom are prepotent. An individual will act to satisfy his physiological needs before his needs for safety, and when both needs for safety and physiological needs are satisfied, the needs for love and belonging become important, and so on. One might quibble with the precise order of importance Maslow gives to the various needs, or with the particular needs he specifies, but the hierarchy is valuable in pointing out that humans do have different kinds of needs, some more important than others; the needs lower in the hierarchical system have to be satisfied before the others come to influence behavior. If a need at the bottom of the hierarchy is unsatisfied, then the individual's behavior will be dominated by the effort to meet that particular need. When the needs that are low in the hierarchy are satisfied, however, then needs such as those to know and understand will have a greater effect on a person's behavior.

Thibaut and Kelley (1959) reason that a person's behavior is based on the result of an analysis in terms of the cost and reward of certain activities. In Charlie's case, for instance, the cost of his activities might be those aspects of reprimands and punishments that he finds distasteful, while the reward might be the attention which he needs. If the reward is perceived by the person as being greater than the cost, he tends to persist in the activity, as did Charlie.

Maslow sees physiological needs, such as food, oxygen, and rest, as being most important for the individual. Then come needs for safety, love and belonging, and esteem. Satisfaction of the need for esteem results in feelings of confidence, worth, and usefulness. The need for self-actualization for Maslow is the need to be or to become the person one can be. Maslow puts desires to know and understand among the less important human motives. Many educators would disagree with this low emphasis on understanding and argue that it largely determines one's ability to cope with the environment, which is extremely high in importance for survival. Some of the needs are related to others; for example, knowledge and understanding may contribute to safety, and the relative strengths of the different needs are likely to differ between individuals. Thus Maslow's illustration considerably oversimplifies the roles of needs in real life, but it is useful to have a demonstration of how different needs might vary in preeminence and in potency for directing human behavior.

Understanding Human Needs

It is reasonably clear that a teacher who understands the principle that human behavior is governed by human needs, and who has some insight into the needs of the individuals in her classroom, can effectively increase control of their behavior in ways which promote effective communication and learning. This may be extremely useful and valuable, especially for the teacher who has problems with classroom control and discipline, although situations in which humans are being controlled by other people clearly have certain dangers. At the very least, behavior that is maintained by another person providing the individual with something he needs tends not to persist when there is no one to provide the reward. The behavior is dependent on whoever rewards it. Hence one person's behavior is controlled, as it were, from the outside, by another individual. At the beginning of this chapter, it was remarked that in an effective person behavior needs to be largely independent of external drives and forces so that control comes from the individual himself. A man whose behavior is largely controlled externally lacks independence and initiative and is unable to make imporant decisions for himself. To use Riesman's terms, the "inner directed" man is less dangerous to himself than the "outer directed" or "other directed" person who lacks the inner controls that make for independence. Many of the most horrifying acts of violence and destruction that have occurred would not have happened were people less efficient at following orders and more able to judge and decide for themselves.

The potential danger in a situation whereby the teacher takes upon herself the function of controlling the behavior of students is that the development of abilities necessary for independence and autonomy may be hindered. No child will learn to make decisions if he is surrounded by people who control his behavior through the external provision of his needs. Some of the examples that John Holt provides in his book *How Children Fail* (1964) illustrate a real failure by many children to develop genuine autonomy concerning their learning activities in school. It seems that this failure is largely due to conscious or unconscious actions of teachers in controlling behavior. For example, Holt gives plenty of examples showing that many children are anxious to appear successful (as defined by the teacher), to get "the right answer," to avoid being wrong, to avoid displeasing the teacher, and so on. The causes often lie in the rewards provided for such behaviors. What seems to happen is that great emphasis is placed on rewards, such as stars and teacher praise, that are both external to the learning task and administered by someone (usually the teacher) other than the learner. At the same time, the activities that are rewarded are likely to be those that give the most obvious indications of successful learning, such as getting correct answers, or that make life easier for the teacher, such as avoiding awkward questions. An emphasis on correct answers may be perpetuated by the reward value they have for a teacher in demonstrating the latter's success as a pedagogue.

The result is that children's behavior is directed to ends which have more apparent than real connection with learning. Errors are bound to occur in learning, and if we are very anxious to avoid errors, we are not likely to learn much. The "right answer" is often not particularly important, and the most important questions rarely have one simple correct answer. As John Holt says:

> Practically everything we do in school tends to make children answer-centered. In the first place, right answers pay off. Schools are a kind of temple of worship for "right answers," and the way to get ahead is to lay plenty of them on the altar. In the second place, the chances are good that the teachers are answer-centered, certainly in mathematics, but by no means only there . . . even those teachers who are not themselves answer-centered will probably not see, as for many years I did not see, the distinction between problem-centeredness and answer-centeredness, far less understand its importance.
>
> (Holt, 1964, page 90.)

Dangers of Behavior Control

We are faced with a paradox. On the one hand, it is clear that the use of certain behavior modification strategies based on an understanding of students' needs makes it possible to control behavior in ways which facilitate their learning. On the other hand, influencing children's behavior by control strategies, whether these be ones which emphasize approval, coercion, or whatever, encourages overdependence on the teacher and interferes with their learning to be independent, self-controlled individuals.

One can argue that humans are being controlled by others all the time, and that there is nothing particularly unusual or evil about people having some degree of control over children. It is also true that certain external control measures may be valuable as means, providing one is careful not to mistake means for ends. If by praising a child the teacher encourages him to engage in activities that result in learning, the child may soon begin to find the learning activity rewarding in itself. In this instance an external method of control is used to initiate a certain sort of behavior, on the assumption that once learning commences, internal controls, such as interest, curiosity, and feelings of success in the learner will take over and direct learning activities.

If a child who is already learning fairly successfully continues to need continual encouragement and praise or material reward, it is worth examining the learning material to insure that it has real value for the learner. This is not to say that teachers should withdraw all encouragement or praise even with children who seem to enjoy learning and are successful at it. In general, once a child has begun to find that school learning can be useful to him and that he can succeed at it, the teacher need rely less on external forms of control.

Thus far the discussion of the relationship of need satisfaction to behavior has involved situations where the needs of some individuals, namely the students, are provided by others, the teachers. This is external control in the sense that the people who meet the needs are not the same as the people who have the needs. The generalization we have made about the relationships between needs and activities applies as well to situations where the needs are provided by the individual who has them; that is, where there is self-control rather than external control. Note that the concept of control is still apt, but there is clearly an important difference between the situation where an individual is able to control his own actions and the situation where an individual's actions are controlled by someone else. Just as an understanding of children's needs may help teachers control the classroom, so may an individual's understanding of his needs enable him to control his own behavior. The distinction between the two types of situations is dramatized when one talks about the issue of "freedom versus control." In fact, the phrase is really used to contrast control of an individual by himself with control of the same individual by someone else. What is changed is largely the locus of the controlling agent, not the basic principles of control.

In order to extend our understanding of behavioral control processes in relation to learning, we need to know more about learning mechanisms as such. Accordingly, the next four chapters examine learning processes, and the discussion of behavior control is resumed in Chapter 7, which considers the role of motivation in human learning.

Chapter 3

Human Learning and
the Role of the Individual Learner

Learned and Unlearned Behavior

Among the various living species humans are supremely efficient at learning, and all complex human behavior is learned. In nature there are instances of such behavior which appear to be relatively uninfluenced by learning, but there is no complex unlearned behavior in man. We might ask why, if complicated behavior is possible without learning, does it not occur in humans? This question can best be answered by examining an instance of complex unlearned behavior in another species. Among insects there are numerous instances of extremely complicated and apparently sophisticated behavior patterns which occur in the relative absence of opportunities for learning. The behavior of a wasp species, a solitary variety called *sphex*, provides a good example. When it is time to lay eggs, the female *sphex* wasp builds a burrow for that purpose and then seeks out a cricket which she proceeds to sting in such a way as to paralyze but not kill it. Then the wasp drags the paralyzed cricket into the burrow and lays her eggs alongside. She closes the burrow and then flies away, never to return. Later the eggs hatch and the wasp grubs feed off the paralyzed cricket, which because it has been paralyzed rather than killed, has not decayed and has been preserved.

This impressive sequence of activity by the wasp *sphex* is highly organized, precisely sequenced, and appears to be similar in degree of sophistication to learned human activities. There is little wonder that observations of behavior in insects showing similar degrees of complexity have led people to suggest that there exists, for instance, social organization among ants. Groups of them behave in armylike fashion with a division of labor making possible the performance of ambitious and complicated activities. Yet when such activities are closely examined, the behavior turns out not to be quite so similar as it first appears to the planned, conscious human behavior which it seems to resemble. This becomes clear if we slightly disturb the highly sequenced pattern of activities in the *sphex* wasp. Recall that at one stage the wasp brings the paralyzed cricket to the burrow, leaves it outside, goes inside as if to see that all is well, emerges, and then drags the cricket in. Very impressive! But observe what happens if, while the wasp is inside making her inspection, the cricket is moved a few inches away. When the wasp comes out of the burrow it brings the cricket back to the threshold, but not inside, and then repeats the procedure of going in to inspect the burrow. Next we repeat the procedure of moving the cricket a few inches away. The wasp goes through the whole sequence again. Once more we move the cricket away, and again the wasp repeats her behavior and never "catches on" to the more useful strategy of bringing the cricket straight in to the burrow. Consequently, the sequence of activities gets no nearer completion.

One patient observer repeated the procedure forty times, always with the same results. The disruption in the sequence of activities spoiled the whole process, and the wasp was never able to get the cricket into the burrow, as it could not adapt to this change.

The behavior of the wasp is stereotyped. When a change is introduced into the usual sequence, there is no way by which it can cope with the new situation. What at first sight seems to be a very organized plan of serial activities turns out to be a sequence of fixed responses to specific stimuli. This sort of complicated yet stereotyped behavior is probably adequate for the survival of a species which exists in a relatively uniform physical environment. However, among species that live in environments where many unpredictable events occur, individual animals are most likely to survive if their behavior can adapt in ways which deal with the changes in the environment.

In some respects complex unlearned behavior is not unlike the functioning of complicated machines. My wife's sewing machine is an impressive example of a precision instrument, but there is no way in which it can be used to make ice cream. It is supremely good at doing its job, but its repertoire is restricted and unadaptive. In the case of an insect, we might say that the mechanisms for controlling behavior are "wired-in" either at birth or shortly after. There is relatively little provision for subsequent changes based on the experience of the individual with his environment.

An animal that can learn has a huge advantage. Learning is one means, and a very powerful one, by which an individual organism can adapt to changes. Humans do not have complex behavior patterns wired-in, and the human brain is correspondingly less specialized to carry out particular activities than is that of any other species. The great adaptability of man, and hence his potential for change and development, lies in the fact that his behavior patterns come about through learning as a result of experience in his environment. Staats (1971) points out that man's nonspecialization, his generalized capacities to adjust by learning, have enabled him to advance beyond other animals.

> It is suggested that man does not inherit in his biological structure any complex human behavior. To inherit specific behavioral skills as a member of the human species would have been maladaptive. A Stone Age man who had a repertoire of higher mathematics, or chemistry, or courtly manners, perfect pitch, ethical behaviors, a pacifist conception of human interaction, or what have you, would have had a useless set of skills. Fortunately, such men had no such

skills, because training that would have produced these skills was absent. Rather, such men learned to shape rocks, fight savagely, throw spears, club prey, make fire, plan group hunts, stitch furs, carve fishhooks, and so on.

The intelligent cave dweller was the man who had the advantage of learning in those areas of skill and profited from them. It is fortunate that we do not inherit most such skills as he displayed, for they would be largely useless and interfering today.

The child is a superb mechanism who can "receive" complex and subtle environmental stimuli, who can learn and retain marvelously coordinated responses, and in whom the stimuli and responses can come to be related by means of the intricate associations provided by the brain and central nervous system. It is the writer's conviction that the individual becomes what he is largely through learning. He would not be the magnificent biological organism that he is were this not the case. It is in large part because of his stupendous ability to learn, to acquire different complex repertoires, that man is set apart from lower organisms.*

Threshold Effects

A question which causes difficulty and confusion, and one which is important in any attempt to examine the specifically human characteristics of human learning, is whether the differences between humans and other animals in learning, and for that matter in other forms of behavior, are qualitative or quantitative; in other words, whether they are different in kind or merely in degree. In a way, both alternatives are correct. To understand this puzzling statement it is necessary to introduce the concept of a threshold. Imagine

* From *Child Learning, Intelligence, and Personality* by Arthur W. Staats. Copyright 1971 by Arthur W. Staats. Reprinted by permission of Harper & Row, Publishers, Inc. Pp. 48–49.

two tribes, one living at the top of a mountain, one living at the bottom. It so happens that at the top of the mountain there is, unusually perhaps, lush vegetation, a pleasant climate, and the amenities of life are relatively close at hand. Because of this the people have enjoyed considerable leisure and have developed a high degree of civilization with great intellectual and artistic accomplishments. The people at the bottom of the mountain are completely different. There the weather is unpleasant, the vegetation is sparse, and it is all the people can do to eke out a miserable existence. Consequently, they have not evolved any advanced or distinctive artistic or intellectual life, and they live at a level of pure subsistence. Thus, the people in the two tribes live completely different lives. If we were to ask whether the differences were qualitative or quantitative on the basis of their achievement, we would have to say they were qualitative. Are these qualitative differences in modes of living based on qualitative differences in the innate capacities of the people? Not necessarily. Going back into the prehistory of the tribes, we find that they were originally one. One one occasion, one of the tallest members of the tribe was able to climb the mountain, and when he got to the top he found the abundant conditions there. He came back and encouraged other people to join him. Climbing the mountain was so difficult that only the healthiest people could manage it, and some had to stay behind. Thus, the original difference between the people who stayed at the bottom and the people who climbed to the top of the mountain was purely quantitative.

The point of this fictional example is that large qualitative differences of kind may evolve from small quantitative differences. A small difference may place different members of a species above and below certain critical thresholds, leading to very large differences in later achievement and capabilities. Something of this sort may have been important in leading to the huge differences that now exist between learning in humans and other species.

The Importance of Tools

What are the threshold effects initially responsible for leading to the differences that now exist between humans and other species? No precise answer can be given, but one important factor was the use of tools. It has been observed by many, from Benjamin Franklin to Jerome Bruner, that man is a tool-making animal. The implications of this are enormous. There are other species which make use of tools, some occasionally, and some quite regularly. Montagu (1965) gives a number of examples, including the British greater spotted woodpecker, which apparently uses clefts in a tree trunk as vices and pushes pine cones into them so that the cones are firmly held while the birds pull out the seeds; and the Arnhem land hawk, a bird which picks up smoldering sticks in its claws and drops them into a dry patch of grass, waits with its companions for the exodus of frightened animals attempting to escape the fire, and then falls on them as they flee.

But the use of tools by animals in no way approaches their use by man. We can define the concept "tool" somewhat broadly to include all artificial means by which man increases his powers, either to carry out activities more conveniently, quickly, or accurately than would be possible without the tool, or to do things that would not otherwise be possible. The primitive man who uses a stone to dig a hole in the ground is carrying out more easily a job which might be possible with the hands and feet, unaided, but the pilot who flies across the Atlantic can do so only because he has tool systems which make possible what otherwise would be inconceivable. Natural selection in man may once have favored the tool-using members of the species in ways which did not occur in other animals. Perhaps the branch of primates that developed into *homo sapiens* lived in conditions where tool-making and tool-using were of greater adaptive value than for other species. Primates, being relatively small, weak, and slow, would benefit from tools in the form of sticks, stones, and simple mechanical artifacts, and if, perhaps through deforestation, some of them were forced to reply on meat-eating, the adaptive value of making weapons would become pronounced. It is likely the forerunners of the species *Zinganthropus*, a direct ancestor of man, not only used tools consistently but were highly dependent on them. Montagu indicates that they had developed beyond using materials, such as sticks and stones, that would make do for ready use as tools on an ad hoc basis, to a stage where things such as stones were consistently and purposefully modified for future use. At this stage one is well on the way to the actual manufacturing of tools, which indicates more sophisticated types of behavior than does the occasional use of objects in the environment.

Over a million and a half years ago primate ancestors of man were living who were consistent makers of tools, although they must have been very different from modern man in physical features. Once there is a species in which the consistent tool-users and tool-makers are favored in natural selection, all sorts of developments become possible. If tool-making is an indicator of learning, we might say that man, rather than being good at learning because he is human, became human because he learned, and the most important and uniquely human tool is language. It is now clear that evolution is much less dependent on solely accidental changes and mutations than Darwin supposed (Koestler, 1967), and learning to make tools has been very important in the evolution of the human species.

Whether they be simple, as in the case of primitive instruments, complex, as in modern technological devices, specific in use, as with machines, or with broad functions, as in a human language, tools make it possible for man to "express and amplify his powers" (Bruner, 1966, page 24). As Bruner says in discussing tools in relation to human culture:

> There are, first the amplifiers of action—hammers, levers, digging sticks, wheels—but more important, the programs of action into which such implements can be substituted. Second, there are the amplifiers of the senses, ways of looking and noticing that can take advantage of devices rang-

*ing from smoke signals and hailers to diagrams and pictures
that stop the action or microscopes that enlarge it. Finally
and most powerfully, there are amplifiers of the thought
processes, ways of thinking that employ language and
formation of explanation, and later use such languages as
mathematics and logic and even find automatic servants to
crank out the consequences.*

(Bruner, 1965, page 1013.)

In short, man's use of tools is more accurately seen as a
cause than as a result of the huge differences in capabilities
that now exist between humans and other species. It is tool-
using that marks man off as a species. When the tools are very
powerful, as in the case of language, the ways in which the
tools come to affect man's functioning are numerous and radical. The relationship between mankind and the tools he uses
is clearly a reciprocal one. Simple tools merely amplify human
powers in a straightforward manner. For example, it is easier to
cut meat with a stone than with human teeth. However, as
tools become more complex they begin to produce changes
in their users. This is seen with human language, whereby the
user becomes introspective, conscious, and correspondingly
able to function or "reason" in ways inconceivable for other
species. The Russian psychologist Vygotskii, who placed great
emphasis on the importance of tools in the evolution of consciousness in man, stressed that with language the changes
that man as a tool-user can make in external things react on
his inner mental processes. Language enables man to think.

We have strayed from the child learning at school in order
to observe some of the unique characteristics of learning in
the human species and to point out a major advantage that
learning can bring. Humans have been unique in developing
tools in order to cope with their needs, and learning in man is
closely related to and dependent on human tools, especially
language. In addition, complex human behavior is entirely
dependent on learning; although complicated behavior is conceivable in the absence of learning, unlearned behavior pat-

terns would be too rigid for human needs. It is largely due to the changes accompanying the use of tools, especially language, that much human learning, and certainly the learning required for the complex abstract abilities stressed in school, is quite different from any learning that occurs in animals. Complex human learning depends on symbolic capacities that are not developed in other animals, and much of the learning that takes place in school is therefore quite different from any learning that occurs in nonhuman species.

A frequent criticism of research by psychologists who study animal learning is that by confining their observations to experiments on tame animals in laboratory situations, they fail to become aware of the more interesting and highly developed parts of the animal's learning repertoire, which can only be seen when the animals are observed in their natural habitat. Perhaps this reasoning is even more apt in the case of human behavior. It is conceivable that laboratory studies of learning have failed to observe some of the more interesting characteristics of learning in humans. If we want to know something about the ways in which humans learn most effectively, we might be wise to complement our studies with natural observation. Such observation is made by anthropologists, but rarely by psychologists whose central interest is learning. The rare exceptions include Jerome Bruner's (1965) comments on learning in a primitive tribe, based on a lengthy film; parts of Phillip Jackson's book *Life in Classrooms* (1968), and a few careful observational studies, such as Eleanor Leacock's *Teaching and Learning in City Schools* (1969).

The Individual in Human Learning

It would be useful to specify variables important in the sorts of human learning that are valuable in education. How does complex learning occur? Do humans learn more efficiently in some ways than others? What are the factors present when human learning is at its best? Common sense has provided many attempts to answer questions such as these. One recurring theme in works by thinkers in education, from

Rousseau, William James, and John Dewey, to modern writers, is that in the school situation the process of trying to impart large bodies of information to students has led to learning being seen incorrectly as a largely assimilative process on the part of the learner who plays a passive role which does not involve much learner participation. They have argued that the traditional classroom situation imposes a somewhat inactive role on learners, and they suggest that the efficiency of learning is thereby restricted to a level far below what is possible when students are able to participate actively and at their own pace in learning activities they choose on the basis of interest. Although most modern teachers would agree with the proposition that passive and rote learning should be discouraged, observation of many classrooms confirms one's suspicion that much learning is certainly of a passive, assimilative kind. The view that effective learning is facilitated by active learner involvement seems reasonable enough, but before accepting such an assertion as an item of fact, one needs to determine whether the evidence supports it.

Let us first look at the results of a simple experiment by Jensen and Rohwer (1963). Subjects were asked to perform a learning task requiring them to learn lists containing pairs of words. Such items are used frequently in psychological experiments on verbal learning and are called "paired-associates." There were two experimental conditions. In one condition, the subjects, who were retarded adults, were simply instructed to learn the pairs of words, and in the other condition, they had to construct sentences in which the two words in each pair were used as subject and object. For instance, if a pair were *scissors-telephone*, an appropriate sentence might be, "The scissors jumped up on the telephone." The subject had to make up such a sentence for each pair of words. Comparing learning rates in the two conditions, the authors found that learners made only a fifth of the normal number of errors by constructing sentences. It is clear that this increase in learning efficiency outstrips any effects of manipulating the variables which have been traditionally regarded as important in experiments on verbal learning, such as distribution of practice and part-whole learning.

It would be valuable to know what made learning more effective in the sentence-making condition. One suggestion is that the learners had to do something constructive with the words perceived; incorporating words in a sentence demands active cognitive processes. The learners must relate the words in a meaningful way; it is necessary to use one's own knowledge and understanding in order to produce a sentence that makes sense. So we can say that learning in the more effective conditions is an active participatory process whereby the learner is engaged in cognitively manipulating the materials to be learned. It appears that learning is further increased when subjects participate actively in another manner, by forming mental images to represent verbal items (Paivio, 1969; Bugelski, 1970). This finding is discussed in Chapter 10.

In a second example, learning more closely approximated that which is typical in classrooms. The experiment was carried out by the author (Howe, 1970d), and since it was partly a replication of a previous study by Kay (1955), in which very similar results were obtained, the findings are highly reliable. Young adults were asked to listen to a prose extract from a modern novel. After they had heard the passage they were requested to write out what they could remember of the meaningful content of the passage. Immediately following the attempts at meaningful reproduction, the subjects again heard the original version. In a subsequent session, exactly one week later, they were again asked to reproduce what they could of the original passage. Once more, immediately afterwards, the subjects listened to the original version. The same procedure was repeated in two subsequent weekly sessions so that each person had listened to the original version five times and had attempted to recall it on four occasions.

One might expect that this experimental situation would provide good conditions for learning to improve from week to week. After all, on each weekly occasion the subjects were given an opportunity to correct errors in their retention. The results showed, contrary to expectations, hardly any week-to-week improvement. More interesting, when one examined exactly what was recalled from one week to the next, it emerged that each subject recalled very accurately what he himself had produced in the previous recall session, and that his successive attempts appeared to be almost unaffected by the repeated presentation of the original. In scoring recall, two judges measured the amount of meaningful content from the original material that was effectively communicated. A high correlation between the scores allocated by the different judges indicated that the method of scoring meaningful recall was reliable. Another way of scoring recall is to count the number of words correctly reproduced. Although on the surface this may seem pointless since we are interested in meaningful retention rather than verbatim recall, it happened that verbatim and meaningful retention were very highly correlated in this study, and the verbatim measure had some useful functions. For instance, when we examined the "additions" (incorrect items that formed part of a subject's recall attempts), it was found that an incorrect addition which appeared in one of a subject's attempts at recall was twice as likely to be repeated in a subsequent recall attempt as a correct item that had been presented on four occasions as part of the repeated presentation of the original version, but had not been previously recalled. It seems that items produced by a learner himself were more likely to be recalled than items he had heard but not produced, even though the latter had been presented on four occasions.

For meaningful recall, an item correctly recalled on Trial One had a .7 chance of being recalled correctly again on the next trial, but items not recalled on Trial One had only a .2 chance of being recalled on the second recall trial. If an item was not recalled in the first three sessions, its probability of recall on the Trial Four was less than .2, despite the fact that by then the subject had heard it no less than four occasions. Note that this is a much lower probability than that for items which had been presented only once but subsequently recalled correctly. In short, items that a subject himself reproduced, or even incorrectly added, were much more likely to be remembered than other items, although the learner listened to the latter on a number of occasions. Learning and retention is most effective for whatever the learner himself constructs or produces.

The results of a further study by the author (Howe, 1970f) also demonstrate the influence of learners' constructive activities on subsequent retention. The investigation originally formed part of an attempt to measure the effectiveness of taking notes. Since the development of inexpensive and convenient methods of reproducing written materials has replaced the traditional function of note-taking, it would be useful to know if note-taking is justified on other grounds. If not, the task of reproducing information can be handled much more easily in other ways. It is conceivable that the activity of taking notes has additional effects which are valuable for the learner, and the study formed part of an attempt to examine this possibility (see also Howe, 1970b).

In the experiment, subjects were asked to write notes which would communicate as accurately as possible the meaningful content of a prose passage they heard. A week later they were asked to attempt written recall of the prose passage. In analyzing the results, judges looked at the notes that each subject had made and measured the extent to which the content was related to the content of the retention test. Is a subject more likely to retain those items on which he had made effective notes than the other items? Comparing recall for items that had and had not appeared in a subject's notes, it was found that the probability of subjects recalling an item that occurred in his written notes was .34, whereas the probability of recalling an item that was not in his notes was .05. In other words, items that were communicated in a subject's notes were about seven times as likely to be recalled than ones that were not. Taking notes on a particular meaningful item seems to require the learner to relate and process the material in order to express it in his "own words." Again, it is clear that what the learner does in the situation has a very strong influence on the effectiveness of his learning activities. It is quite likely that taking notes results in some items receiving inadequate attention, which would influence the results. Even so, a difference in retention of the order of seven to one remains extremely striking.

These sets of experimental findings are all strikingly consistent with the view that the individual learner has a most important active role in the learning process. It seems that people do learn most effectively in situations in which they are required to participate in a constructive manner. These are likely to be situations in which the learner is highly interested in what he is doing, where the task is perceived as relevant to him, and in which there is a high degree of learner involvement. In the absence of these conditions it is unlikely that the learner will consistently bring into play the constructive activities that were found to be so effective.

Constructive Functions in Learning

The emphasis on the role of the individual's cognitive processes in learning is by no means new. Sir Fredrick Bartlett (1932) stressed what he called "Construction" in seeing, hearing, and remembering. He also discussed "effort after meaning," stressing that in coping with the environment the individual seeks to find ways of integrating the available data in terms of his cognitive structure, which is largely formed by his learning experiences in the past. In saying that something is "meaningful" to us, we mean that it can be related to things we already know; we have a frame of reference which gives meaning to the new information. Bartlett found that when students tried to reproduce stories they had listened to or read, which contained elements that were unfamiliar and relatively devoid of meaning in terms of the learners' cultural background, the reproduced versions were much more conventional, in both content and style, than the original in relation to that culture. Content that could not be interpreted in terms of the listener's culture either became distorted or was forgotten. In some of Bartlett's experiments a story containing many unfamiliar concepts was read by one student, who then reproduced it and passed his account to the next student. He read that version and in turn reproduced it, and so on, through a chain of perhaps seven or eight people. As Hunter (1964) observes, in the process of the story being passed from one subject to the next, "the story becomes, in a word, conventional. It retains only those characteristics which can be readily assimilated to that background of past experience which all members of the chain share in common" (Hunter, 1964, page 144.)

If the material is perceived as being important, attitudinal and emotional factors may strongly influence the manner in which the learner processes the material. Attitudinal factors influence what a person perceives; what he sees is affected by what he wants to see and what he expects to see. Allport and Postman (1947) in *The Psychology of Rumor*, point out that Bartlett's emphasis on "effort after meaning," whereby people appear to transform their perceptions in ways that are meaningful and "make sense" to them, applies particularly strongly when there is ambiguity about knowledge of great potential and importance to individuals. Rumors are likely to occur in such situations, and they thrive on lack of reliable information. From the previous discussion we can deduce that the accuracy with which a person can perceive and communicate information will depend on the adequacy of his cognitive structure or frame of reference for accommodating the incoming information without serious distortion. Without relevant previous experience the individual will lack an adequate frame of reference for integrating the material or interpreting it accurately. In that event, what happens will depend on how important he perceives the information to be. If the individual thinks it unimportant, he will probably pay little attention to any part of the material that cannot readily be assimilated. If the same individual does perceive the information as being important to him, and at the same time has insufficient background of knowledge and experience for him to perceive or interpret it accurately, it is likely that the incoming material will be distorted and altered by the perceiver. In Bartlett's experiments, materials that were not meaningful in terms of the observers' common experience tended to be distorted or lost, but the circumstances giving birth to rumors are different in that the lack of experience or frame of reference is, on these occasions, accompanied by a much higher degree of interest in the content of the information than in the case of the somewhat artificial circumstances of Bartlett's laboratory experiments. Rumors are most likely to thrive in situations where a satisfactory frame of reference is lacking, but where information is seen by the participant as being important. Allport and Postman examined the spread of rumors in war situations in which information was, on the one hand, very scarce and, on the other hand, extremely important. Here ambiguity and importance are present together, and under such conditions, distortions and alterations occur when information is transmitted, giving rise to many wild rumors.

Another way of viewing the situation in which a lack of adequate cognitive structure for processing information prevents interpretation is to regard the human brain as having a number of "codes" (Biggs, 1968). The codes represent cognitive capacities for dealing with incoming information, and if information arrives for which no satisfactory code is available, a number of things can happen. First, the information may be lost or forgotten. Second, the material may be distorted so as to fit an existing code or codes, and this is what happens in the case of rumors and in the various distortions observed in Bartlett's experiments. A third and more exciting possibility is that a new code may be formed, or that a number of existing codes which on their own were not satisfactory for handling the incoming information may be combined in some manner so as to form a new code which is capable of dealing with the information. In this situation we can say that learning is taking place. The individual is genuinely adapting to the situation, and as a result of the cognitive reorganization he will be prepared for dealing with such information on future occasions.

Neisser (1967) points out that approaches whereby cognition is seen as basically constructive rather than receptive or simply analytic have historical antecedents in Brentano's *Act Psychology* and Bergson's *Creative Synthesis*. Discussion of such constructive activities as searching through memory, adopting strategies, filtering, censoring, retrieving, and decision-making, raises questions about who or what carries them out: *who* searches, retrieves, filters, and so on? "Is there," asks Neisser, "a little man in the head, a *homunculus*, who acts the part of the paleontologist vis-à-vis the dinosaur?" Neisser considers that it is not possible to ignore such a notion, but feels that while behaviorist psychologists have strongly attacked the inherent "mentalism," their own theories leave the problem unsolved. It is conceivable that there is something akin to an "executive routine" in computer programming, whereby a hierarchy of subroutines end their operations by transferring control to an executive, and the latter "decides" when the other routines are appropriate. S. H. White's (1965) description of hierarchically arranged learning mechanisms with "temporal stacking" and Miller, Galanter, and Pribram's (1960) approach, which extends the notion that behavior is guided by a series of feedback loops, provide interesting attempts to deal with some of the problems relating to the processes by which constructive activities are directed.

We can summarize the preceding few pages by saying that learning is a highly constructive activity on the part of the individual learner, so that what the learner himself brings to the learning situation is exceedingly important in determining the outcome of his attempts to learn. Even the simplest perception depends on far more than the ability to receive information. There is complex interpretation and processing in terms of the content of the learner's previous experiences which both give rise to and are influenced by attitudes, expectancies, and the like. To use Bruner's phrase, the individual who receives information goes "beyond the information given." In a very real sense one can say that the information that is perceived depends on the individual who is perceiving it, and by necessity, what is learned depends on this. By implication, the teacher can encourage learning in school by helping to bring about situations wherein the constructive learner activities that we have shown to facilitate learning come into play, and these are inevitably situations where the learner has a reasonable degree of control over the learning activities and involvement in the learning materials.

Learners' Roles in Simple Learning

It has been shown that interpretive, constructive activities are important in relatively complex human learning. As a matter of fact, there is evidence that a considerable amount of constructive activity on the part of the individual learner occurs even in simple learning situations. In the case of what is called "simple stimulus-response learning," it appears that the learner has a strong role in determining what the effective stimulus shall be. Koestler (1967) points out that in simple tasks such as discriminating by ear between words such as *big* or *pig* and *map* or *nap*, what is heard depends very largely on the context in which the words are spoken. Research in Russia by E. N. Sokolov and others (see Razran, 1961) on the "Orienting Reflex" shows that even in simple animal learning the state of the animal determines what is to become a stimulus. An interesting instance of this is provided.

> *A cat's auditory nerve was wired to an electric apparatus so that nerve impulses transmitted from the ear to the brain could be heard in a loud speaker. A metronome was kept going in the room, and its clicks, as transmitted by the cat's auditory nerve and amplified by the apparatus, were clearly audible, but when a mouse in a jar was brought into the room, the cat not only lost interest in the metronome, as one would expect but its impulses in its auditory nerve became feebler or stopped altogether.*
>
> *(Koestler, 1967, page 101.)*

This dramatic example makes it clear that even such an apparently simple process as the reception of straightforward stimuli can be largely controlled by the perceiver, in this instance a cat.

By now we have come some way towards understanding several of the most important processes involved in human learning. It has been shown just how important the learner is in learning, and in succeeding chapters we will go further into attempts to understand more precisely the nature of the coding, interpreting processes that take place. It is interesting to find that there is a certain measure of agreement between the implications of the previous chapter and the present one, although they are concerned with apparently different problems. In the previous chapter it was concluded that since education requires a person to learn not only to acquire information but to be able to use it, to make decisions, judgements, and the rest, it is necessary to give learners considerable experience in actually making decisions and in acquiring the ability to control and determine one's own learning. The evidence of the present chapter points to a similar conclusion, but for entirely different reasons. Here we find that complex human learning depends on the learner as an individual, whose constructive activities largely determine the outcome of the learning situation. Hence it is reasonable to advocate the use of learning situations in which the learner can have a great deal to say in determining the nature of the activities. It is a cliché that nobody can learn anything for anyone else, but we are now more aware than before of just how true this is.

Before proceeding, in Chapters 4 and 5, to pursue in greater detail the mechanisms and processes of meaningful human learning, a brief digression will be made to examine two issues that are raised by some of the experimental findings described in the present chapter. The first concerns the role of errors in human learning, and the second, the value of taking notes.

The Problem of Errors

In the experiment by Howe (1970d) on repeated presentation and recall of prose materials, the major finding was that the contents of each of a subject's successive recall attempts were extremely similar to the others, despite the repeated presentations of the correct passage, which might have been expected to provide excellent opportunities for revision in the direction of increased accuracy. This high degree of stability in the reproductions produced by subjects is certainly advantageous when the reproductions are correct, but when a subject has made an incorrect attempt at recall, the stability of the contents of such an attempt is something of a liability. Presentation of the correct material apparently does not, in this situation, provide sufficent opportunity for the learner to correct his erroneous internal version of the data.

The experimental situation is not unlike that in which a teacher tests his students on some items they have been attempting to learn. After the test, the teacher reports the correct answers on the assumption that in instances when a student's test answer was incorrect, his error will be corrected. The present results indicate that this assumption is quite wrong; merely providing correct answers is not a sufficient procedure for students to rectify errors they have made, even in the case of primarily factual prose material. There arises the question of what should be done when errors occur, since we have found that simply providing correct answers is insufficient to ensure they will be learned. Of course, as we have noted, the presence of correct answers is not always a guarantee of learning, and we could add that for many important questions there is not one unambiguously correct answer. Nevertheless, to be correct is often important; two plus two does not make five, and the person who believes it will find himself somewhat handicapped by his error in his pursuit of arithmetical competence.

One conceivable solution to the problem of what to do with learner's errors is to provide learning situations in which errors are avoided entirely. This is to some extent possible when learning materials are presented in very small, carefully graduated steps, as in the case of some forms of programmed instruction. It is possible to devise instructional sequences,

following procedures devised by B. F. Skinner, in which gradual step-by-step presentation ensures a very low error rate,
with the result that the problem of how to rectify learners'
errors is largely removed. However, some important problems
remain. First, it is doubtful that *all* errors can be prevented,
however gradual the introduction of new learning materials.
Second, there are probably some areas of instruction in which
small step presentation cannot be used. Third, even when it is
possible to apply such instructional methods they may be
undesirable despite the fact that the problem of errors is thereby avoided. Many learners may be bored when items are presented in this manner and regret the lack of challenges encountered with other types of presentation. In addition, when
learning is made easy by very gradual progression, students
may suffer from not having to exercise skills that are required
for using and applying what has been acquired. In short, then,
although it may sometimes be possible to avoid the problems
involved in correcting errors made by learners by the simple
expedient of devising learning sequences whereby very few
errors occur, this solution is not always desirable. Certainly it
may be possible to "cover the content" of, say, physics, in a
small-step manner, but it is doubtful whether a learner who
proceeded by such a method alone would develop all the skills
that are expected to result from the study of physics. It seems
unlikely that learners will get much opportunity in gradual
small-step learning to practice the types of independent, constructive activities that are important in meaningful learning.

Perhaps we can best solve the problems involved in helping learners correct errors by first examining how the errors
came about. To do this, it is necessary to see how the material
to be learned was processed by the learner. The precise cause
will be specific to a particular error, but in general it would
appear that the learner's cognitive processes that are responsible for coding and interpreting information are involved in
the (incorrect) processing that underlies an incorrect response.
As the souce of the error lies in the cognitive processes of the
individual learner, the correction of the error also requires the

learner to carry out active cognitive operations at a corresponding degree of complexity and involvement. It is clear
that merely providing the correct answer by no means ensures
that this will happen, and it is therefore not surprising that
repetition of learners' errors occurs despite the repeated presentations of the correct prose passage. On the other hand, if
the learner is placed in a position where he can again process
the original material, integrating it and relating it in terms
of his existing cognitive structure, correction of the error
should result in his having a stable version of the correct
answer. In a classroom situation this might be made possible
by having the student work through the material again.

In summary, the persistence of errors in some learning
situations indicates a real cause for concern. However, the
solution of preventing errors by trying to avoid them totally
does not appear to be entirely practicable or desirable, and it
would seem that the best general remedy is to ensure that the
degree of involvement of the learner's higher cognitive processes at the time of remedying errors is equal to that present
at the time of original, incorrect learning.

The Value of Taking Notes

The second of the two issues that were raised by experimental findings concerns the role and value of the practice of
taking notes for human learning. It will be recalled that one
of the results of the study by Howe (1970f) was that when
adult students were asked to take notes as they listened to
meaningful prose material, the probability of subsequent correct recall was more than six times higher for a meaningful
item that was included in a particular student's written notes
than it was for an item that he had not included in his notes,
despite the fact that subjects had no opportunity to peruse
their notes after writing them. This finding would appear to
suggest that the practice of taking notes can be most valuable
as a practical aid to learning, but there are some problems in
interpreting the results. For instance, it is quite possible that
the major effect of note-taking activities was to prevent atten-

tion to material that was being presented at the same time, in which case the finding of more accurate recall among the recorded items than among the others might be used as a basis for recommending that students take no notes at all and concentrate on attending to all the material. At any rate, findings indicate that it would be worthwhile to examine the value for human learning of the common practice of taking notes.

When a practice has been common in education over a long period of time, we tend to take for granted that it has useful functions. However, as changes occur, it is often wise to examine established practices, and in the case of note-taking it might be useful to ask both whether it remains the most effective way of fulfilling its original functions and whether those functions are as valuable as they once were (see Howe, *in press*).

Traditionally, a reason for the taking of notes by learners has been that it provides them with a permanent and convenient record of information and knowledge that would not otherwise be available. By writing down required parts of the contents of a lecture or of printed material, the student provides himself with necessary information. However, modern technology can now provide inexpensive and convenient alternative ways of recording and reproducing information, which have the advantages of freeing students from the time-consuming activity of taking notes and presumably of allowing more time for learners to attend and communicate in ways that are educationally useful. Certainly there will always be some situations in which the most convenient method of reproducing information is to take brief notes, but on most occasions the student who is provided with a reproduced version of the material he needs to consult will be freer to interact with the teacher in ways that facilitate learning.

Thus there would be little justification for the continued practice of note-taking on a wide scale if their sole function were to reproduce the content to be learned. The fact that note-taking continues to be a common practice would seem to indicate an assumption that taking notes does have a value for learning in addition to that of recording information. It is often assumed that note-taking somehow facilitates learning, although the reasons underlying such an assumption are rarely made explicit. There are a number of possible ways in which note-taking might aid learning, other than by providing a written record of information. For instance, it is conceivable that the activity of taking notes might help learners attend to the material at hand and to carry out processing and integrating operations that tie the material to the learner's cognitive structure. Another possibility is that the notes made by a particular student, being a version of the content as perceived and processed himself and hence meaningful to him, might provide a more useful aid when subsequently consulted than would a version of the material prepared by another person.

Experimental research should be able to provide the knowledge needed to answer the question of whether or not note-taking activities can influence students' learning of written materials. In the case of this common educational practice, one might hope that there would be a considerable body of research evidence available concerning its value. In fact, research in this area has been very sparse. In one of the few experimental studies carried out to examine the importance of note-taking, McClendon (1958) asked college students to listen to 14-minute lectures describing various aspects of communications. Three experimental groups were respectively asked to make no notes, detailed notes, or to take notes in their customary manner. The students were tested for retention of the material, either immediately afterwards or after a five-week interval. Neither in the immediate nor in the delayed test did the note-taking instructions have any effect on the accuracy of retention. In another study, by Eisner and Rohde (1950), some of the university student subjects took notes during a 30-minute lecture, and others were required to write notes on the lecture after it was finished. Subsequently, a true-false recognition test was given immediately afterwards, and there was a further test three weeks later. On neither test was there a statistically significant difference in performance between the students who had taken notes during the lecture and those who made notes after it had ended.

McLeish (1968) describes a study by P. S. Freyberg, in which it was observed that adult subjects who listened to a lecture and took no notes at all performed better on recall tests immediately after the lecture and two weeks later than did students who were instructed to take either detailed or outline notes. In another study (Ash and Carlton, 1953), it was found that taking notes during the presentation of a film did not improve students' retention. This seems hardly surprising, since note-taking activities might well have interfered with attending to the film. Finally, Poppleton and Austwick (1964) measured the performance of high school students and postgraduate university students who learned statistics by two methods. Some of the students were presented with the material in programmed instruction format, and the others read the same material in regular text form, and these students were allowed to take notes. The two methods of instruction were equally effective for the postgraduate students, but among high school students, the subjects who used programmed learning were more successful than those who received the material in text form, which they used in conjunction with note-taking.

In summary, experimental research on note-taking does not appear to provide evidence supporting the claim that note-taking activities have positive effects on learning, apart from its function of recording information. The results seem to indicate that there is little justification for the widespread practice of note-taking. However, we can question this conclusion, since the experimental studies leave some important questions unanswered. For example, in none of them was there any real attempt to control the precise form of the note-taking. It is quite possible that some types of notes are more effective than others, but the experimental studies have provided no clear evidence about this, nor has there been differentiation between the note-taking and what learners *do* with the notes they have made. Even if note-taking does not affect learning directly, it may provide the learner with material that is more valuable to him than the original version, since the notes, being coded by the learner in his own words, "make sense" to him in ways not otherwise possible. In the experimental studies reviewed in the previous paragraph, the procedure was to examine the effects of the note-taking per se, which leads to artificial comparisons, since a realistic evaluation of note-taking must also take into account the *use* made by subjects of the notes taken by themselves.

Another reason for questioning the negative conclusion about the function of note-taking evidence is that evidence gained in experiments other than those directly examining note-taking would suggest different conclusions. The experiments described earlier demonstrated that when learners engage in complex cognitive activities and are required to deal with meaningful verbal information—coding, interpreting, and the like—learning is thereby facilitated. In addition, Bartlett's (1932) discussion of a learner's "effort after meaning" in processing incoming information, and Allport and Postman's (1947) emphasis on each individual's "frame of reference" as determining how people perceive and transmit knowledge, point to the great importance for learning of attempts by students to relate and integrate new information in terms of what is already familiar to the individual.

What are the implications of this evidence for note-taking? Briefly, one can say that taking notes can be an activity that demands the types of constructive cognitive transformations by learners which have found to be effective. However, this is not necessarily the case, and this fact forces us to look rather carefully at the precise nature of notes that are taken, and at the underlying cognitive processes. A student's notes that simply provided a verbatim record of prose information would not necessarily require much involvement on the part of the learner, and hence the preparation of such notes might make little contribution to learning. However, notes in which the precise wording and phraseology were constructed by the learner would require interpretive activities on his part, and hence might substantially affect learning. Therefore, research on note-taking needs to be carried out in which greater attention is paid to the precise nature of the note-taking activity than in the existing experimental studies. Hartley and Cameron (1967) compared the contents of notes made by students with what the lecturer actually said, noting that the agreement of the contents of the notes with a set of "ideal notes" prepared by the lecturer was around 70 percent in the first ten minutes of a 50-minute lecture, but dropped to about 20 percent in the final 10-minute period. However, there was no measure of retention, so the results do not show the effect on learning of the degree of correspondence in content between the lecture and students' notes. The author's experiment (Howe, 1970f), which was described earlier and which introduced this discussion of the value of note-taking, provides data that goes some way towards filling the gap. It will be recalled that students listened to an extract from a novel, and they were asked to take notes communicating what they considered to be the meaningful content, and one week later they attempted written recall. After the note-taking session, the notes had been handed to the experimenter, who scored the extent to which twenty meaningful ideas in the passage appeared in each subject's notes. In addition to the finding that items forming part of a student's notes were almost seven times as likely to be recalled as items that did not appear in notes, it was observed that different subjects varied in their note-taking strategies of the individual subjects. One can hypothesize that an "efficient" note-taking strategy is one in which the maximum number of meaningful content units is communicated in the minimum number of words. Accordingly, for each subject the number of meaningful items reproduced in the notes was divided by the number of separate words used in the notes, and the correlation was calculated between this ratio and the number of meaningful units recalled. There was a statistically significant correlation ($r = +.53$) indicating that accuracy of recall is positively related to the "efficiency" of note-taking.

In another experiment, Howe (1970b) attempted to examine the effects of both different types of note-taking strategy and the use made by students of their own notes. Instructions to each subject were one of three alternatives: (1) to attempt as nearly as possible word for word reproduction; (2) to make brief notes, communicating the meaningful content; and (3) to make no notes at all, and simply concentrate on listening. Afterwards, half of the subjects in each of the three conditions were allowed four minutes to review the material, using their notes, and the other subjects were given a distracting task which prevented rehearsal. A number of administrative problems resulted in loss of data, and perhaps as a result of this, the differences in recall scores between the groups given the different note-taking instructions were not statistically significant, but subjects allowed to review did recall significantly more items than the others. It would be useful to replicate this study.

In general, it appears that some note-taking activities lead to types of cognitive activities on the part of learners which have been found to facilitate learning. Further experimental research on the role of note-taking is required, and future research should examine different types of note-taking strategies, rather than confining itself to the simple comparison of conditions in which notes are taken and are not taken. The research should also look into the use by students of notes they have made.

Chapter 4

Types of Meaningful Learning

Meaningful Learning

Learning, if it is to be valuable, should be as meaningful as possible. What do we mean by meaningful? One educational psychologist, D. P. Ausubel, has looked into this question rather systematically, and he makes a distinction between "meaningful" learning and what he calls "rote" learning. The phrase rote learning is generally used by Ausubel (1968) to denote situations where what is learned is a pattern or sequence of words with relatively little attention to the meaning. An illustration of the difference between rote and meaningful learning is provided in a short account which apparently was told by John Dewey. It appears (Bloom, 1956, page 29) that Dewey was visiting a school, and went to observe one of the classrooms. At one point he asked the pupils a question, "What would happen if you were to dig a deep hole into the earth?" Dewey waited for an answer, but was met with silence and blank stares. After an embarrassing pause the teacher muttered something about Dewey having asked the wrong question. The teacher then turned to the children and said "What is the state of the center of the earth?" Immediately all the children responded together, "igneous fusion."

Clearly, the question which the teacher asked was basically the same in meaning as Dewey's, yet on one occasion the children knew the answer, and on the other they had no idea.

The children had learned the form of words that provided the correct answer to the question about the state of the center of the earth, but they had not learned it in a meaningful way. If they had, they would have had no difficulty with Dewey's question. What had been learned was simply a meaningless sequence of words. It is true that the sentence that the state of the center of the earth is one of igneous fusion is a meaningful one; clearly it was to the teacher, and it is to most educated adults. The important point is that it was not meaningful to the children in that classroom. All that had taken place for them was the rote acquisition of a particular sequence of words.

We should be somewhat wary of a simple distinction between meaningful and rote learning. Reality is not quite so simple; there are degrees of meaningfulness. Even in the situation described by Dewey, the learning about the state of the center of the earth was not quite so meaningless to the children as the sequence "fusion state igneous of" would have been. Probably, even to those children, a statement in correct English would make sense in a way that random word sequence does not. A related but not identical distinction to the rote-meaningful one is that between what Biggs (1965) calls "structured" and "unstructured" learning. In structured learning the parts are clearly related to each other, whereas in unstructured learning they are not. As in the case of the rote-meaningful distinction, it would probably be wiser to think in terms of a continuum rather than a dichotomy.

Even within relatively meaningful materials, it is useful to think of various degrees or levels of meaningfulness. For instance, the phrase "Caesar crossed the Rhine" has some meaning to anyone who can understand the English language. Someone who knows to whom "Caesar" refers, and who is aware that the Rhine is an important European river will find the sentence more meaningful; he can understand more clearly what happened. The sentence will be yet more meaningful to a person who is acquainted with European history; for him the event can be fitted into the perspective that his knowledge provides. In this instance, the information is relatable to what the learner knows at a higher level of abstraction. The same sentence would be still more meaningful to a scholar who was well versed with the travels of Julius Caesar in Europe. Thus, although it is useful to make distinctions between meaningful and rote learning, and between structured and unstructured learning, it is clear that we are really dealing with differences of degree, and not absolute differences.

The foregoing discussion helps to make clear another point, and this is one to which Ausubel (1968) attaches particular importance. For meaningful learning to occur, it is not only essential that the material be logically meaningful, in the sense that there are people to whom it can make sense, but that the material should be meaningful to the particular learner. However meaningful something is, if the learner himself does not find it so, it is impossible for meaningful acquisition to occur. As a result we have to be able to see the learning situation from the learner's perspective in order to be able to make any predictions about the possibility of meaningful learning. One might argue that this is a rather obvious point, but in classrooms it is sometimes neglected, nevertheless.

It was shown in Chapter 3 that learning is most efficient when the learner is capable of relating new material to the contents of his previous experience or cognitive structure. Ausubel, likewise, insists that for meaningful learning the knowledge to be acquired and the existing body of ideas, skills, and experiences must be relatable in a nonarbitrary fashion. He also states that the learning must have the quality of substantiveness, by which he means that the learner's understanding is not altered if a changed form of wording is provided. Clearly, this condition was not present among the children whom Dewey questioned. The fact that a correct response did not occur when the question appeared in a form slightly different from the original, indicates that the quality of substantiveness in learning was absent.

A concrete analogy which may help to clarify the distinction between rote learning, in which there is no substantive nonarbitrary relating by the learner of new material to exist-ing cognitive structure, and meaningful learning, is provided by imagining a brick wall. In this analogy, meaningful learn-ing of new subject matter can be visualized as a new brick being incorporated into the wall. The fact that the new brick be-comes part of the wall both gives stability to the new brick, and at the same time the new brick itself adds strength to the existing whole. Having gained a new element, the whole wall is changed; it is now a different wall than before. Rote learn-ing, on the other hand, might be visualized as a situation in which a loose brick is placed on the top of an existing wall. There is little stability for the new brick; it might be blown or knocked off quite easily, and the existing wall does not itself gain anything from the presence of the new brick. It does not become a different wall.

We can also say that meaningful learning involves change. That is to say, change in the aggregate of capacities and knowl-edge possessed by the learner. I once overheard a couple of university students talking about their forthcoming vacation. One of them said that he was looking forward to being able to go away and forget what he learned in his course. The point about meaningful learning is that one cannot simply forget it; the person who has meaningfully learned something is different from what he was before. Perhaps this is to over-simplify and to dramatize the distinction between meaningful learning and rote learning. Nobody can recall perfectly all the knowledge he acquired some years ago, however meaningful. Much forgetting takes place. However, such learning produces some changes that in turn influence future learning, so that although total recall is not possible, learning which is mean-ingful cannot be entirely discarded.

People are very much more efficient at learning materials that are meaningful than they are at rote learning. Ausubel illustrates this point by mentioning that the typical adult can re-member approximately seven random digits presented sequen-tially on one occasion, whereas he can acquire and retain complicated arguments at a single hearing. As we might expect, there is a close relationship between the finding that people can retain larger bodies of knowledge and learn much more effectively when learning involves constructive rather than purely assimilative processes (Chapter 3), and the fact that meaningful learning is much more effective than rote learning. It is in conditions where the material being learned is meaningful, in the sense that it can be related and integrated in terms of the learner's existing structure of experience, that it becomes possible for his cognitive structure to be utilized in constructive and interpretive activities. In short, only when the material has meaning to him can the learner as an individual carry out those constructive mental activities that are so effective for human learning.

Some Handicaps to Meaningful Learning

Meaningful learning, when we define meaningful in terms of the learner's understanding, is the whole point and focus of the educational enterprise, yet one still encounters instances where rote learning and memorization are required of students, not only in schools but in universities as well. Presumably, most teachers try to make learning as meaningful as possible, but it is sometimes difficult to detect that material which is clearly meaningful to the teacher is not so meaningful to the learners. Ausubel's emphasis makes clear that it is the responsibility of the teacher to make sure that students really can understand material that is apparently meaningful to them, and the Dewey incident shows the results of failure to do this.

There are a few situations where learning that is important must inevitably be of a rote nature. When there is little opportunity for the material to be firmly related to the learner's cognitive structure that incorporates previous learning experiences, and there is little structure in the material, memorization that involves relatively little engagement of active cognitive processes on the part of the learner may be required. For example, in the case of second language learning it is essential to acquire a large number of vocabulary items, and meaningful learning may be restricted both because the relationships between foreign words and their native language equivalents are often somewhat arbitrary, and because there may be little in the way of structure or relationships between the different second language items. In other areas of learning, it may be useful to supplement meaningful learning with skills gained from rote memorization that promote useful immediate or automatic responses. For example, the shopkeeper who needs to calculate prices or make change quickly might find it useful to memorize multiplication tables; he will then be in a position to realize without delay that seven nickels make thirty-five cents. On the other hand, such memorization of multiplication should follow and not precede the acquisition of a meaningful understanding of number principles involved in multiplication. Learning multiplication tables is no substitute for such understanding. Even in those instances where essential learning must be of a relatively rote nature, there are devices known as mnemonic systems that can introduce some lower-order meaningfulness into the learning, and these are described in Chapter 10.

The knowledge that rote memorization procedures can sometimes be valuable does not justify their widespread use. It is still not uncommon to encounter situations in which children are required to memorize names of presidents, kings and queens, mountains, and capital cities. Occasionally, one finds teachers who demand that their students memorize poems "by heart" or "by rote" (verbatim). It hardly needs to be said that the main effect of such tasks is to produce in children a strong dislike of poetry, and this may generalize into a dislike of learning in school environments.

Even when learning tasks are apparently meaningful, children at school sometimes rely on strategies of rote memorization. There are a number of possible reasons for this. One is that some children acquire the belief that all learning is unpleasant, or at least all school learning, and for that reason a task that seems to demand learning is something to be got out of the way as soon as possible. Thus, a great deal of anxiety is often attached to learning situations. The learner has a need to reduce his anxiety, to get away from a situation which he finds unpleasant and frustrating, and he does this in the way which he has found most effective for him. We can see this happening in an illustration given by John Holt (1964).

> *Remember when Emily, asked to spell "microscopic," wrote MINCOPERT? That must have been several weeks ago. Today I wrote MINCOPERT on the board. To my surprise, she recognized it. Some of the kids, watching me write it, said in amazement, "What's that for." I said, "What do you think?" Emily answered, "It's supposed to be microscopic." But she gave not the least sign of knowing that she was the person who had written MINCOPERT. . . .*

> *What does she do in such cases? Her reading aloud gives a clue. She closes her eyes and makes a dash for it, like someone running past a graveyard on a dark night.*
>
> *(Holt, 1964, page 9.)*

Writing of another child, Holt says "She seems to find the situation of not knowing what to do so painful that she prefers to do nothing at all, waiting instead for a time when she can call for help the moment she gets stuck" (Holt, 1964, page 9). These learning situations are clearly perceived by the children simply as unpleasant situations to be avoided or from which to escape as quickly as possible. In this circumstance, a rote learning strategy might be more effective for dealing with the children's needs than meaningful learning. It is certainly sad that some children should find learning at school as unpleasant as they undoubtedly do, and learn that learning is something to be avoided, but this is inevitable when past failures diminish a student's confidence in his ability to learn at school. Glasser (1969) who sees the cause of many serious human problems in experiences of failure at school believes that schools have too often been guilty of needlessly exposing to experiences of failure children who have come to school eager to learn and confident in their ability. Ausubel points out that because of anxiety or a history of failure in a subject, some students feel that they cannot learn meaningfully and hence perceive no alternative to panic, except rote learning. The highly anxious learner's dominant need may be to escape from the situation as quickly as possible, and if the learner has little confidence in his learning ability, it is unlikely that meaningful learning will result. In addition,

> Some pupils may develop a rote learning set if they are under excessive pressure to exhibit glibness, or to conceal rather than admit, and gradually remedy, an original lack of genuine understanding. Under these circumstances it seems easier and more important to create a spurious impression of facile comprehension by rotely memorizing a few key terms and sentences than to try and understand what they mean.
>
> (Ausubel, 1968, page 38.)

We have shown that for meaningful learning to occur the material must be logically meaningful and the learner must be able to perceive it as being meaningful. Ausubel (1968) points out one additional requirement, that the learner has a meaningful learning set so that he regards the task as one requiring meaningful learning rather than as a memorization talk. This serves to indicate another reason why children in school may sometimes use a rote strategy even with content that appears to be highly meaningful to them. The students may have learned from sad experience that substantially correct answers, which happen to be dissimilar in precise wording to the original version, are not acceptable to some teachers. By the way of illustration, there is a scene in the film *No Reason to Stay* made by the National Film Board of Canada, in which the teacher asks "What were the four reasons I gave you yesterday for the spread of Christianity, in the order in which I gave them to you?" It is clear that if students are required to demonstrate not only meaningful learning of a particular idea or concept but precise word by word correspondence with the form in which material was presented by the teacher, they will be encouraged to learn by rote memorization. What they learn thereby may have little value for the students, but at least it keeps the teacher satisfied. Even in cases where it is genuinely important to know the correct answer to a particular question (and some educators think there is no one correct answer to most questions of real importance), it is usually absurd to insist on a particular wording. On the contrary, an effective way to aid meaningful learning is to express in one's own words what is acquired. The cognitive processes that are required in order to do this make it likely that the learner will effectively integrate the information in a meaningful manner, and serve as a check that the individual really understands what is being learned. The findings of experiments on note-taking, reported in Chapter 3, support this reasoning. We can hardly express something in different words if we do not understand it. Hence, it might be wise to actively discourage rather than encourage learners from aiming at verbatim correspondence with the form of learned materials.

Ausubel's suggestion that overemphasis on children getting "the right answers" may encourage the tendency to conceal lack of understanding is repeated by Holt (1964), who draws a distinction between "producers" and "thinkers."

> Schools and teachers seem generally to be as blind to children's strategies as I was. Otherwise, they would teach their courses and assign their tasks so that children who really thought about the meaning of the subject would have the best chance of succeeding while those who tried to do the task by illegitimate means, without thinking or understanding, would be foiled. But the reverse seems to be the case. Schools give every encouragement to producers, the kids whose idea is to get "right answers" by any and all

means. In a system that runs on "right answers," they can hardly help it. And these schools are often very discouraging places for thinkers.

(Holt, 1964, page 25.)

If adults place too much emphasis on right answers, rather than taking the more difficult course of trying to determine whether learners really do understand what they are being taught, children inevitably get the idea that what is most important is to produce the right answer, and not to undertake the active thinking and reasoning activities that are necessary for meaningful learning.

Organizers

What can be done in situations where learning would be valuable for an individual but where some of the conditions required for meaningful learning are absent? Meaningful learning necessitates the learner being able to relate new materials to his existing cognitive structure. In instances where this cannot be done, it is sometimes possible to provide additional material that will effectively "bridge the gap" between the new learning and the learner's existing knowledge. There are limits, of course. A 4-year-old child is unlikely to be able to learn meaningfully advanced calculus because he not only has insufficient specific knowledge to which the new information can be related, but also because the basic reasoning skills available to him are not sufficient to cope with this sort of learning. For less extreme situations, Ausubel has proposed the use of what he calls "Advance Organizers." Advance organizers are intended to serve a bridging function, to connect or relate what the learner already knows to new to-be-learned materials. The advance organizer is a body of material that *can* be related to the learner's existing knowledge, and which in turn provides a framework to which the knowledge that is to be acquired can now be connected. Another way to visualize advanced organizers is as forming relevant "anchoring" ideas. The organizers provide the learner with a sort of cognitive anchor to which new knowledge can be attached. In general, the organizers consist of "sets of ideas which are presented to the learner in advance of the body of (meaningful) material to be learned, in order to ensure that the relevantly anchoring ideas will be available" (Ausubel and Robinson, 1969, page 145).

There are two types of situations in which Ausubel advocates the use of advance organizers. First, when material that is unfamiliar but which is potentially meaningful is to be learned, an organizer will have a useful function if specifically relevant ideas are not presently available in cognitive structure. Secondly, there are some instances where the learner already has available ideas and skills that are relatable and relevant to the new material, but where the learner is not yet aware of their relevance. In this case, the role of the organizer is to make explicit to the learner the connection that can be made between the new material and what is already known.

Ausubel has carried out research on two distinct kinds of advance organizers. The first kind, which he calls "expository," is appropriate to situations where the new learning material is entirely new to the learner. The instance he gives is one in which the learner is expected to acquire knowledge of Darwin's theory which is initially quite unfamiliar to him. In this instance, the organizer might be a short body of knowledge whose content is intended to show how Darwin's ideas are related to the learner's general knowledge, and provide a framework of Darwin's major ideas, to form anchoring concepts for the detailed exposition of the theory. The second type, "comparative" organizers, are applicable in situations where the new learning material is not entirely novel. For instance, if the learning task was to acquire detailed knowledge of one technique of life-saving, and the learner already knew about a different method, the organizer might point out some of the similarities and dissimilarities between the two. Hence, in the following detailed presentation of the new technique, the learner would be able to make greater use of his existing knowledge about the other method than might formerly have been possible. This would help him relate and integrate the new knowledge.

A number of experimental studies have tested the effectiveness of each type of organizer. Ausubel (1968) carried out an experiment on the use of an expository organizer in connection with a prose passage which described properties of various types of steel. The passage to be learned was 2500 words in length and dealt with the metallurgical properties of plain carbon steel. It emphasized basic principles, such as the relationship between metallic grain structure and temperature, carbon content, and rate of cooling. The passage included both principles which were applied to technological processes, such as heat treatment and tempering, and important factual information, for instance, the exact critical temperatures involved. The topic was not familiar to the undergraduate students who participated in the experiment. For one group of subjects, the passage to be learned was preceded by an advance organizer, 500 words in length, containing background material for the learning passage presented at a higher level of abstraction, generality, and inclusiveness than the actual passage to be learned. The object of the advance organizer was to serve as an organizing or anchoring focus for the steel material and to relate it to existing cognitive structure, but the organizer contained no information that would give a direct advantage in answering the test questions on the steel passage. For the other subjects, who served as a control group, the 2500 word passage to be learned was preceded by a 500 word body of prose, consisting of historically relevant background material. Each group of students was allowed 35 minutes in which to study the 2500 word description of properties of carbon steel, and subjects' retention was tested three days later. It was found that the group of students who received the advance organizer performed better on a multiple-choice test than the other subjects, scoring on average, 16.7 out of 36, compared with 14.1 for the control group. One reason for using a historically relevant passage for the control group was that this is commonly done in textbooks in this area, presumably with the intention of increasing the student's interest. The results of the experiment suggest that the value of this sort of material is significantly less than that of the expository advance organizer.

A similar experiment was carried out to test the effectiveness of comparative advance organizers. In this study (Ausubel and Youssef, 1963), the subjects were required to learn passages containing information about Buddhism and Zen Buddhism. Advance organizers pointed out the principle similarities and differences between Christianity and Buddhism for the Buddhism passage, and between Buddhism and Zen Buddhism for the Zen Buddhism passage. As in the previous study, there was a control group of subjects who were given historical and biographical material prior to each passage. Again, the findings were that both passages were more accurately retained in the condition which incorporated an advance organizer than in the control condition, although with only one of the two types of material was the difference statistically significant.

In short, the findings of experiments testing advance organizers indicates that they can be effective in facilitating learning. The implication is that if pains are taken to relate new knowledge to the existing cognitive structure of the learner, more efficient learning will result. The primarily verbal character of the organizing materials typically used by Ausubel makes them most appropriate for relatively mature learners. For younger and less sophisticated learners, organizing experiences that take a concrete form would probably be more effective.

Bloom's Taxonomy

So far, although we have discussed the importance of active and constructive learner functions in interpreting, coding, relating, integrating, and the like, functions which have in common the emphasis on what the learner himself brings to, and how he himself influences the learning environment, we have been somewhat vague about the precise nature of these cognitive activities. Part of this vagueness is inevitable; it is possible to make guesses and hypothesize about the cognitive processes that underly human performance, but since cognitive processes cannot be directly observed the validity of the hypotheses remains in doubt. Certainly, various kinds of cognitive processes are involved in learning. To start, we can deal with information about the environment at lower or higher levels of abstraction. Transformations can be relatively simple or relatively sophisticated, and the kind of learning that occurs is related to the form of cognitive activity and to its degree of complexity. As a way of beginning to look into this question, it is useful to give a brief description of the "Taxonomy of Learning" devised by B. Bloom and others (Bloom, 1956). This taxonomy is not directly concerned with cognitive processes, but it describes learning outcomes in a manner which is consistent and helpful when one tries to infer such processes, and it has quite often been used and referred to in published investigations into school learning.

Bloom's taxonomy is in part an attempt to arrange educational behaviors from simple to complex. It contains six major classes arranged in order so that the behaviors at one level seem likely to make use of and be based on those of the lower levels. These are the major classes:

1. *Knowledge*
2. *Comprehension*
3. *Application*
4. *Analysis*
5. *Synthesis*
6. *Evaluation*

It is immediately apparent that the various levels roughly correspond to the degree and complexity of involvement by the learner in the task situation, although the categories refer primarily to *results* of cognitive processes rather than to the processes per se. We can say, for instance, that the learner has to carry out further and more complex reasoning activities in the instance of synthesis than in the case of simple acquisition of knowledge. Also, as Bloom emphasizes, the types of activities necessary for acquisition of knowledge are also necessary for the higher order activities. In one sense, levels of learning outcomes are hierarchically arranged; the ability to carry out the complicated types of operations are dependent on the performance of simpler types of tasks.

Bloom defines "knowledge" as involving the recall of specifics and universals, the recall of methods and processes, or the recall of a pattern structure or setting. If I can remember that William of Normandy invaded Britain in 1066, I have demonstrated knowledge, at least. An example given by Bloom of a question which tests the availability of knowledge is the following:

> *The Monroe Doctrine was announced about ten years after the*
>
> *1. Revolutionary War*
> *2. War of 1812*
> *3. Civil War*
> *4. Spanish-American War*
>
> *(Bloom, 1956, page 79.)*

Of course, understanding might go much deeper. Demonstration of knowledge about a topic by no means implies the absence of further capacities related to learning and thinking.

The second category in Bloom's taxonomy, "comprehension," relates to relatively simple understanding. This would include the ability to understand the literal message contained in a communication; to carry out simple translations, for example, translating mathematical verbal material into symbolic statements and vice-versa; to interpret, in the sense of reordering or rearranging meaningful material; and to extrapolate, for instance, in predicting continuation of trends. An example of a question used to test abilities at this level is the following:

> *A group of examiners is engaged in the production of a taxonomy of educational objectives. In ordinary English, what are these persons doing?*

A. *Evaluating the progress of education.*
B. *Classifying teaching goals.*
C. *Preparing a curriculum.*
D. *Constructing learning exercises.*

(Bloom, 1956, page 99.)

Bloom points out that this exercise involves translation of "taxonomy" to "classification," the less abstract term. Another example given by Bloom is in the form of a cartoon strip which portrays an episode in the life of its major character. The student is asked to explain the activities portrayed, first translating or interpreting in more abstract form the highly concrete events portrayed.

The category of behaviors that are labeled "application" refers to situations in which learners are required to use abstractions when no mode of solution is specified. Applying knowledge to new situations is one aspect of the phenomena called "transfer of training" to be discussed in Chapter 5, and Bloom and his collaborators (Bloom, 1956) consider that the general consensus is that training will transfer to new areas most readily if the learner is taught in such a way that he acquires effective methods of attacking problems. Examples of educational objectives that demonstrate application include:

The ability to apply social science generalizations and conclusions to actual social problems.

The ability to apply the laws of trigonometry to practical situations.

To develop some skill in applying Mendel's laws of inheritance to experimental findings on plant genetic problems.

The ability to relate principles of civil liberties and civil rights to current events.

(Bloom, 1956, page 124.)

A large number of questions are provided to demonstrate ways of evaluating learners' application skills. The following question is to be used in a situation whereby students are learning about the principles involved in the production of steam. In this question, it is necessary to make use of this knowledge in determining how the principles might apply to the possible circumstances described in each of the choices.

> When a geyser first begins to erupt, hot water over-flows at the orifice and this is followed by a rush of steam, mingled with hot water. The first overflow of hot water aids in the production of steam, because
> A. Less water needs to be heated.
> B. More water can seep into the fissure from the surrounding rocks.
> C. The higher the pressure, the greater the steam produced.
> D. The lower the pressure, the lower the temperature at which the steam is produced.
> E. The water which overflows is necessarily below 212°F in temperature.
>
> (Bloom, 1956, page 139.)

The other classes of learning outcomes, analysis, synthesis, and evaluation require progressively more complex capacities. As we have said, the various classes are not intended to relate directly to the cognitive processes involved; they are more closely based on the actual goals, the performance of the learner. The latter are clearly related to underlying cognitive processes involved, but are not identical. One might well quibble with some of the details of Bloom's taxonomy. Particularly at the higher levels, that is, analysis, synthesis, and evaluation, it is often very difficult to decide in which category to place a particular task, and it sometimes appears that tasks which Bloom places in the same category require extremely different types of thinking and learning. Perhaps a universally acceptable taxonomy is impossible at this stage. In any case, whether or not we accept the detailed points and ordering of Bloom's taxonomy, the general principle by which tasks, and by implication the underlying cognitive processes, can be arranged in varying orders of complexity, and hence of the involvement of the more complex cognitive processes, is most valuable. Of course, questions have a number of functions in learning besides those considered by Bloom, and a broader discussion of questions and the role of inquiry is provided in Chapter 10.

Cognitive Involvement

In describing situations where the most complex and sophisticated cognitive processes available to the learner are involved in a task, we might say that the learner is "cognitively involved" in what he is doing. Hence, cognitive involvement is defined in terms of both the degree of complexity of the task at hand, and the extent to which the learners most highly developed reasoning processes are brought to bear on the task.

Degree of cognitive involvement, as an indicator of the complexity of processing activities, is thus an important determinant of the effectiveness of learning activities. In other words, the greater the prominence and complexity of constructive learner activities in coding, interpreting, integrating, and otherwise dealing with information in the environment, the more powerful the effect is likely to be, measured in terms of learning. Cognitive involvement is not intended to be the kind of concept that provides precise measures of learner processes. Its function is to draw attention to the fact that there are close relationships, albeit ones that cannot at present be precisely measured or specified, between a person's cognitive activities and the learning outcomes.

The nature of learning outcomes under different degrees of cognitive involvement will be roughly related to the categories in Bloom's taxonomy. Cognitive involvement is similar in denotation to "activity" in learning, but it is distinct in that the adjective "cognitive" excludes activities which have indirect rather than direct effects on learning. Other activities, such as underlining words in a textbook, may help the learner pay attention to a task, and thus facilitate learning. Some of these activities that learners carry out in forms of programmed instruction (see Chapter 10), such as providing one-word answers or pressing buttons, may contribute to learning because they fulfill the function of gaining or maintaining the attention of the learner. The concept of cognitive involvement is not intended to include such functions.

Discovery Learning

Ausubel makes a distinction between "discovery learning" and "reception learning." He uses the term discovery learning to refer to situations in which the learner to a large extent comes on what is acquired by himself, in other words makes some sort of a discovery. In reception learning, the material is presented to the learner in a relatively complete form. Ausubel points out that reception learning, by this definition, is by no means necessarily meaningless, nor need it be acquired by the learner in a rote or passive manner. He suggests that because reception learning situations have often been ones in which the learner has a particularly passive role, and in which there is often no great effort to ensure that the learner does much to process the information in ways that result in deep understanding, educators have tended to equate reception learning with rote learning and memorization. However, reception learning can be highly meaningful, and discovery learning, while it can be quite valuable, is often very wasteful. If everyone had to discover all knowledge and skills for himself, there would be no cultural transmission of knowledge from one generation to the next, and the advances that have taken place in civilization would simply not occur. We might add that it is precisely because reception learning is possible, that is to say because we have available ways of learning in addition to discovery learning, that civilization and the increase of knowledge and understanding from one generation to another can take place. In short, the fact that we have escaped from dependence on discovery learning alone has led to culture and civilization.

Certainly, there is nothing in any way new about discovery learning. What is perhaps new is the increasing realization of the fact that when other methods of acquisition are used, it is very easy for knowledge to be presented in a way which is perceived by the learner as being sterile, or irrelevant, so that the learner does not become cognitively involved with the material. We can certainly increase the efficiency of communicating knowledge when we avoid relying solely on discovery learning, but at the same time, it is necessary to be careful that what is being communicated is in a form that remains highly meaningful to the learner.

Logically, it would appear that discovery learning approaches are most appropriate in situations where reception methods are unlikely to bring about a high degree of cognitive involvement on the part of the learner, leading to meaningful learning. For instance, when learners are very young, or when the subject matter is quite unfamiliar it is likely that the abstract form of verbal presentation that is associated with reception learning would not be perceived as highly meaningful to the learner. In such a situation, a discovery approach, involving concrete experiences for the learner, is more likely to be understandable to the learner and engage his interest and involvement. On the other hand, in the case of a mature student presented with learning material for which he has already adequate background knowledge, presentation of materials in a form appropriate for reception learning, as in book form, may be perfectly adequate to ensure the learner's interest and hence engage active cognitive processes. In this case, reception learning might well be much more economical than a more time-consuming discovery approach.

The concept of discovery learning has never been sharply defined, and this explains some of the ambiguity and confusion that is present in discussions on the role of discovery learning in education. The meaning of the term "discovery" is simple enough, but its application to educational practice is less simple. One problem is that in a learning situation discoveries can vary from those which are relatively spontaneous on the part of the learner, requiring little structuring and support by the teacher, to those in which the situation is carefully prepared so that the student is placed in a situation whereby he is led to make a "guided" discovery. Thus, the nature of the student's discovering activities is strongly affected by the amount of structure in the learning situation. In school, few if any learning situations are completely unstructured; simply placing a few books in the classroom provides an element of structure, and unless the teacher is entirely silent, her activities are likely to suggest directions in which learning will take place.

The preceding remarks make understandable Bruner's (1966) wry comment that

> I am not quite sure I understand anymore what discovery is and I don't think it matters very much. But a few things can be said about how people can be helped to discover things for themselves.
>
> (Bruner, 1966a, page 101.)

Glaser's (1966) attempt to provide a definition at first appears uncomfortably circular.

> Learning by discovery is defined usually as teaching an association, a concept, or rule which involves "discovery" of the association, concept or rule.
>
> (Glaser, 1966, page 14.)

However, he is able to point out two important aspects:

> When one examines the task situations and instructional sequences that have been called discovery and that have been contrasted with discovery, what are the outstanding features. . . . First, a learning-by-discovery sequence involves induction. This is the procedure of giving examples of a more general case which permits the student to induce the general proposition involved. . . . Second, in using the discovery method, the imposition of a structured instructional sequence is minimized in order to provide a relatively unguided sequence onto which the individual imposes his own structure.
>
> (Glaser, 1966, page 15.)

One might object that inducing a proposition from examples provided by the teacher constitutes a somewhat narrow, restricted form of discovery, and that avoiding structured instructional sequences does relatively little on its own to facilitate discovery. Glaser, however, does a useful service by providing some guidelines in this area.

The question is sometimes asked, and experiments have been designed to try and answer the question, is the discovery method better than some other method? There are a number of difficulties with the question itself. First, there probably are as many methods of discovery as there have been things that have been discovered. Secondly, the method which is better depends on what one wants to do. It is rather like asking whether guns are better than butter. If one wants to make cakes butter is likely to be more useful, but it is not effective for killing people. In education, careful specification of objectives is important.

For these reasons it is not surprising that the findings of experiments comparing the effectiveness of discovery and other approaches to learning have often been inconclusive. Gagné and Brown (1961) carried out an experiment comparing different methods for the learning of number problems. Students in all groups received an introductory program providing prerequisite basic skills and principles. Next, one group was provided with rules, together with specific examples. A second group was required to discover the principle for solving the problems, with relatively little guidance, and the third group used guided discovery, going through a series of steps designed to help them find the principle for solving the problems. A problem-solving test was used to evaluate learning, and it was found that the guided discovery group had the best scores. The other discovery method was more effective than giving rules and examples, and the authors suggested that the effectiveness of the guided discovery group lay in the fact that it required learners to state and practice the concepts necessary for solving new problems. Corman (1957) varied the amount of guidance given in learning to solve matchstick problems, providing no, some, or much information about the method and principle needed for solution. He found that success in learning the principle was directly related to the amount of information about the principle provided, and this result also applies to ability to verbalize the principle. Generally, providing information facilitated application of the principle to new problems, but Corman found that the effect of information varied with problem difficulty and with the ability of the subjects. For the more able subjects, instructions which included much information were most effective, but less able subjects performed equally well in the different conditions.

Of the other experimental studies in this area, some report findings which favor discovery approaches, some favor relatively structured teaching methods, and perhaps the majority report no consistent differences. The rather confused state of research in this area is indicated by Ausubel's and Robinson's (1969) statement:

> There is no simple way of "adding up" the results of the various experiments. The principal difficulty is that these studies vary in many significant details, the most important of which are probably the amount of actual guidance or direction in the "guided discovery" treatment, and the taxonomic level of the task involved (for example, comprehension, application, problem solving). In addition, it is not always clear—even in the published research reports, unfortunately—whether all treatment groups received an equal amount of learning time or, if they did, how the most "directed" group could have been profitably employed on the task to be learned while the most "undirected" group went through the time-consuming task of formulating the principles themselves.
>
> (Ausubel and Robinson, 1969, page 499.)

There are some problems concerning the appropriate criteria of success following different methods. Discovery learning implies more than a method by which knowledge is acquired. By discovery one does not merely acquire knowledge, but one learns about acquiring the knowledge. If the only reason for having scientific knowledge was to make available the particular body of information and facts that were known, discovery learning could be justified only if it contributed effectively to the acquisition of such knowledge. On the other hand, if among the reasons for encouraging students to learn, say, science, is the feeling that knowing about processes in scientific development and thinking in the ways that lead to scientific understanding are valuable things to learn, there might be justification for such emphasis on the use of discovery methods.

As is the case with several fashionable phrases in education, discovery learning means slightly different things to different people. Rather than asking whether discovery approaches are good, bad, or indifferent, it might be more useful to examine the processes that seem to be present in situations to which the phrase is applied, and see how these relate to our knowledge of the conditions that are useful and effective in learning.

The discovery method is generally used in connection with rather concrete physical activities. Perhaps the phrase is in some respects an unfortunate one, implying rather dramatic goings on, with sudden "Eureka" effects, and the like. One often uses the word to describe situations where learners are doing things with their hands, and physical contact and concreteness are certainly valuable for some types of learning, particularly with children.

It is possible to use the word discovery more broadly to include discovery that is purely "in the mind." One difficulty with the phrase discovery learning is that it largely describes the situation "from the outside" of the learner. What is needed are descriptions of what is happening in the mind of the learner, and this may be largely independent of whether another person would describe the learning method as discovery learning, reception learning, or whatever. In short, what we are suggesting is that what matters is how the learner acts in the situation, the extent to which he is cognitively involved. Insofar as concepts such as discovery learning and reception learning tend to draw attention to the externals of the teaching situation, we may gain by temporarily putting them aside, and attempting to view more directly the mental activities of the learner.

The reasons why some discovery learning situations are effective are largely the same as the factors stressed in the earlier discussion of constructive cognitive activities in learning. Compared with other methods, discovery learning situations are more effective when they bring about a higher level of cognitive involvement in the learner, and the extent to which a discovery method contributes to cognitive involvement will depend on the particular method and subject matter, and on characteristics of the learner, but as a broad generalization we have suggested that the frequently concrete, physical and occasionally "dramatic" activities that are associated with discovery learning methods tend to be more effective the younger a learner is, and the more naive he is in respect to the principles or concepts being discovered. In conclusion, it is what happens inside the learner that is important; discovery approaches may sometimes provide the best means of bringing about a high degree of learner participation and involvement, but reception methods of presentation may be equally or more effective in instances when learners can understand material presented in written form.

Chapter 5

Structure and Transfer in
Human Learning and Development

In this chapter we extend the description of human learning, looking more closely at the organization and structure required for the acquisition of complex knowledge and skills. This leads to a discussion of transfer of learning. In turn, human development depends on learning appropriate skills in an order that makes it possible for new learning to build on existing capacities.

Hierarchies and Organization

In the previous chapter, discussing Bloom's taxonomy, we pointed out that success at the higher levels of learning objectives depends on prior competence in the more simple capacities. A person cannot synthesize unless he has some knowledge, any more than one can run before he can walk. We can say that cognitive abilities are vertically organized, and in this respect the concept of "hierarchical" organization is helpful. There are many different kinds of hierarchies, but a hierarchy can be closely defined as a system in which there is organization at different levels, and in which events at a higher level are dependent on the lower levels, but cannot be predicted solely on the basis of knowledge about the lower levels. An army is an example of a hierarchically organized system. The chain of command goes down through various levels, starting at the top. Events at the lower levels are to some extent governed by decisions made at a higher level, and at the same time the lower levels will influence what is done at higher levels. (The commander with an army of starving, ill-trained soldiers will make different battle decisions than those made by the leader of a crack corps.) On the other hand, however much we know about the lower levels of organization, we can never exactly predict activities at the higher levels. (The commanding officer always has some freedom of choice.)

Hierarchical organizations are commonly encountered in scientific investigations of complex phenomena. We observe hierarchical organizations in physiology. The patterns of activity in simple "instinctive" animal behavior are often hierarchically organized (Tinbergen, 1951), and there is hierarchical organization in the decisions and plans by which men govern their activities (Miller, Galanter, and Pribram, 1960). One of the criticisms of behaviorist psychology (see, for example, Koestler, 1967) is that confining scientific data to observable, quantifiable, behavioral responses restricts one to studying the lower levels of phenomena that are organized in hierarchies. Since one cannot predict activities of a higher level on the basis of the knowledge of lower levels alone, we may impose a restriction on the sorts of understanding that are obtainable. To return to the military analogy, although detailed knowledge about the quality of the various private soldiers that make up an army will certainly be valuable in understanding military organization, that knowledge alone is insufficient. Or to use a different analogy, if we want to understand the principles of building brick houses, knowledge about bricks, although certainly valuable, is not sufficient. It is also necessary to know about the ways in which the bricks are organized. Assuming that the observable responses in human behavior often form a lower level of hierarchically arranged activities, and thus have a place within the governing hierarchy somewhat analogous to that of the private soldiers in an army, or the bricks in a building, one can appreciate that there is a limit to the utility of knowledge about simple behavioral responses, as a basis for understanding all aspects of human psychology.

Hierarchical organization provides a number of advantages in situations where complicated organized functions are necessary. A thoughtful discussion of the roles and characteristics of hierarchical structures in living matter is provided by Koestler (1967). Among his conclusions is that "the whole lifetime of the earth would be insufficient for producing even an amoeba—unless one proceeds hierarchically from simple sub-assemblies to more complex ones" (Koestler, 1967, page 47.) He concludes, "We can safely assume that wherever there is life, it must be hierarchically organized."

Gagné's Approach

Hierarchical organization is especially important in the cognitive activities that are necessary for learning. To say that learning must be "structured" for the acquisition of knowledge is something of a cliché, but it is important to consider the "vertical" nature of structures in learning. Ausubel's discussion of "Advance Organizers" indicates the need for materials that provide a bridging function between the learner's existing knowledge and cognitive skills and the desired learning objectives, but it is important to avoid underestimating the complexity of the connections. Rather than a simple unidimensional bridge, it might be more realistic to think in terms of multidimensional connecting structures with different levels of learning dependent on the availability of simpler skills. Learning, as it were, builds upwards as well as across, as Gagné (1965) indicates.

> In order to determine what comes before what, the subject must be analyzed in terms of the types of learning involved in it. The acquisition of knowledge is a process in which every new capability builds on a new foundation established by previously learned capabilities. . . . A student is ready to learn something new when he mastered the prerequisites; that is, when he has acquired the necessary capabilities through preceding learning.
>
> (Gagné, 1965, page 25.)

Figure 2 is an illustration by Gagné showing how some subskills required for reading might be hierarchically organized. The figure is practically self-explanatory. Success at the skills on each level requires the prior ability to perform the tasks at the level below, which, of course, depends on achievement at the lower levels.

Gagné has described eight different types or *varieties* of learning. He proposes that each variety begins with a different state of the organism and ends with a different capability for performance. He takes pains to emphasize a point we have made in Chapter One, that there are large differences between different types of learning. He considers that great confusion has arisen from the erroneous assumption in educational psychology that all learning is basically the same. Gagné's varieties of learning are

1. *signal learning*
2. *stimulus response learning*
3. *chaining*
4. *verbal association*
5. *discrimination learning*
6. *concept learning*
7. *rule learning*
8. *problem solving*

Clearly, these are not entirely unrelated to the categories in Bloom's taxonomy, although the latter is more directly concerned with behavioral objectives, in terms of performance and tasks, whereas Gagné's varieties relate to conditions of learning. Gagné's eight types of learning differ from each other in the prerequisite learnings required. Each type depends on the availability of simpler learning capacities. Problem solving, for instance, requires a prior understanding of rules, and involves the combination of ideas.

Concept learning involves the classification of events so that a learner is able to make a common response to a whole class of stimuli, and to do this necessitates distinguishing the

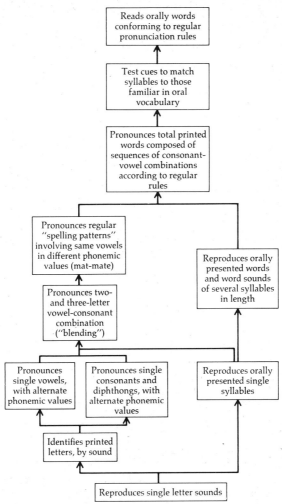

**Figure 2. A learning hierarchy for a basic reading skill
("decoding") devised by R. M. Gagné**

From *The Conditions of Learning* 2nd edition by Robert M. Gagné.
Copyright © 1965, 1970 by Holt, Rinehart and Winston, Inc. Reproduced
by permission of Holt, Rinehart and Winston, Inc.

properties of objects, a form of discrimination learning. In general the eight types of learning are distinct but interdependent, the simpler varieties being prerequisites for the more complex types.

Most of the elements of learning hierarchies for relatively advanced skills, such as the structure shown in Figure 2, require the more complex varieties of learning, such as rule learning and concept learning. Pointing out that the topics of school instruction possess hierarchical organization, Gagné (1970) states that learning the rules that form instructional objectives requires the previous learning of other rules, in addition to prerequisite learning, in the form of concepts, discriminations, verbal sequences, and down to simple connections.

In discussing the implications of hierarchical organization for learning in schools, Gagné says:

> The subjects of school instruction possess hierarchical organizations with respect to required types of learning. Each can be analyzed to reveal prerequisite learnings that grow progressively simpler as one works downward from principles to Ss→R connections. The learning of the principles that are usually the most obvious objectives of instruction requires a previous learning of other principles, and these in turn require prerequisite concepts, multiple discriminations, verbal sequences, chains, and Ss→R connections. The implications for the design of instruction are quite clear. If learning at any level is to occur with greatest facility, care and attention must be paid to the prerequisite of such learning. It will be difficult for the child to learn the definitions (principles) of geometry unless he has previously acquired all the concepts of line, angle, triangle, intersection, and so on. It will be difficult for a learner to acquire the principles of any specific signs unless he already knows some more basic principles of classifying, measuring and inferring. The systematic planning of instruction in the elementary school grades in terms of such capability

will probably have a marked positive effect on facility of learning the more advanced principles of all school subjects.
                                                          (Gagné, 1965, page 202.)

Gagné suggests that as a practical step in trying to use one's knowledge about the organization of learning to devise appropriate instructional strategies, it might often be useful to proceed backwards by analysis of the final task, working down through the various necessary levels in hierarchical organization. We can start with the required end product of learning, and ask what kinds of capabilities would the individual learner have to possess in order to perform the learning or problem solving task successfully on the basis of straightforward instructions. The need for careful specification of objectives, indicated by Mager's (1962) statement that "if you're not sure where you're going, you're liable to end up someplace else" becomes especially clear when methods of programmed instruction are used (see Chapter 11).

Having specified learning objectives, one can proceed by asking what in turn would be required for the subordinate stage to be possible, and so on. Starting with the required goal it is possible to work back to the knowledge and capacities that the learner already has available. When we do this, asking at each stage what kind of capability the individual would have to have in order to perform the task, the answer indicates a new kind of task which is probably simpler and more general. Gagné would say that by this procedure we have identified "subordinate knowledge" which is essential for the performance of the more advanced task, and we can repeat the procedure again with the newly defined surbordinate task, asking once more what would the individual need to know in order to be capable of *this* task, given only instructions. Gagné suggests that by proceeding in this way from level to level, a hierachy of subordinate knowledge is defined, growing increasingly simple and at the same time increasingly general as the defining process continues.

Multilevel hierarchies of knowledge occur most often in

areas, such as science and mathematics, where understanding depends on the learner proceeding in a relatively fixed sequence from simple concepts to more and more complex rules. Skills that are dependent on such hierarchies are unlikely to be acquired in the absence of careful instruction. An example of such a skill, that *can* be learned by most 4-year-old children, but frequently is not acquired until much later, is telling time. Abilities that do not depend upon multilevel hierarchies of learning are more likely to be acquired without specific instructions. For instance, the young child in a foreign language environment will gain language skills on his own. In this instance, learning does not depend on hierarchically structured rules and skills being presented in a particular sequence.

In order to gain real benefit from ideas applying to curriculum development that have been put forward by learning theorists, the teacher needs to *use* them in a practical context. The experience of putting into practice knowledge about Gagné's descriptions of learning hierarchies, or Bloom's taxonomy, or Ausubel's advance organizers, for example, will give the educator much more insight into the strengths and limitations of the various proposals than can be gained simply from reading about them.

It is possible to carry out experiments which test the validity and utility of Gagné's thinking and descriptions concerning hierarchical organization in learning. For instance, we can test the validity of a particular hierachy by finding out whether children who can perform correctly on the end goal can also carry out the subskills described in the hierarchy. Also, we can predict that the ability to carry out one of the subskills described in a hierarchy designed to describe a particular learning performance will be necessary for carrying out tasks at higher levels. Wiegand (1970), who constructed a learning hierarchy of subordinate capacities for a task which consisted of a science problem, found that the subjects who could successfully perform the highest order skill could also perform the simpler related skills in the hierarchy, and he showed that complex scientific concepts can be acquired fairly quickly if all the necessary subordinate capacities are acquired. Presentation of subordinate knowledge in turn facilitates the learning of facts (Gagné, 1969; Gagné and Wiegand, 1970), having a function in some respects similar to that of the advance organizers used by Ausubel.

Related to the emphasis on hierarchical organization in learning are Bruner's (1960) remarks on the role of structure. He has developed Dewey's insight that "Education is by its nature an endless circle or spiral" (Dewey, 1929, page 77), in formulating what is called the "spiral curriculum." Bruner thinks that areas of knowledge, such as mathematics, biology and language, have certain structures which it is important for students to understand, since

> *Grasping the structure of a subject is understanding it in a way that permits many other things to be related to it meaningfully. To learn structure, in short, is to learn how things are related.*
>
> (Bruner, 1960, page 7.)

Starting with the hypothesis that any subject can be taught to any child in some honest form—a hypothesis which has caused a great deal of controversy, at least some of it based on misunderstanding—Bruner considers that there are many areas to which children should be introduced at an early age. They could return to or revisit the same topics and areas at later stages, making use of their developing powers for abstract understanding, and for integration on the basis of progressively more complex bodies of knowledge. Taking the teaching of literature as an example, Bruner considers it desirable for children to gain awareness of the meaning of human tragedy and a sense of compassion for it. He asks:

> *Is it not possible at the earliest appropriate age to teach the literature of tragedy in a manner that illuminates but does not threaten? There are many possible ways to begin: through a retelling of the great myths, through the use of children's classics, through presentation of and commentary*

> *on select films that have proved themselves . . . what mat-*
> *ters is that later teaching builds upon earlier reactions to*
> *literature, that it seeks to create an even more explicit and*
> *mature understanding of the literature of tragedy. Any of*
> *the great literary poems can be handled in the same way,*
> *or any of the great themes—be it the theme of comedy or*
> *the theme of identity, personal loyalty, or what not.*
>
> *(Bruner, 1960, page 53.)*

The emphasis on the importance of building on previous knowledge is common to the thinking of Gagné and Bruner. Gagné shows how learning can be ordered for the acquisition of precise, structured skills, as in science and mathematics. Bruner's statements indicate the possibility of extending the same broad principles to areas, such as literature, which do not have such a precisely structured form. He makes clear that in literature, history, and the arts simple concrete understanding can form a basis for higher and more abstract levels of comprehension.

Transfer of Learning

Psychologists and educators have expended a lot of energy worrying over problems and matters having to do with what is generally called "transfer of learning" or "transfer of training." Underlying the interest in such problems is the assumption that what is learned in the classroom is transferable to other situations and is useful in acquiring new learning, and the concern to ensure that such transfer really takes place. Transfer is generally assumed to occur when some prior learning influences subsequent learning (Kelly, 1967). Defined as such, the concept of transfer is somewhat broad, and since virtually any learning by an individual can influence some future learning, it is questionable whether the concept has a meaning which is both unambiguous and distinct from that of the simple word "learning."

At all stages of education we make assumptions, sometimes explicit, usually implicit, about the transferability of what is learned in school. In their most simple form, such assumptions have been expressed in the argument that the mind has certain mental "faculties"—reasoning, will, memory, and so on —which can be improved by training. Suggestions that learning Latin or memorizing poetry are useful for developing "reasoning abilities" or "the memory" are based on this sort of thinking. In fact, quite apart from the naïveté in the logic of such reasoning, there has been ample empirical evidence to refute it before 1900.

William James (1890) carried out an experiment to determine whether the activity of memorizing large amounts of poetry would result in increased generalized ability to memorize poetry. James and his students started by memorizing a poem by Victor Hugo, and measured the time it required. For the next month, they gave themselves daily practice in memorizing works by other poets. To determine the effectiveness of this practice, at the end of the month they memorized another poem by Victor Hugo, of identical length and similar form to the first one, and again measured the amount of time required for memorization. In fact, there was a tiny decrease in the time required to learn the poem, but it was not substantial enough to give support to the idea that one can gain any general increase in memorization ability from practice in memorizing. James concluded that one's native retentiveness is unchangeable.

In the light of modern knowledge, questions about transfer of learning have to be formulated more precisely. In asking whether learning A transfers to the situation B, we have to specify the exact tasks and knowledge gained or required in the two situations, and we have to be precise about the nature of what is transferred. For instance, it is clear that learning the alphabet may "transfer" to reading skills, since knowledge of letters is a prerequisite for reading. Also, a person who has experience driving a car will have greater initial competence driving a tractor than someone who has no such experience. In each instance, it is true that something has "transferred" from one situation to the other. On closer examination, it is apparent that the nature of that which transfers differs so much between the two situations, that the word "transfer," which they share, serves to mask somewhat fundamental differences. Again, in the learning hierarchies described by Gagné, achievement at one level depends on "transfer" of prerequisite abilities, but the nature of the transfer is very different to that of the other examples. It is clear that to avoid ambiguity one has to carefully specify the type of transfer that is under investigation.

When we ask questions about transferability of learning, we are usually interested in finding out the extent to which what is being learned or acquired in one situation is affecting performance in circumstances other than those of the particular situation in which the knowledge was acquired. First, we might want to know the extent to which the knowledge acquired can be used in a variety of situations. Here, the basic concern is with what Ausubel (1968) calls the "substantiveness" of learning. The children described in Chapter 4 who knew that the state of the center of the earth is igneous fusion, but who could not say what they would find if they dug a deep hole into the middle of the earth, did not have substantive knowledge, in that they were unable to answer a question when its precise form was altered. Another type of phenomenon is illustrated by a student who can use mechanical principles in his reasoning to answer a problem in an engineering course, but who cannot use the same principles in a situation to which their applicability is slightly less explicit, for instance, in fixing his own backyard. One has to learn not only to use knowledge gained from one situation or discipline in circumstances that are superficially different from that in which learning took place, but also to gain skills and habits involved in seeking ways to utilize knowledge in a variety of situations, thus extending the range of instances in which various capabilities can be used.

Another type of transfer occurs when knowledge or skills become a basis for further knowledge or the development of further skills. The fact that we build on previous knowledge is basic to our thinking about learning in education, and the contributions of psychologists as Ausubel and Gagné have been largely concerned with specifying the conditions in which this type of transfer occurs. All learning is change in the sense that the acquisition of new learning alters the learner's existing structure of cognitive capacities; the wall with a new brick is different to what it was previously. If a particular change in cognitive structure is important for a particular future situation, the previous learning will influence the learning that will occur in the new situation. Hence, instead of asking whether transfer of learning occurs, it is more helpful to discover whether the change that accompanies a specific learning experience is one that will influence what happens in a particular new circumstance. Some changes in cognitive structure resulting from learning are more far-reaching than others. My knowing that there is a green sheet of paper on the corner of my desk just might slightly alter my behavior in a small range of potential situations, but for practical purposes it is unlikely that this knowledge will affect future learning. On the other hand, a young child who learns that he can attract attention and praise by using the word "Mommy" may make considerable use of this learning, both in extended use of the particular word and in language development more generally. In addition, in speaking of transfer it is useful to distinguish between situations where what is learned has direct applicability to other contexts, and those in which the transfer is indirect. Knowledge about physiology has direct utility in a physiological examination, but its application to medical practice is less direct.

In summary, the confused issue of transfer of training is best considered by looking at the various sorts of changes that constitute learning, and asking what effect these changes will have on future situations. Such changes are likely to be particularly important where learning is hierarchically structured. For instance, if the final goal is to be able to calculate volumes of liquid, and a requirement in the hierarchy of skills subordinate to that goal is to be able to measure length and height, we can assume the ability to make these measurements is a necessary prerequisite for calculation of volume.

Skills for Human Learning

Granted the naïveté of discussing cognition in terms of various faculties, and the related "mental discipline" approach, it is conceivable that there are certain rather general skills that can be utilized in a range of situations requiring, for instance, thinking or problem solving. Is it realistic to talk about "improvement of thinking," for example? Can we develop "critical-thinking" abilities? If a skill or capacity that can be explicitly defined is likely to be useful in a wide range of learning situations, students should be encouraged to learn it. However, concepts such as "problem solving," "critical-thinking," or "reasoning," are broad and imprecise, and each involves a large number of different skills. Rather than talking about improving thinking, it would be more useful to specify the various underlying skills and capacities that are required, and to ensure they are learned. It may be useful to have labels to describe broad outcomes of learning, but to make decisions about learning in school, it is necessary to be more exact. The fairly precise categorization of learning processes and outcomes provided in Bloom's and Gagné's systems have considerable value here. If a term such as "critical-thinking," could be given a precise operational definition in terms of the specific capacities required, the definition might form a basis for developing curricula that lead to mastery of the necessary skills and capacities. However, terms such as "critical thinking" or "problem solving," are often used without adequate definition, and it is then impossible to provide criteria for the adequacy of the learning experience. Precise specification of learning outcomes is very desirable. Skills required in thinking and reasoning cannot be learned *in vacuo:* one cannot learn problem-solving skills without solving particular problems, and partly because of this, the acquisition of skills required in problem solving and reasoning often occurs simultaneously with the acquisition of specific knowledge. Although it is very useful to discriminate between different varieties of learning outcomes and different types of processes involved in learning, in reality the learning of several skills and processes as well as the acquisition of knowledge, may take place simultaneously.

Research by Harlow (1949) on "learning sets" illustrates a type of experience whereby learning skills can transfer to a variety of situations. Harlow carried out a range of experiments on learning sets, using children as subjects in some, and monkeys in others. A typical study was one in which monkeys were presented with three objects, two of which were similar in some dimension, and the third different. The task was to respond consistently to the different or "odd" object, a situation not unlike the "one of these things is not like the other" problems on Sesame Street. After the first task, a different set of objects would be presented, but again with two similar and one different. It was found that after a few oddity problems, the monkeys could solve other problems of the same form very quickly. The animals had learned a skill which is applicable to a whole class of problems.

Bruner (1957) has drawn attention to transferability of learning skills in situations similar to those which involve learning sets. If a rat learns to wend its way through a maze by a route that goes *Left, Right, Left, Right*, it is subsequently likely to learn, in a shorter time, the sequence *Right, Left, Right, Left*. We can ask whether this learning to alternate is specific to spatial tasks, or whether a more generalized alternating ability has been acquired. Has the organism a general alternation code that can be applied to all alternation tasks, or not? To answer this question one might set up a situation demanding nonspatial alternation, such as a maze in which the correct path is defined by alternate color choices, *Black, White, Black, White*, where color is independent of spatial position in the maze. Early success in this task would indicate the presence of a generic code. Bruner points out that although this can be described as an example of "transfer of training," in one sense nothing is really being transferred. In effect, the rat is simply learning a code that has applicability to a range of situations.

Transfer and the Structure of Complex Learning

Much recent curriculum reform has been explicitly concerned with transfer. The growing realization that the world is one in which things change and in which people have to make their own decisions has begun to lead to reduced emphasis on "coverage" of acquired knowledge and greater emphasis on acquisition of the skills required for independent inquiry. There is less concern with acquisition of factual information and greater concern with basic skills that are needed for understanding and learning.

Scandura (1969) claims that "knowledge had by a learner affects future learning *only* when this knowledge is prerequisite to the to-be-learned material." It is certainly true that this type of transfer is important, especially when learning sequences are hierarchically organized. Ausubel and Robinson (1969) use the phrase "vertical transfer," for instance, whereby learning at one behavioral level, for example, comprehension, facilitates learning at a higher behavioral level, for instance, problem solving. However, knowledge can also affect future learning in situations where the knowledge is not a vital prerequisite. Ausubel and Robinson discuss two other varieties of transfer. In "sequential transfer," the learner draws on past learning so that "an idea taught today will typically have some relationship to an idea taught tomorrow, and both ideas will have some relationship to the ideas taught the next day" (Ausubel and Robinson, 1969, page 138). The transfer is essentially "horizontal," the learner remaining at the same behavioral level in making the transfer. This is also true in the case of the third category "lateral transfer." To illustrate lateral transfer, Ausubel and Robinson (1969) provide the example of a child who has been taught addition and subtraction with classroom materials, such as blocks and beads, and who can transfer his understanding to home situations as when calculating the number of eggs are left in a one-dozen carton when five are removed. Ausubel and Robinson suggest that lateral transfer is the most common kind of transfer to occur when skills and knowledge taught in school are used by the learner outside the school.

The three categories of transfer—lateral, sequential, and vertical—to some extent overlap the different varieties of transfer we have previously described, and some transfer circumstances cannot be placed exclusively in one of the three. However, as a simple means of categorizing varieties of transfer according to some major dimensions, this is a convenient and useful system.

Learning and Human Development

The progression from an account of transfer of training to a discussion of the role of learning in human development represents a change of emphasis rather than one of content. In discussing transfer, the stress is on relatively short-term, specific effects of learning; developmental issues are concerned with broader, long-term influences of experience.

Both biological and environmental factors undoubtedly contribute to human development, but there is considerable controversy existing about the relative importance of these two determinants. They interact in complex ways, so it is not possible to provide a simple numerical value for the weighting of each of the two. By analogy, in cake-making one cannot numerically describe the relative "importance" of the flour and the eggs ("the flour is twice as important as the eggs") because the resulting cake is not simply the sum of its constituents, but the end-product of complex processes in which they are both involved; likewise with human development. On the other hand, questions about the roles of learning and biological factors in development can be meaningful and important. To return to the cake analogy, although the effects of flour and eggs cannot be simply measured, it is true that six eggs and a pound of flour will produce a different outcome than a dozen eggs and half-a-pound of flour. In addition, it might be useful to know whether varying the amount of flour has greater or less effect on the outcome than varying the quantity of eggs. In short, changes in ingredients have large effects upon the end-product, however complex the interactions, and in the case of development in humans, it is particularly desirable to understand the effects of the various determinants, especially learning.

Although there is by no means universal agreement about the role of learning in human development, the last few years have seen an increasing tendency to recognize the central place of experience (learning) and to examine experience in studies of development. One influential factor has been the growing awareness of the effects of early experience on later abilities. Although, since Freud, it has been generally appreciated that the first years of life are in some respects crucial for later emotional growth and personality, it is only comparatively recently that experience in the early years has come to be seen as having equally crucial effects on subsequent intellectual capabilities. Fowler (1969) was unable to find one instance of any individual of high ability who did not experience intensive early stimulation as a central component of his development. In studies of "geniuses," when evidence exists, it is invariably found that the individual had an unusually vigorous early environment, often incorporating intensive early training (Engelmann and Engelmann, 1966).

A second cause of the increasing awareness of experience as a factor in child development has been the evidence that infants and young children are capable of learning many things earlier than they are customarily acquired (Staats, 1971), and that considerable learning can take place at a very early age (B. White, 1971). In the past, descriptions of average child development (for example, Gesell and Ilg, 1943) have been used as if they were yardsticks of "natural" development. In fact, there is no reason to assume that all infants will progress at a given rate, unless development is conceived as largely a biological process. For instance, Staats (1971) claims that given the appropriate environment, children can learn to speak much earlier than is normal, and he argues that such acceleration is desirable in view of the importance of language skills as a basis for further learning.

Those who stress biological determinants in development would argue against the acceleration of learning on the grounds that when learning precedes certain kinds of physiological maturation, it gives the learner no real advantage over other individuals. In an often cited experiment by Gesell and Thompson (1929), it was found that although a six-week perod of training in stair-climbing given to one member of a pair of twins resulted in an initial advantage over the other twin, the latter soon caught up, after receiving a shorter period of training at a later age. Similarly, McGraw (1940) observed that the one member of a pair of twins who was given early toilet training achieved no permanent advantage thereby. The implication drawn from such studies is that there is little point in accelerating early learning, since the appropriate age for learning is determined by physiological maturation. Against this, it is argued that although physiological maturation may be a limiting factor in some *motor* activities, such as stair-climbing and toilet-training, such maturation does not limit performance in *intellectual* skills among human infants. Hence, using such examples as a basis for advice about other types of learning may be unjustified.

Some of the strongest advocates of a position stressing the potency of environmental over biological factors in learning would recommend that in certain circumstances early learning is desirable even where, due to biological maturation, that same learning could be accomplished more easily at a later age. Thus, Staats (1971) argues that it would be worthwhile to teach infants to walk earlier than they customarily learn to do so. He does not deny that infants can learn without specific training, but claims that the child whose walking skills are accelerated will thereby have gained an ability that will help him cope with various aspects of his world.

> *Why be concerned about the development of such behaviors. . . . ? The answer is that these are basic skills which,*

*when acquired, will allow the child to learn other things
equally important to later adjustment and later learning.
The child who walks early, for example, can be introduced
to other experiences that will produce valuable learning,
social as well as intellectual, sensory-motor, and so on.**

Thus, an effect of the early learning of one skill may be to
open the child to experiences that are important for growth in
other areas. In the case of the stair-climbing and toilet-training
examples described earlier, the accelerated learning did not
bring about any such opportunities, and hence did not benefit
the children concerned. However, one can imagine a hypothetical example whereby climbing stairs brings the child into
contact with various new and valuable experiences. In such
circumstances, early practice in stair-climbing might be justi-
fiable, even if it were true that at a later age the child could
learn more quickly to climb stairs.

Some of the same considerations apply to the issue of
learning to read at an early age. Granted that there have been
some exaggerated or baseless claims about the possible results
of early learning, for instance that children can learn to read
before the age of two years, there is little doubt that most
children are capable of learning to read at the age of four
years given the appropriate training, and that children who
learn to read early maintain their lead in achievement over
school classmates of the same mental age who did not begin
to read until the first grade (Durkin, 1966). The argument
that children who learn to read early would suffer at school
from being bored or confused is not supported by the results
of Durkin's extensive study.

Just as in the case of stair-climbing or learning to walk, the
value to the child of being able to read at an early age will
depend on the use made of the skills. In reading, it is likely

* From *Child Learning, Intelligence, and Personality* by Arthur W.
Staats. Copyright © 1971 by Arthur W. Staats. Reprinted by permission of Harper & Row, Publishers, Inc. P. 58.

that most children who are sufficiently motivated to learn to read outside the structured school situation will also want to use their reading ability.

The possibility of accelerated early learning in young children raises problems concerning the desirability of such accelerations and the implications of knowledge about early learning for education at preschool levels. Detailed discussion of these issues is outside the scope of this book. Briefly, on the one hand are those who argue that although acceleration of intellectual growth through early learning is possible, it is nevertheless undesirable. They say that childhood is a time for freedom and play without the stress and pressure imposed by efforts towards early education; that precocious intellectual development without parallel social development is harmful; that Western culture already overvalues intellectual skills at the expense of affection and other capabilities, and that the child whose intellectual skills are ahead of those of other children of his age will be an embarrassment to his school teachers and will not be accepted by his peers. Those people, on the other hand, who favor increased early learning can claim that there is no definite evidence for any of the dire consequences of acceleration predicted by their opponents. Certainly, a parent's desire to increase the rate of learning in her child can result in the child feeling "pushed" or "pressured," but there is absolutely no reason why this has to be so, and there will remain ample opportunities for free play. Indeed, the mothers of young children know that children suffer from boredom in unfilled time, and the child who has a large number of skills will have available correspondingly large resources to fill his time. There is no doubt that "pushing" children to engage in activities that do not interest them is harmful. It is interesting to note Durkin's (1966) remarks about children who read early:

> Young children are much more responsive to help with reading that is the consequence of their own questions rather than of their parents' ambition or insecurity—or

whatever it is that prompts parents to make an arbitrary decision to teach preschoolers to read, without regard for the child's interest or the possibility of strain developing in the parent-child relationship.

(Durkin, 1966, page 135.)

Against the claim that accelerated early learning can cause a harmful discrepancy between intellectual and social development, it might be argued that there is no solid evidence for such a claim, and the implication that one can dichotomize between social and intellectual learning may be incorrect. Perhaps social and intellectual skills are to some extent interdependent and are acquired simultaneously. However, there is a large knowledge gap in this area. A similar lack of knowledge surrounds the question of whether the advanced learner faces more problems at school than his peers. Again, there is no real evidence, and on the side of the pro-early learning position, it can be argued that the child who has the most skills is likely to be resourceful and adaptive and less at the mercy of vagaries of individual teachers than his classmates. However, this is only conjecture. Against the objection that Western society already places too much emphasis on intellectual competence, it might be argued that the child will have to live in that society, and that whatever the individual teacher or parent might want to do to change it, it should not be at the child's expense.

All that is clear is that there are a number of separate arguments on this issue. Some of them can be resolved on the basis of existing evidence (for example, intellectual acceleration is possible), some would be answerable if evidence were available (for example, whether early learners have more difficulty in adjusting to present-day schools than other children), and some arguments reflect different opinions and philosophical positions concerning desirable roles for learning in human life (for example, how much value should be placed on intellectual capacities?), and are not decidable on the basis of any conceivable scientific evidence.

The work of Jean Piaget has provided a very large contribution to knowledge of intellectual development. He has made many studies incorporating vast numbers of observations of young children in naturalistic conditions, and the theories built on such observations have been extremely influential in child psychology. Since Piaget's research is largely directed at describing development and not at the role of learning, a description of his contributions is outside our present scope, but readers who are interested in the thinking of children and infants should seek out his books or consult some of the many interpretations, commentaries, and discussions of his work that have helped to communicate Piaget's ideas. A recommended presentation of Piagetian psychology is the book by John Flavell (1963). Some of Bruner's works help communicate Piaget's thought. Bruner has interpreted Piaget's thinking and has developed related ideas which more directly concern the role of learning in development (Bruner, 1960; 1966). Also, Bruner has developed separate theories which are strongly influenced by Piaget's contributions to investigate intellectual development (Bruner *et al.*, 1966).

The Role of Learning in Developmental Changes

Piaget describes various stages of human development, and although he has remained open about the extent to which learning influences development from one stage to the next, it has sometimes been assumed that the notion of developmental stages is incompatible with an approach that gives learning an important role in development. However, it is conceivable that some of the principles which have been useful in describing relatively specific learning achievements that occur over short periods can be extended to the types of long-term changes that we associate with development. For instance, some of the principles of hierarchical organization put forward by Gagné, described early in this chapter, apply to the lengthier sequences of learning by which children develop over longer periods of time. Gagné (1968) has noted that in situations where changes in capacities are studied with respect to relatively specific forms of behavior over limited periods of time, one generally calls the processes "learning" and "memory." The word "development" is used to refer to changes of capacity observed over a longer period of time. The processes are clearly related, although the distinction is useful. Gagné draws attention to the importance of inquiring into the relation of the types of change called learning, on the one hand, and those called development, on the other. Development, claims Gagné, is a result of an interaction of growth and learning, and within certain limitations behavioral development results from the cumulative effects of learning. Gagné suggests that learning makes cumulative contributions to the intellectual development of the human being, and he sees the child as progressing from one point to the next in his development as he learns an ordered set of capabilities which "build upon each other in progressive fashion through the processes of differentiation, recall, and transfer of learning" (Gagné, 1968, page 181). Much of what we learn takes the form of complex rules which require the existing understanding of simpler rules, and as might be expected from the earlier discussion of Gagné's ideas, the organization is seen by him as largely hierarchical. In fact, the principles which Gagné (1968) brings into use in discussing the cumulative role of learning in intellectual development are largely those which occur in his discussion of hierarchical organizations in relatively short-term learning situations. The differences in the underlying structural changes in learning and development are differences in generality and in the extent to which different sorts of learning are integrated, that is, they are differences of degree rather than kind. As Gagné says:

> The "stage" in which any individual learner finds him-
> self with respect to the learning of any given new capacity
> can be specified by describing (a) the relevant capabilities
> he now has; and (b) any of a number of hierarchies of
> capabilities he must acquire in order to make possible the
> ultimate combination of superordinate entities which will

achieve the to-be-learned task. In an oversimplified way, it may be said that the stage of intellectual development depends upon what the learner knows already and how much he had yet to learn in order to achieve some particular goal. Stages of development are not related to age, except in the sense that learning takes time.

(Gagné, 1968, page 189.)

This statement about the role of learning in far-reaching developmental changes gives weight and clarity to Ausubel's remark that,

If I had to reduce all of educational psychology to just one principle, I would say this: the most important single factor influencing learning is what the learner already knows. Ascertain this and teach him accordingly.

(Ausubel, 1968, frontispiece.)

Gagné (1968) provides a detailed account of the stages of learning required for a child who has initially available simple conceptual understanding of such things as a length of straight lines and width, to become capable of solving correctly the sorts of problems whose solution is regarded as indicating the stage that Piaget calls "conservation." Such a description takes a form similar to the Figure 2 on page 97, except that it is more complex in terms of the number of levels in the hierarchy, and in the degree of integration between different parts. Basically, however, what Gagné does is to task what children need to have learned in order to respond correctly to situations designed to test the abilities appropriate to that stage, and then he asks what prerequisite skills the child must have acquired in order to obtain the latter capacities, and so on, level by level. The lower levels require progressively less complex cognitive capabilities as one goes downwards, until one arrives at levels of functioning already available to the child.

By way of example, consider the ability to judge that the volume of a liquid is unchanged when a liquid is poured from one container to another container that is very different in shape. Many children below the age of about 7 are not able to judge volume independently of the shape of the container, and are said by Piaget to be unable to "conserve" in this situation. Gagné sets out to describe the specific intellectual skills that are necessary for a correct solution. He starts by stating that in order to "conserve" in a situation involving judging the volume of liquid in containers the child must know that volume is a function of length, width, and height. This understanding depends on knowledge of progressively simpler rules. Each of the simpler rules or skills is a prerequisite for understanding more complex rules. The result is a hierarchy similar in form to that shown in Figure 2. Whereas Piaget would describe the child who can perform correctly on the final task as a "conserver," Gagné (1968) would be inclined to state simply that the child has certain rather specific intellectual skills. Of course, it may be possible for the child to use those skills in situations not identical to the circumstances in which they were learned. Hence a child who can, in Piaget's term, "conserve" in a task involving water in rectangular containers will have acquired most of the skills to judge a similar task with sand and circular containers. Whereas a Piagetian would be inclined to state that the child can solve a range of "conservation" problems because he has reached the conservation stage, Gagné would prefer to describe the state of affairs by stating that the child has the skills that are required in common for solving various problems.

The word "readiness" is often invoked in discussing the education of young children. In learning to read, for example, it is claimed that there is little point in trying to teach some of the advanced skills until the child has reached a stage of "readiness" to learn them. There is nothing in the least objectionable about this, and it is certainly true that the ability to acquire complex skills depends on the learner having acquired simpler, subordinate skills. Unfortunately, the role of readiness in development has often been confused with that of biological determinants of maturation. One is told, for instance, that a given child is not being taught to read because he has not yet arrived at reading "readiness," the implication being that one must wait for some spontaneous growth process to occur, after which the teacher can go ahead with helping the child to learn to read. The point to realize is that for the vast majority of cognitive skills learned in schools, readiness does not arrive in the absence of learning, so the lack of readiness can generally be interpreted as indicating a need for additional learning, and not as an excuse for inactivity. There are *some* instances where skills depend on maturational processes to the extent that very early learning experiences have relatively little value, but by the age at which a child reaches school the physiological maturation necessary for cognitive learning has already occurred, and lack of readiness is remedied only by learning. As Gagné (1970) points out, the stage of developmental readiness for a learner depends on the skills he has already learned and on the capacities he has yet to acquire to meet particular objectives. It is certainly true that a child may be unable to acquire a skill or understand some principle before he has learned prerequisite skills or principles, and there is no objection to using the phrase "readiness training" to describe the necessary learning, as long as one is careful to distinguish between readiness and maturation. As was made clear in the earlier discussion of learning in young children, rate of learning largely depends on a child's experiences; previous learning by the individual is a major determinant of his degree of readiness for learning particular new capabilities.

Chapter 6

Intelligence, Language, and Human Learning

Intelligence

It has been made clear that learning and development are closely related. In any individual, each is also related to intelligence. The concept of intelligence is one that has been frequently confused and misused, and it is arguable whether intelligence testing in schools has been more harmful than beneficial in its ultimate effects (Hoffmann, 1964). Prior to any discussion of intelligence in learning, it is important to know something about the concept of intelligence, that is, how it is defined. In particular, it is necessary to understand that intelligence is *not* the type of explanatory concept that it is often taken to be.

Intelligence is often regarded as a personal attribute in the same sense as eyes, fingers, and legs. An individual is said to learn fast *because* he is intelligent, implying that high intelligence is a cause or explanation of performance. People sometimes ask whether intelligence tests really measure intelligence, implying that there is a fixed, tangible thing called "intelligence," and that deficiencies in intelligence tests are largely a matter of inaccurate measurement. Intelligence is regarded as some capacity or potential that underlies performance but that is distinct from what a person can actually do or learn. In fact, intelligence as measured is simply an indication of how well a person performs in certain tests, and it is by no means an explanation of why an individual performs well or badly. It may be useful to *describe* the individual who performs well as intelligent, but to say that the individual does well in the test because he is intelligent is akin to saying that the object outside my window is a car because objects of that nature are called cars, or that a certain car goes fast because it is a high-performance car.

It might be objected that if an intelligence measure is only a description of performance in a test, there seems to be little value in such a concept. Actually, it is very useful. If it is possible to devise a test containing items that measure an individual's capacity to perform skills that are required for success in a given culture, it may well be that scores on the test can be very useful in giving information about how well the testee will be able to cope with the situations he encounters, in short, to predict his success. In addition, if success within that culture requires considerable learning ability, it will be useful to have a test that includes items relating to skills required for learning. Intelligence tests are of this nature. Generally speaking, the function of intelligence tests is to sample intellectual skills, and the score that an individual obtains may provide a valuable indication of how the individual can perform in his environment. This score is the measure of intelligence. In short, intelligence is simply a measure of performance in certain tests, and not an explanation of anything. The concept is automatically culture-bound, since the tests that are used are deliberately chosen as one on which performance is predictive of performance on tasks that have a definite function within the culture. In a different culture, one in which different abilities are valued, the most useful test would be one which predicted performance at those abilities, and hence what is measured, whether or not we choose to call it "intelligence," would be correspondingly different. Vernon (1969) states:

> The group of skills which we refer to as intelligence is a
> European and American middle-class invention—something

which seems to be initimately bound up with puritanical values, with repression of instinctual responses and emphasis on responsibility, initiative, persistence and efficient workmanship. It is a kind of intelligence which is specially well adapted for scientific analysis, for control and exploitation of the physical world, for large-scale and long-term planning and carrying out of materialistic objectives. It has also led to the growth of complex social institutions such as nations, armies, industrial firms, school systems and universities. But it has been notably less successful than have the intelligences which are better adapted than ours for coping with the problems of agricultural and tribal living.
(Vernon, 1969, pages 89–90.)

It is conceivable that there may be differences between individuals in "potential" for learning or in rate of learning that are independent of what the individual has learned. It is possible to discuss such a notion, and to use concepts to label this hypothetical potential (Vernon, 1969). However, such a potential is not to be confused with measured intelligence, which is, as we have stated, simply a measure of how well an individual performs on test tasks that require intellectual skills. Defining a person as intelligent is not intended to specify how the individual acquired the intellectual skills that produced his score on the test. Since such skills are bound to be a result of previous learning, to speak of a person's intelligence being independent of what he has learned is absurd, but we shall return later to questions concerning the relationship between intelligence and learning.

Heredity and Learning as Determinants of Intelligence

The fact that intelligence is a measure based on learned skills by no means rules out the possibility that individual differences in intelligence test scores may be caused by biological factors. It is conceivable, for instance, that inherited differences in the function of brain cells lead to differences in learning rate. Also there are numerous other ways in which inherited factors might affect learning, and hence determine intelligence.

There has long been controversy over the question of whether environmental or hereditary influences contribute most to individual differences in intelligence. In some respects the question resembles the one concerning the roles of flour and eggs in a cake, given earlier as an analogy in the discussion of the roles of learning and biological factors in development; both are involved, and the result is not a simple summation of the two. Nevertheless, it would be valuable to know whether alterations in the environment affect intelligence more or less than hereditary differences. The debate over this question has become especially heated since the publication in 1969 of an article by Arthur Jensen. The article has been severely attacked, misinterpreted, and erroneous implications have been drawn from it; Jensen has been accused of being a racist, which he is not.

Jensen (1969) brings together the evidence from a number of studies that attempted to investigate the relative potency of hereditary and environmental determinants of intelligence. Some of these studies used identical twins on the assumption that hereditary factors are identical in the members of each pair. It is then possible to examine the effects of variations in the environment. For instance, if environmental factors are important determinants on intelligence test scores, one would predict that identical twins brought up together would be more similar in intelligence than twins reared apart, and that the larger the difference in the environments in which the twins are reared, the greater difference there would be in intelligence test scores. On the other hand, if environmental factors exert a much weaker influence than hereditary determinants of intelligence, the scores of identical twins would be very similar regardless of differences in the environments in which they were reared.

Much of the evidence from twin studies of this nature appears to support Jensen's position, which is that hereditary causes are much more important than environmental influences in producing differences in intelligence. For example, Vernon (1969) indicates that the similarity in intelligence test scores beween intelligence of identical twins brought up apart is much higher than that among unrelated children brought up together who have a similar environment for learning. Jensen's (1969) data similarly shows much greater similarities in intelligence between pairs of identical twins than between unrelated children experiencing similar environments. For instance, the intelligence of identical twins reared together is very similar (the correlation being $+.97$), and the correlation is not much lower when identical twins are brought up apart ($+.87$). On the other hand, pairs of unrelated children brought up in the same home environment have, on average, considerably less similarity in intelligence test scores, the correlation being $+.27$.

This and other evidence is claimed by Jensen to indicate that genetic influences are more important than environmental ones in leading to differences between individuals in intelligence. A controversial implication of such a proposal is that the differences in intelligence scores between racial groups in the United States are largely due to hereditary factors, and hence are only partly modifiable by movements towards equality in educational opportunities. However, there are a number of reasons for seriously questioning the assumption that existing evidence indicates hereditary factors to be more powerful than environmental influences, and these questions inevitably challenge the implications that have been drawn.

First, further evidence from studies of twins appears to disagree with that produced by Jensen. Bloom (1964) describes a study in which the quality of the educational environment was found to be closely related (the correlation being $+.79$) to the intelligence test scores of identical twins who were separated during the first three years of their lives. Nineteen pairs of identical twins reared apart on which data were available were divided into eleven pairs in which the children had been in similar educational environments, and eight pairs in which educational environments were less similar. It was found that the similarities in intelligence, expressed as correlations, were $+.91$ for the former (similar environments) compared with $+.24$ for the latter (less similar). In other words, the results of the study were that among identical twins environmental factors had a much larger influence upon intelligence than is apparent in the data presented by Jensen. Further evidence that appears to suggest conclusions different to those of Jensen is discussed by Deutsch (1969). He points out that some twin data indicate greater differences in scores between identical twins reared apart than Jensen acknowledges, and hence Deutsch claims, as does Bloom, that even in the most genetically similar individuals the environment may powerfully influence intelligence test performance. For instance, Stone and Church (1968) report differences of up to 24 IQ points between identical twins, and they show that the magnitude of such differences is positively related to differences in educational and social advantage.

The second reason for seriously questioning Jensen's conclusion is that studies comparing environmental and hereditary effects have generally used poor measures of environmental quality. It is generally assumed, quite correctly, that higher social-class homes provide an intellectually richer environment, on average, than lower social-class homes. However, the correlation between social class and environmental quality, though positive, is rather low (Miller, 1970), and hence one cannot really justify using social class data as a *measure* of environment. Bloom (1964) points out that the general index of social or economic status has obscured many very important differences among environments. He remarks on the dearth of adequate measures of environments, suggesting that this has led to an underestimate of the environmental effects in behaviorial science research, and points out the need for more precise and specific measures. Despite some recent research in the area (for example, Miller, 1970), this need still exists.

The third reason for questioning the claim that hereditary factors are more powerful than environmental ones arises from the fact that biological differences can sometimes produce differences in environment. This may lead to results that overestimate the strength of hereditary influences, at the expense of environmental ones. In the case of children brought up in the same home, it might appear that the objection raised about using social class as a measure of environment, does not apply. However, the effective environment may be different for two individuals in the same home since people may react differently to them. The fact that identical twins look very similar may lead to people responding very similarly to each, thus producing for the twins effective environments that are more alike than those encountered by children who look different. In addition, as Staats (1971) suggests, the placement in foster homes and adopted homes of the twins who were measured in the studies we have mentioned may have been influenced by knowledge of their hereditary background; that is to say, environmental placement may have been partly determined by biological factors. Staats provides an illustration:

> *Because of the biological conception of human behavior that is commonly held, placement officials actually try to place a child in a home that coincides with the child's supposed biological inheritance. A case occurred several years back in New York where temporary foster parents were not going to be allowed to permanently adopt a child they had grown to love, with the child reciprocating the affection. The reason was that the parents were considered to be unsuited for the child. She was a blond, blue-eyed child of northern European descent, and the foster parents were dark-haired, brown-eyed, and of southern European descent. According to a biological conception of human behavior, it would be important to provide the child with parents of her own "kind."**

* From *Child Learning, Intelligence, and Personality* by Arthur W. Staats. Copyright © 1971 by Arthur W. Staats. Reprinted by permission of Harper & Row, Publishers, Inc. P. 23.

In addition to the three reasons outlined, there are a number of other factors indicating the need for caution in interpreting data on the effects of environment and heredity. Generally speaking, environmental differences in twin studies have been rather small, and this may combine with the poor measures of environment to lead to underestimates of environmental effects. Related to this is the fact that there has been little long-term research on the effects of a highly enriched environment on children's intelligence.

Learning and Intelligence

In view of the fact that intelligence tests measure skills that are acquired through learning, learning is clearly a determinant of intelligence. On the whole, in devising intelligence tests, there has been an attempt to use items on which performance is relatively unaffected by specific learning experiences, and which measure skills that are basic for learning. However, performance on intelligence tests can be sharply increased by practice. Vernon (1969) provides evidence of large practice effects on scores in various tests administered in a number of different countries.

The existence of large practice effects cast some doubt on claims that intelligence scores provide stable measures of basic intellectual capacities. Even more damaging to such claims is the evidence from studies in which students have received coaching on the types of items used in tests. Guinagh (1971), for instance, used the Raven's Progressive Matrices Test (a very popular, "culture-free" test of intelligence) to test children from a low socioeconomic environment, and then provided some of the children with three hours of training on the skills required for the test, avoiding the particular items used. Then the Raven's test was administered again. Some of the control groups showed slight gains, presumably due to practice, but among the children in the experimental groups who received the training, there were very large gains in test scores, varying between 50 percent and 100 percent in different subgroups. These results indicate that either such tests do not really measure basic intellectual skills, or that such skills can be enormously increased by a three-hour training program, and both of these possibilities indicate the need for careful thought about the nature of intelligence and intelligence tests.

Further evidence about the contribution of learning to measured intelligence is provided by Schmidt (1966) whose study is described more fully in Chapter Twelve. Briefly, he found that within a subculture where allocation of children to schools was made on a basis independent of other environmental variables, intelligence tests scores were closely related to number of years of schooling. Staats (1971), who proposes that differences between individuals in intelligence are largely, if not entirely, due to differences in environment, and not to hereditary factors, argues that the child described as intelligent is one who has learned the skills that are tested, and as a result has a good basis for acquiring further skills. It would appear that the extent to which schooling will influence such test scores will depend on the extent to which the necessary skills can be acquired in the school environment, and also on the inavailability of opportunities for acquiring those skills in other environments the child encounters.

The Potency of Learning

The extreme environmentalist point of view can be expressed in the sentence "the person *is* what he learns." It is undeniably true that learning extends beyond the acquisition of skill and knowledge; individual differences in motivation and personality are at least partly the results of learning. Bandura (1969) and Staats (1971) suggest that many abnormalities commonly thought to be biological in origin are more often due to deficiencies in learning experiences. As the following account by Staats indicates, the nature of the diagnosis strongly influences attempts to solve the problem.

> *It is common to have a physician diagnose a child as minimally brain damaged if the child does poorly in school*

and has very low academic achievement test scores, but does not evidence the more general behavioral deficits that lead to the label of mental retardation . . . the diagnosis of the child may be made entirely on the basis of the child's behavior—with no evidence of unusual brain structure or function that has been causally related to the behavior in question.

Such a diagnosis is likely to lead to very different attempts to solve the problem than would analysis that concluded that the problem was the child's past history of experience and his present environmental conditions. That is, detailed accounts of the child's behavior might reveal that the child has never paid attention in school, in the way that successful children do. It might be the case that since his very earliest schooling when the teacher began formal presentations of academic material, the child in question would not look at the stimuli presented, would not make the responses involved—at least in most cases—and would occupy himself with other matters.*

It is easy to see how, in a situation such as this, one thing may lead to another. The child does not attend; consequently, he does not learn; consequently, he receives little attention or encouragement from the teacher; consequently, he finds school an unrewarding situation; consequently, he does not attend, and so on, in a vicious circle. Staats shows how the organic conception of mental retardation may lead to a similar chain of events.

The organically oriented conception [results in] . . . the child who is backward in learning [being] placed in a group of similar children, and thus receives training that is less rich than children who have already learned more . . . it . . .

---

* From *Child Learning, Intelligence, and Personality* by Arthur W. Staats. Copyright © 1971 by Arthur W. Staats. Reprinted by permission of Harper & Row, Publishers, Inc. Pp. 15–16.

*helps produce a cumulative decrement (retardation) in the child who was backward to begin with. It must also be remembered that much of the child's learning comes from his peers. Thus, the child who is backward behaviorally, who needs a superior learning situation, is instead associated with other backward children who provide him with an inferior learning context, and he again receives a less rich learning experience.**

Staats writes of a "downward spiral" of learning, in describing how lack of one learned skill may lead to deficiencies in progressively more skills.

> *Let us take the case of the child who does not gain his initial repertoires as rapidly as most other children because of poor learning conditions for one reason or another . . . we can expect to see a downward spiral of relative performance. The child who acquires his basic behavioral repertoire more slowly than others is not ready as soon to succeed in the task of learning the next more advanced skill. Moreover . . . he will find himself in a less propitious social circumstance of reward for learning; thus his attentional and working behaviors will be poor, and his learning will be at a less rapid rate than would be the case in better motivating conditions. . . . The less advanced the performance, the less the reward. The less the reward, the less the maintenance of learning behaviors. The less advanced the learning, the greater the decrease in the reward, and so on. The mental retardate can expect to find himself in such a downward spiral of relative progress in learning.***

Clearly, where an organic diagnosis for retarded learning performance might lead to advice to parents or teachers of

* From *Child Learning, Intelligence, and Personality* by Arthur W. Staats. Copyright © 1971 by Arthur W. Staats. Reprinted by permission of Harper & Row, Publishers, Inc. P. 17.
** From *Child Learning, Intelligence, and Personality* by Arthur W. Staats. Copyright © 1971 by Arthur W. Staats. Reprinted by permission of Harper & Row, Publishers, Inc. P. 314.

the "wait until the child is ready" variety, the explanation provided by a psychologist agreeing with Staats would lead to very different suggestions, indicating the need for massive enrichment. Such suggestions might include close interaction with the child, considerable encouragement, attention, and other reward-producing activities in an effort to put the child in situations where learning can occur successfully, so that he can acquire both basic skills and appropriate motivation for further learning, reversing the "downward spiral" effects.

Comments on Language Skills

Man's language affects and is in turn influenced by his reasoning, and hence there are close relationships between learning, language, and intelligence. The "Sapir-Whorf hypothesis" states that the language of a society both reflects and determines its ideas, the individual's experiences being largely affected by cultural predispositions to make particular choices and interpretations of phenomena. There is little agreement about the magnitude of the relationship between language and thought or about the directions of causality, but there is no doubt that they are related. The situation is rather complicated. On the one hand, there is no doubt that the way in which we use language and the ways in which we think, reason, and learn are closely related. On the other hand, we cannot say in any simple way that language causes learning and reasoning or that reasoning improves language ability.

Most programs designed to combat cultural deprivation have emphasized language deficiencies, and see development of language skills as being very important. Much of the content of Sesame Street, for example, is designed to promote the use of language. An extensive compensatory program developed by Bereiter and Engleman (1966) is based on the premise (for which they provide considerable evidence) that

> It is the lack of verbal learning, in particular the lack of those kinds of learning that can only be transmitted from adults to children through language, that is mainly

responsible for [learning] deficiencies. Thus, there is justification for treating cultural deprivation as synonymous with language deprivation.

(Bereiter and Engelman, 1966, page 42.)

Some writers have questioned the assumption that children from "disadvantaged" environments are necessarily deficient in their ability to use language. Baratz (1969) points out that most of the evidence indicating that such children are deficient comes from studies in which middle-class and lower-class children were placed in typical middle-class testing situations, and their utterances were counted. Baratz suggests that theories developed by Bernstein (1959) have been wrongly interpreted as implying that the presence or absence of particular standard English word forms indicate not only linguistic but conceptual deficiencies. Certainly, there is no doubt that ghetto children do not perform well on tests of standard English, but that is hardly a fair measure of their linguistic competence. Baratz suggests that the "errors" in standard English made by cultural minorities indicates not a failure to have learned the rules in a standard English linguistic system, but that different rules have been learned. To test this suggestion, Baratz carried out an experiment comparing the language behavior of standard and nonstandard speakers when asked to repeat standard and nonstandard sentences. If children in the (Negro) minority group tested are learning a well-ordered but different system from that used in the white culture, it would be predicted that white children will make as many errors in repeating nonstandard sentences as the Negro children make in repeating standard English. In that case the white children might be classified as "deficient" in language, if the nonstandard system is used as the criterion of development.

Each child in the experiment attempted to repeat 15 standard and 15 nonstandard sentences. The children were from grades three and five. These are examples of the actual sentences used: (Standard) "The teacher gave him a note about the school meeting to give to his mother." (Nonstandard) "De teacha give him a note 'bout de school meetin' an he 'posed to give it ta his movah ta read" (Baratz, 1969, page 893). The results of the experiment clearly support Baratz' suggestion: the Negro children did significantly better than the white children on the nonstandard sentences, and the converse was true for the standard sentences.

The findings of Baratz' study strongly question the assumption that Negro children, and by implication children in linguistic minority groups generally, are necessarily deficient in linguistic abililty. On the other hand, it is true that although the dominant culture uses standard English as the medium of expression, children who are deficient in ability to use standard English have a strong disadvantage.

Whether the child in a minority group has more to gain or lose from learning the language of the majority culture is a question that arouses considerable heat. On the one hand, he acquires skills that are needed in the majority culture. On the other hand, the individual's sense of identity may be damaged by changes in his language, which could lead to unrewarding changes in his way of life. In this dilemma, some might echo Shakespeare's words, quoted in a discussion of language by Postman and Weingartner (1969):

CALIBAN
You taught me language; and my profit on't
Is, I know how to curse. The red plague rid you
For learning me your language!

The Tempest

It is conceivable that too much stress has been placed on the undeniably close interdependence between language and reasoning. Lenneberg (1967) points out that with deaf preschool children,

Unless there is also generalized neurological or psychiatric disturbance, the almost complete absence of language in these children is no hindrance to the most imagina-

tive and intelligent play appropriate for the age. They love make-believe games; they can build fantastic structures with blocks or out of boxes; they may set up electric trains and develop the necessary logic for setting switches and anticipating the behavior of the moving train around curves and over bridges. They love to look at pictures, and no degree of stylizing renders the pictorial repersentation incomprehensible for them, and their own drawings leave nothing to be desired when compared with those produced by their hearing contemporaries.

(Lenneberg, 1967, pages 362–363.)

Information obtained by anthropologists on color naming in various tribes has been interpreted as providing strong evidence for powerful relationships between language and cognition, especially in perceptual discrimination. However, it is possible that there have been some misinterpretations of evidence, or the methods of collecting evidence have been faulty. Lenneberg (1967) provides evidence from studies of the deaf to show that both among children and adults, the differences between hearing and deaf subjects in perceptual discrimination are sufficiently small as to render questionable some of the asssumptions about the central role of language and linguistic habits in this type of cognitive capacity.

This is not to deny the important fact that language is indispensable for the symbolic types of learning which are important in making man so different from other species. Lacking in language skills, deaf children do appear to be handicapped in the complex abstract types of learning required for advanced intellectual development. Bereiter and Engelman's (1966) examination of the evidence leads them to the conclusion that, because of language disabilities, deaf children are culturally deprived, regardless of home background, in much the way that some lower-class children are deprived. Of all the "tools" that man has available, and uses to increase his power, language is clearly the master. One can hardly imagine meaningful language that is not closely related to reasoning. The Russian psychologist Vigotskii noted that a word which means nothing is not a word at all, and he suggests that language has enabled man to internalize his cognitive processes, so that thinking becomes not merely a matter of certain functions that enable man to deal with the external world, but a means of manipulating the cognitive functions themselves, in short, of thinking. Words such as "awareness" and "consciousness," indicate the presence of this type of functioning.

The manner in which language is used clearly alters as the user's age increase. Bruner (1966) notes:

> It seems to be the use of language as an instrument of thinking that matters, in internalization, to use an apt but puzzling word. The very young child uses language almost as an extension of pointing, and recent work shows that the likelihood of a word's use in the early linguistic career of the child is vastly increased if the object is either in hand or in direct sight. It is only gradually that words are used to stand for objects not present, and it is a still longer time before such remote referring words are manipulated by the transformational apparatus of grammar in a manner designed to aid the solution of mental problems—tasks requiring that a barrier be overcome. And it is even later that words become the vehicle for dealing in the categories of the possible, the conditional, the counterfactual conditional, and the rest of the vast realm of mind in which words and utterances have no direct referent at all in immediate experience.
>
> (Bruner, 1966, page 14.)

Biology and Learning in Language

Controversy exists as to the possible existence of biological factors that predispose humans to use language. Many researchers in the field of psycholinguistics, following Noam Chomsky, consider there may be biological endowments in man that make the type of language used by humans uniquely possible for the human species. An excellent account of language development as interpreted by psycholinguists is provided by McNeill (1970). Advocates of the latter point of view present a number of reasons for the likelihood of biological endowments (Lenneberg, 1966; 1967). One is that there appears to be anatomical and physiological evidence for specialization of certain parts of the human brain for language functions. Another reason is that the onset of language is somewhat regular in its appearance and relatively uniform in the sequence of events by which different linguistic skills appear. A third reason is that language in humans appears difficult to suppress, there being relatively small delay in learning to speak among children subjected to conditions of gross deprivations and neglect, and congenitally blind and deaf children are able to acquire language skills surprisingly easily in view of the apparent difficulties. Speech, of course, is considerably hindered by deafness. A fourth reason supporting the point of view that humans have biological endowments for language is that there are a number of "universals" whereby the languages of different peoples in civilizations that have had no contact, nevertheless share attributes in common.

None of these reasons, however, provides really conclusive evidence for biologically transmitted specific language mechanisms. Researchers favoring learning theory approaches consider that learning plays a much larger role in the development of language skills than the psycholinguists admit. Representative of the approach that emphasizes learning is the work of Staats (for example, 1971). A common argument against explanation of language development purely in terms of learning is that there is simply not enough time for a child to acquire all the necessary language skills by simple associative learning. However, this argument ignores the fact that it is possible to learn general rules and principles, so that learning does not have to depend solely on the acquisition of vast quantities of simple associations.

Language in Nonhumans

One of the arguments in favor of the viewpoint that biological endowments are of major importance in language acquisition used to be that no nonhuman species can learn human languages. Certainly, animal species have various kinds of languages, but these are extremely different in function and potency to human languages. However, recent work has provided findings indicating that at least some human language skills can be acquired by primates. Of course, anatomical reasons prevent speech in nonhumans, but one chimpanzee acquired the ability to use, with apparent understanding, 34 words (Gardner and Gardner, 1969). Another chimpanzee acquired 120 words, which were represented by pieces of colored plastic, varying in shape, size, color, and texture (Premack, 1970). The chimpanzee learned a number of the linguistic functions used in human grammar and was clearly able to understand functions involving combinations of words where the meaning depended on order; the language skills extended well beyond the use of specific words.

Some of the problems involved in attempting to discover all there is to be known about how language and learning affect one another are enormously complex, and solutions are a long way off. But, as we have tried to show, modern researchers have at least begun to make the questions more explicit, and there is beginning to be excitingly fast progress in this area.

Chapter 7
Motivation and the Independent Learner

Introduction

In the previous four chapters we have advanced towards understanding the processes by which students gain knowledge and skills that contribute to intellectual development and education. Among the most important broad principles is that learning is effective when the learner's mind is actively engaged in a task, and conditions that help bring about such engagement facilitate learning. Important among them is the necessity for the learning task to be presented in a manner that ensures understanding on the part of the learner.

A further condition for learning was discussed in Chapter 2. Human behavior is largely determined by human needs. When classroom behavior has results that are rewarding for the young student, such as teacher praise, such ("reinforced") behavior tends to be repeated. Behavior that does not have rewarding consequences is likely to diminish, or "extinguish." In fact, it is also possible to provide reinforcement when there is direct evidence of learning as an alternative to reinforcing student behaviors that are compatible with learning, such as attention. Staats (1968) and his associates have carried out a number of studies in which reinforcement directly followed responses that indicated learning, such as reading words correctly. This procedure is generally effective when the rewards handed out meet the needs of the experimental subjects. Programs have been devised which resulted in the acquisition of reading skills by an older student with long records of failure at reading (Staats and Butterfield, 1965) and by a 4-year-old culturally deprived child of low IQ who would customarily be described as "not ready" for learning (Staats, 1971). This boy's progress in reading was roughly equivalent to that of another similarly aged child whose IQ was 130. Staats considers that this fact provides an indication of the limitations of intelligence test measures as indices of basic human capacities.

The difference between rewarding "constructive" classroom behaviors that are compatible with learning as typically takes place in studies of "behavior modification," and providing direct rewards for evidence of learning as is customary in Staats' experiments, is a small one. When rewards follow a student's attention to a learning task, the reinforced behavior ("attending") is a basic skill required in learning. Attending is particularly crucial for learning based on observation, and this is important in a variety of learning situations that will be discussed later in this chapter. One advantage of providing reinforcement when there is evidence of young students using a basic skill, such as attention, rather than waiting for direct evidence of learning as such, is that one avoids the ill-effects of encouraging pupils to be "producers" rather than thinkers (Holt, 1964). Holt observed, it will be recalled, that when praise, encouragement, and other rewards are provided only when students give correct answers, the latter tend to become "answer-oriented," adopting strategies that are incompatible with the careful and relaxed reasoning necessary for meaningful learning.

Internalizing the Control of Behavior

A basic limitation of the behavior modification situations described in Chapter 2 is that the control of student's behavior is largely in the hands of the teacher. Since control is largely external, students are largely dependent on the teacher, and for two related reasons it is necessary that, so far as possible, learners should have control over their own behavior. The two reasons, in brief, are that students need to be independent in order to function effectively as learners in the modern world, and that, as the intervening chapters have made clear, individuals learn most effectively when they manifest a degree of cognitive involvement present when decisions and choices about learning are largely under learners' own control.

Having explored some of the processes involved in meaningful human learning, we are now ready to consider the ways in which determinants of human behavior come to be largely internalized, and thus cease to be entirely dependent on the controlling actions of external agents such as teachers.

In Chaper 2, we indicated the need to think hard about what the learner needs to do with what knowledge he acquires. The learner has to use whatever knowledge he has gained, in evaluating, choosing, comparing, and deciding. In almost all the situations where acquired knowledge is important, it is necessary to know how to use this knowledge, and the skills required for making the best use of what we know have themselves to be learned. In addition, abilities that constitute "learning how to learn" are essential in a rapidly changing world. We pointed out that if children are to leave school with the necessary skills to make the knowledge they have gained there really useful to them, it is worth their spending considerable time and energy to acquire the various skills and abilities essential for making use of information.

In the following chapters, it became apparent that the activities of the learner himself, as an individual, are extremely critical in determining what is acquired. Learning is a very learner-centered process. The things that the individual brings to the learning situation are vital; his "efforts after meaning," his interpreting, coding, and other constructive activities, whereby he deals with the situation before him. The greater the extent to which the learner is encouraged to carry out these functions, to participate in a highly active manner, to be "cognitively involved," the greater the learning.

Independence as a Goal

Effective education encourages the learner to be independent, but agreement with this sentiment leaves room for disagreement about the methods of achieving independence. On the one hand, there are teachers who agree with A. S. Neill, who believes that very young children in his Summerhill School should be encouraged as early as possible to make the widest reaching and most important decisions for themselves. There is great freedom from external controls at Summerhill, and as long as a child does not do things that interfere with the freedom and convenience of others, he is free to do exactly as he wishes. Others, on the other hand, would argue that although it is important for children to acquire independence, initiative, and responsibility, Neill's is not the best method of achieving this. They might claim that the 6-year-old child is just not ready to make a wide range of decisions for himself, and perhaps the onus of having to make major decisions at such a tender age may itself be cruel and frightening. Perhaps young children need and desire considerable support in making choices, and maybe the necessary abilities are best acquired rather gradually rather than by a child's being "thrown in at the deep end," as seems to be the case at Summerhill. No child is expected to learn how to read overnight, and perhaps the equally important learning necessary for a child to make effective decisions and choices should be gradual and carefully structured. Certainly the goal of independence in learning is a fine one, but there is a difference between the independence as an *outcome* and giving complete freedom as a method of achieving that goal.

Conditions for Independent Learning

1. Acquisition of Necessary Skills

Given some agreement about goals of education, however, it does become easier to look for ways of using scientific investigation and rational discussion to help achieve the goal. A first start might be to define "independent" in a manner that makes the desired outcomes more specific. As a beginning, we could say that the objective is to help the young child to acquire, as early as possible, the appropriate abilities and skills necessary for him to make a range of decisions both about the way in which he is going to learn, and about what he is to do with what he has learned. Next, it would be helpful to list some specific skills that are required. It would be possible to classify a number of such capacities, varying in specificity and in the extent to which they require prerequisite skills. For independent study, a student must be able to use a dictionary, use indexes, and be able to find needed information in a library, among other things. One could extend this list to include the majority of the capabilities required for a student to work on his own. Some of the necessary skills are less specific than the ones we have mentioned; for example, the ability to develop and formulate questions so that they become sharpened in a manner that facilitates inquiry. The school ought to be able to provide opportunities for students to develop the necessary capacities for independent study. A learning environment actively encourages independent learning to the extent that it provides such opportunities. It would be interesting to compare a school like Summerhill with other institutions to see if they differ in the extent to which opportunities are provided to gain capacities for independent learning.

Some of the basic skills can be acquired by young children. In the previous chapter, we pointed out that the child who learns to read gains a measure of independence from adults in acquiring information from books. Learning to count change and tell time can similarly add to the self-reliance of the young child, freeing him from close dependence on adults. In defining capabilities appropriate for any age, an important step is careful specification of the desired outcomes of learning, and a taxonomy, such as the one devised by Bloom and his associates (Bloom, 1956), can be of great value to the teacher who is arranging learning experiences.

We noted in Chapter 2 that some of the problems that arise in discussions about ways of achieving independent learning capacities have been oversimplified by viewing the issue as one of "freedom versus control." The title of a recent book by Carl Rogers (1969) is *Freedom to Learn*. In education, the freedom versus control question can be refined to one that asks "who does the controlling?" When the issue is expressed in this form, one can answer that the learner must be largely in control if learning is to be really effective. It is worth noting, incidentally, that there is nothing particularly new about people being controlled by others. It is customary to suggest that people in the past were much freer than now, while today bureaucratic governments and agencies control people's lives. There is some truth in this, but the extent to which most humans were controlled by other people was at least as great in the past as now. The mechanisms of control then were less subtle: if the fourteenth-century peasant did not work for his master, he starved, and his family with him. Hence, he did what he was told, the mechanism of control being crude but effective.

2. Perceived Value of Learning

Up to now, we have discussed one essential necessity for students to become relatively independent of external sources of control so that learning becomes largely under the control of the learner. This is that the learner acquire certain skills required for study on his own. There are two other necessary conditions. Of these, the first is that what is being learned is perceived by the learner as relating to his needs, that is, to be relevant.

Learning is a result of certain forms of human activities, which in turn, are determined by the needs of the individual. In Chapter Two, it was suggested that a healthy state of affairs for learning is one in which the activity that produces learning and the need that directs the activity are closely and directly related. For instance, when a person does something because he is interested, it is more likely that his activity will lead to learning than if he does something because he has been told that he will be rewarded with a gold star. If there is a need for a gold star, and the activity that achieves this need is reading, there is a somewhat indirect relationship between the activity and the need. To complicate matters, perhaps the real need is not for the gold star itself, but for the attention or feeling of success or security that goes with it. In this case, we might say that an individual performs some activity, after which another person provides something which contributes towards meeting a need of the first person. Clearly, there is a rather cumbersome chain connecting need to activity. The distinction is often made between internal and external (or "extrinsic") motivation, and it is a useful distinction, but it is necessary to add an additional dimension, the "direct-ness" of the relationship between the activity and the need. Of course, the presence of an external factor, another person, is in itself a cause of indirectness since it provides an addi-tional link in the chain between activity and satisfaction of the need. However, the interal-external and direct-indirect dimensions for need satisfaction are not precisely synonymous when we discuss motivation. Hence, the second of the three necessary conditions for independent learning requires two components. The first is that the sequence connecting the learner's activity to the meeting of his need be, so far as possible, independent of any external rewarding person. In-sofar as such a person is necessary in the sequence, the maintenance of that sequence is "dependent" on that person, and not within the autonomous control of the learner. Sec-ondly, and related to the first component, the chain between the learner's actions and the provision of his needs should be as short and direct as possible. That component is clearly present when a person does something because it is interesting to him; one can then say that the learning has a clear and direct function for the learner (see Chapter 8).

3. Identification

The third necessary condition for independent learning is that the control of behavior is internalized via processes usually called "identification." As we have said, identification is in part a result of the other of the two conditions being met. The concept of identification is somewhat inexplicit, but generally speaking, it refers to processes whereby a learner comes to internalize the sources of control over his activities so that such controls become part of his own identity.

We can clarify the meaning of identification in the following way. The behavior of a young child is determined by a relatively small number of simple needs. The adult's needs are much more numerous; he has what is called a conscience, a sense of right and wrong; he has certain values, attitudes, feelings that determine his behavior. All these constitute needs which are as real as those of the child, but they are clearly more complex. The growth of complex needs is important for socialization in the developing person. Freud's account of the superego is the prototype for identification, the process whereby needs and motives that were originally manipulated and controlled by external factors come to be internalized as part of the person. A young child learns that certain activities meet approval and certain other actvities meet disapproval or punishment, but he gradually comes to avoid behaving in certain ways, not because he fears external punishment, but partly because he "identifies" with the sources of the disapproval. We might speak of this individual as a "socialized human being." There is no need to punish him for doing things that do not fit in with society because he has internalized the various taboos and sanctions that society demands.

Bruner (1966) has described some attributes of identification. He states:

> The fact of identification is more easily described than explained. It refers to the strong human tendency to model one's "self" and one's aspirations upon some other person. When we feel we have succeeded in "being like" an identification figure, we derive pleasure from the achievement and conversely, we suffer when we have "let him down." Insofar as the identification figure is also "a certain kind of person"—belongs to some group or category—we extend

our loyalties from an individual to a reference group. In effect, then, identification relates one not only to individuals, but to one's society as well.

(Bruner, 1966, page 122.)

The process of identification enables motives and needs which originally were external to the individual to be internalized so that external controls are no longer necessary. The nature of identification depends on the individuals in a child's environment, and for the young child, the teacher is often a critical figure.

As Bruner says,

The term identification is usually referred for those strong attachments where there is a considerable amount of emotional investment. But there are milder forms of identification. . . . They are "on the job" heroes, reliable ones with whom we can interact in some way. Indeed they control a rare resource, some desired competence, but what is important is that the resource is attainable by interaction . . . in the process of teaching a skill the parent or teacher passes on much more. The teacher imparts attitudes towards the subject and indeed, attitudes toward learning itself. What results may be quite inadvertant. Often, in our schools, for example, this first lesson is that learning has to do with remembering things when asked, with maintaining a certain undefined tidiness in what one does, with following a train of thought that comes from outside rather than from within and from honoring right answers.

(Bruner, 1966, page 123.)

Schooling and Motivation

Bruner's suggestion that the teacher may be an important figure in the identification process may provide a clue to some of the questions that arise about the effects of years of schooling on students' motivation to learn. In particular, identification processes may help explain some differences between boys and girls in their attitudes to school.

Critics of current education are fond of making comparisons between the child at the age when he enters school eager, curious, adventurous, excited, anxious to learn, and always asking questions, and the same child after three or four years at school: apathetic, bored, listless, and no longer asking questions. The critics argue that the child who has been in school for a few years is *less* rather than more anxious to learn, which is surely a bad state of affairs. Others have countered that not all these changes can be blamed on the school. Bruner and others point out that curiosity in the form shown by the very young child is not in itself sufficient for advanced learning, and the young child, however curious, is extremely distractable. To some extent this is true, but the argument is not entirely convincing. A child, aged 5, 4 or even 3 years of age watching a television cartoon that interests him, is not at all distractable; his attention is fully engaged for periods of time far in excess of what might be expected for any learning in school. It is also argued that when a child goes around asking questions, apparently interested in gaining knowledge and finding out about the world, many of the questions are not as genuinely knowledge-oriented as they seem to be. The child who asks, "Where did I come from?" may be less interested in finding out about his own creation than in gaining his mother's attention or just in expressing himself. Again, there is some truth in the reasoning, but that should not blind us to the genuine extent to which many children really are curious, and when occasion demands, extremely attentive for long periods of time.

Another argument that is raised as a counter to the complaint that children become less and less interested in learning the longer they stay at school is that this decrease in curiosity occurs as children get older, regardless of what the teachers do at school. The very young child at school is anxious to gain attention and praise from his teacher, and that if learning is one way of getting this, then the child will put a lot of energy into what the teacher tells him to do. On the other hand, the older child is less interested in the reaction of the teacher, more interested in the approval of his peers, and has more interests outside the school so that classroom activities have less influence in commanding his interest. In other words, the older child is less interested in school learning because he has changed for reasons connected with his getting older that have nothing to do with the quality of the teaching he encounters. Once again, there may be some truth in this argument, but it does not really seem to account for all of the reduction of interest and curiosity that often occurs in children at school.

There are several possible reasons for children's disenchantment with school as they become older. Some boys may have problems at school adjusting to what is predominately a female-dominated society. Bruner notes the observation by anthropologists that "the basic values of the early grades are a stylized version of the feminine role in the society, cautious rather than daring, governed by a ladylike politeness" (Bruner, 1966, page 123). Inherent in the "ladylike politeness" is not only the motion of a feminine world, but of a middle-class one, and a child who does not come from such an environment is unlikely to feel happy or at home there. Unless the teacher is able to create an environment in which middle-class feminine values and styles of behavior really do not get unnecessary predominance, the school will fail to meet the needs of many children. Also related to this "ladylike politeness," is the emphasis described on producing rather than thinking, and on getting correct answers at the expense of understanding. The conforming behavior and propriety of young girls, rewarded though it may be in the classroom, can later prove a handicap even to themselves. Such rewards can be too successful so that "in later years it is difficult to move girls beyond the orderly virtues they learned in their first school encounters" (Bruner, 1966, page 123).

In addition, some other effects of the socialization that identification helps bring about may not be entirely beneficial in the individual. Taboos that are internalized may have no other function than avoiding societal disapproval. In the case of attributes, such as prudery and the puritanical fear of pleasure, it appears that individuals have internalized unreasonable and ritualistic demands made by society on them. In some instances, what has been internalized by one person may have been useful to others, or to society in general, although lacking values for the individual. Thus, we have heroism, ultrapatriotism, and so on. Leonard (1968) speaks of "internalizing the whip":

> Too often, indeed, such terms as conscience, dignity, stoicism, heroism, honor or even glory have constituted ultimately indefinable variations on a single theme: man's endeavor to act and speak in a manner aversive to him without the prod of external punishment. During the entire period of civilization, a large measure, perhaps a majority, of an individual's education was devoted to teaching him how to be less than he could be and to perform this feat with the aid of no external task master whatever. The whip securely tucked inside, Lord Raglan's rider could charge the cannons at Balaclava with a narrow smile and a quip. And Central High's honor student can sit day after day, mute and almost uncomplaining, as his perceptions, his world, himself, are sliced into little pieces.
>
> (Leonard, 1968, pages 76–77.)

The Role of Imitation in Identification

For identification to occur, it is important that learning takes place through observation of people and events. A simple but important principle of learning is that people learn from what they observe, and such learning often involves *imitation* by the learner. The person being observed and possibly imitated is known as a *model*, and the word *modeling* is sometimes used to refer to learning of this kind.

Imitation is important in learning at all ages, and has been observed in infants as early as 10 to 20 days of age (Church, 1961). Complex forms of imitation require various subskills, central among which is the capacity for paying attention. Important as attentional skills are for learning, detailed discussion is outside our present scope, but the following quotations from Staats (1971) indicate their crucial role in learning.

For further learning to be effected in many different training circumstances, it is important that certain stimuli come to more strongly control attentional responses than do other stimuli. The untrained child will not differentially respond in this way—and this may mean that no new learning occurs.

A child who continues to respond to other stimuli in a situation where an adult is speaking to the child will be considered dull, or autistic, or uncontrollable. . . . A child in a preschool or kindergarten group who does not respond with attention to the teacher's voice as do the other children will be considered backward or abnormal. Furthermore, he will not receive the same training circumstances as the other children, and will not learn as well. . . . Although attentional skills are usually taken for granted as something the child gets from physiological maturation, it is suggested such differences arise from the child's learning history. Moreover, lack of appropriately controlled attention is a frequent underlying reason for the label of mental retardation.

This repertoire of attentional behaviors under appropriate stimulus control is basic to early cognitive learning. For one thing, this repertoire is what the teacher's instructional procedures rely upon. Where children have this repertoire well developed, the teacher need only present the verbal stimuli (instructions) to control the correct attentional behaviors. The children will thus sense the appropriate stimuli in their necessary sequences, and will learn. Where the attentional repertoire has not yet been developed by the pupil, it must be trained or the child will not sense the stimuli, and consequently will not learn.

If the child does not attend to the stimulus, if the adult's words do not control appropriate looking and listening responses, the child does not see or hear the stimulus and learning does not occur. After a period of this the child will not only appear to be but he will be "retarded" or "disturbed."*

Bandura (1969) points out that what is learned by an invidual through observation depends on the particular environment to which he is exposed. Some environmental differences are related fairly reliably to cultural factors, such as difference in social class. A child in a home where reading is a common activity will encounter an environment that differs from a bookless home not only in the presence or absence of books. For instance, he may observe his parents reading; they provide models to imitate. The fact that the parents appear to enjoy reading may be vicariously rewarding to the child. In addition, parents who are themselves keen readers are more likely to encourage (reinforce) their child's attempts, so the child repeats his first reading attempts and thereby learns skills and acquires habits required for reading. The sequence of events forms a lengthy cycle involving various factors that favor learning in which opportunities for observing parent behaviors, and hence for imitating them, are important. An individual's learning is largely determined by the experiences to which he is "exposed." If variables, such as social class, reliably indicate differences in the various environmental factors that cause learning, it is hardly surprising that such variables are related to differences in learning and in intelligence.

Whereas writers such as Bruner (1966) describe identification processes as somewhat distinct from those of other and simpler kinds of learning, Bandura (1969) considers that the phenomena labeled identification can be accounted for by the

* From *Child Learning, Intelligence, and Personality* by Arthur W. Staats. Copyright © 1971 by Arthur W. Staats. Reprinted by permission of Harper & Row, Publishers, Inc. Pp. 174 and 180–181.

same principles that explain the acquisition of other learned skills and ways of responding. Some of the complexity and mystery found in Bruner's description disappears if one accepts Bandura's point of view by which observational learning, incorporating the imitation of models and the effects on behavior of incentives (reinforcement) following learner activities, can account for identification in human learning.

Imitation as a Learning Mechanism:
The Example of Aggression

The importance of observation and imitation in human learning, and the manner in which reinforcement principles contribute to such learning has been made clear in a number of experimental investigations. By way of illustration, it is interesting to examine some instances in which the experimental findings also have clear social implications. Some studies on the effect of aggression shown on film and television upon children's behavior have especially important findings. Bandura and his associates have carried out a large number of experiments examining the effects on children of exposure to situations in which people (models) behave aggressively. For example, Bandura (1965) showed children films in which models exhibited a number of physical and verbal aggressive responses. There were a number of different experimental conditions. In some instances, the model was rewarded for being aggressive, and in others, he was punished or received no consequences. Children who had seen models rewarded for aggression imitated the aggressive response more often than children who had not seen models rewarded, but the difference was rather small, and there was considerable imitation even among those children who had observed models punished for aggressive responses. Following the observation of imitative aggressive response, the children were offered attractive incentives (reinforcement) for imitating the responses seen in the field. Under these circumstances, children in all groups behaved aggressively, and the result of providing incentives was to remove entirely the previous differences in aggressive behavior between the three groups. Bandura (1969) interprets this result as indicating that the extent to which children *learned* aggressive ways of responding was equivalent in the different groups. The effect of the different consequences to the models was simply to influence the *performance* of the children.

Bandura and Walters (1963) describe the findings of a number of experiments showing that children acquire aggressive ways of behaving by learning it through observation. The findings strongly suggest that far from being a *natural* consequence of frustrating situations, aggressive behavior is largely a learned manner of responding. This body of research has strong and clear implications. For example, they make it absolutely clear that the experience of watching violent behavior on television *is* likely to increase the probability of aggressive behavior in the viewer. More broadly, the child who is exposed to violent behavior at home, in the form of physical punishment, learns to behave violently himself, and that aggression is legitimate, in certain situations, as a way of controlling the behavior of others. Parents may limit their use of physical aggression to a narrow range of circumstances, but their children are likely to learn the violent means of behavior very easily, and the ability to subtly discriminate between occasions on which aggression is and is not appropriate, may be acquired much later, if at all. As one might expect from the foregoing discussion, research has shown that the amount of aggressive behavior in children is closely related to the extent to which aggression occurs in the home (Bandura and Walters, 1963; Cohen, 1971).

At this point it is useful to make a brief summary. In the present chapter, we have described the following conditions by which students become motivated to learn independently: (1) Necessary learning skills must be acquired. (2) Learning must be seen by the learner as having clear functions for the learner. These may be practical and material, but "interest" may be sufficiently motivating, meeting Maslow's "need to understand." (Chapter 2.) (3) Partly as a result of (1) and (2), the learner must "identify" in a manner which makes possible the internalization of motives for learning. Imitation is a particularly important condition for such learning, and this in turn requires certain attentional skills.

A large number of factors are involved in human motivation, but the desire of people to understand and control the environment they live in is prominent among humans of all ages. It has already been suggested that when a learner perceives interest or relevance in a learning task, a fairly direct relationship exists between the learning activity and the human need that is filled by learning. It seems likely, on the basis of this type of learning experience, that an individual will come to value learning in its own right; the motivation becomes "intrinsic" to the learning activity. In this context, we can speak of the learner's "autonomy" in motivation. Similarly, the experiencing by a learner of many situations in which school learning rather directly meets needs for the individual, provides instances by which the learner comes to regard learning as a way of achieving "competence" in dealing with the environment, and R. W. White (1959) has pointed out the importance of such a need for "competence" as a motivating factor.

Other Aspects of Motivation:
Ausubel's Analysis of Achievement Needs

It would be naive to regard learning as being exclusively motivated either by factors, such as interest, relevance, and the need for competence, or exclusively by the provision of needs, such as for approval or money, which are less directly related to learning behavior. Ausubel (1968) indicates that different needs which may vary in strength may combine, as elements of a general "Achievement Motivation" in learners. He suggests that achievement motivation in school settings has at least three components. One of these he terms "Cognitive Drive," using this phrase to refer to the motivational effects of a learner finding the task interesting and relevant, or requiring "competence." These are, of course, factors that contribute to "cognitive involvement" by the individual. The cognitive drive is said to be "task-oriented" in the sense that the motive for becoming involved in the task that results in learning is intrinsic to the task itself.

The phrase "ego-enhancing" is used to describe Ausubel's second component of achievement motivation. Ego-enhancing refers to status, feelings of adequacy, self-esteem, and success. It is clear that insofar as factors such as these provide motivation for learning, their relationship to learning is indirect and provided externally, through praise, marks, and other rewards. These factors are not likely to contribute to the development of independence and self-control in the learner.

The third component of achievement motivation to which Ausubel draws attention is "affiliative," and oriented towards assuring the individual of the approval of a person or group with whom he identifies. The person who acts in a particular way in order to be "one of the boys" is demonstrating this affiliative component. The need to gain acceptance from a person or a group may influence the individual in various situations; this influence may complement or oppose the effects of the other components of achievement motivations.

Ausubel's three elements, "cognitive," "ego-enhancing," and "affiliative," all contribute to achievement motivation, but they can vary in at least two ways. First, their relative *strengths* may differ from one situation to another, and as a person becomes older changes occur in the relative strengths of the three components. For example, affiliative drive is very important in young children who need the attention and encouragement of adults. With increasing age, affiliative drive may become relatively less prominent and ego-enhancing factors more prominent as components of the need to achieve. Secondly, accompanying the changes in relative *strength* of the components of achievement motivation, there may be variations in the *directions* of the drives. For instance, in young children affiliative drive may be largely directed towards parents. Later, a teacher may come to exert an influence, and in the older students the affiliative drive may be directed less towards parents and teachers, and more toward a student's peers. Desire for peer approval may provide a motivating factor for achievement at school, but if the peer group does not value such achievement, academic achievement may be depressed.

It is suggested by Ausubel (1968) that the present century has seen changes in the prominence of the three components of achievement motivation. In Western civilization generally, ego-enhancement is the dominant component of achievement motivation among adults, especially in middle-class males. However, continues Ausubel, for roughly fifteen years succeeding World War II, the affiliative drive became relatively more important. This trend was epitomized in the "organization man," in whom the highly regarded properties were affability, "getting along," conforming and "playing it safe," rather than values that Ausubel regards as being traditionally dominant in North American culture, initiative, competence, individualism, forthrightness, and moral courage. Ausubel feels that these attributes have now staged a cultural comeback, partly in response to the challenge of Soviet achievements, and the evidence given for this return of "traditional" values takes the form of his impression that there now exists an almost cult-like veneration of intellectual achievement and creativity.

The Complexity of Motivation in Learning

The complex interaction between the various cognitive and personality components of achievement motivation is evident in the findings of a project by Cloward (1967). Negro and Puerto Rican backward readers in grades four and five were tutored for several months by paid volunteer high school students who were themselves deficient in reading skills. The children, who received four hours tutoring per week over a five month period, gained, on the average, six months growth in reading competence compared with an average 3.5 month's gain for control subjects. At the same time, the tutors showed very marked gains in their reading skills, gaining 3.4 years in reading proficiency over seven months compared with 1.7 years for controls. The large gains in the high school students' skills appear to be due in part to the influence on learning of motivational factors related to self-esteem and self-concept, which accompanied new roles as tutors. Noncognitive needs clearly played a large part in this learning situation. For the high school students, the project may have provided an escape from learning roles in which they considered themselves to be failures. In their new role, they were able to move ahead at a faster rate.

Among Ausubel's three components of achievement motivation, the cognitive drive, by virtue of the direct relationship between learning and need fulfillment, is more central than the others in developing the students' independence at school tasks. Yet, ego-enhancement is also important, at least within the framework of Western cultural values. Desires for status and prestige have contributed to some notable achievements even at the highest levels in science and the arts. Therefore, although in one sense activities which are partly motivated by a need for ego-enhancement are less "pure" than those motivated by cognitive drives alone, it would not necessarily be wise to discard all uses of ego-enhancement (for instance, by banning all forms of competition) in school. Another reason against banning all manifestations of ego-enhancement as a drive for classroom learning is that some valuable learning tasks do contain elements which are arduous, lengthy, and unexciting for many learners, and it would be wasteful to completely deny the use of a potentially useful additional source of motivation. However, to oppose the complete rejection of all forms of ego-enhancing drives in the classroom is not to encourage its predominance. To question the desirability of eliminating all competition, for instance, is not to deny that we might do well to place less emphasis on it than is now customary. Holt (1964) has made it clear that overemphasis on competition in the school and more generally in the culture of Western society is one reason for children's becoming "producers" at the expense of their genuine learning and thinking abilities. Competition necessarily results in losers as well as winners, and its negative effects on the motivation of the former may be disastrous.

Some Effects of Learning on Motivation

Although motivation largely determines learning activities (Piaget says that effect is the energy for development), it has been suggested that the direction of relationship may sometimes be reversed. For instance, if a child who is initially unmotivated begins to learn something, as directed by the teacher, the feelings that he experiences in connection with his learning, may in turn generate motivation for further learning. Thus, as Ausubel (1968) points out, the relationship between motivation and learning is sometimes reciprocal.

One implication for the teacher is that one should not studiously avoid attempting to teach a child anything unless he is already interested. Interest may not develop until some learning has taken place. This argument does not justify a teacher's forcing children to spend much of their time at school doing things that they dislike on the assumption that they will be "grateful" in later years. ("In ten years time you'll be glad you learned Latin.") This kind of reasoning is generally wrong. On some occasions, it is useful to encourage a student to do work which is initially distasteful on the assumption that learning will provide motivation for further progress. Yet the continuous or extended use of learning activities that are distasteful to a student is most likely to lead to antipathy to school learning.

Generally speaking, "Anything indifferent or apart becomes of interest when seen as a means to an end already commanding attention" (Dewey, 1913, page 25). Dewey's statement indicates the value of doing all that is possible to engage the learner's existing interests. In this way, the student may be encouraged to use existing interests as a basis for developing further interests. As Dewey says,

Many a student, of so-called practical make-up, has found a mathematical theory, once repellent, lit up by great attractiveness after studying some form of engineering in which this theory was a necessary tool.

(Dewey, 1913, page 22.)

This discussion of the role of learner interest as a major determinant of motivation for school learning, is continued in Chapter 8, which considers relevance as factor in meaningful learning.

Chapter 8

Relevance in Learning

When the class said that they were learning Roman Numerals, I asked them what use there was in knowing Roman Numerals. After a long discussion, we could arrive at nothing more than that Roman Numerals were used to number chapters in some books. Nevertheless, the class felt that they should learn them because they were taught by their teacher, an excellent teacher with whom they were closely involved. In my desperation to try and get the class to think about the relevance of what they were learning, I asked, "Do they use Roman Numerals in Rome?" Brightening considerably, the class decided that if Roman Numerals were used in Rome, it might be a good idea to learn them; they would then be prepared if they ever went to Rome. This seemingly good idea did not last long, however, because one boy had been to Rome the previous summer. He told the class that, all the time he had been there, he had never seen a Roman Numeral. The class was upset by this unexpected information, although the teachers thought it very funny.*

* From *Schools Without Failure* by William Glasser, M.D. Copyright © 1969 by William Glasser. Reprinted by permission of Harper & Row, Publishers, Inc. P. 55.

The Sabre-Tooth Curriculum

The above quotation might well come from *The Sabre-Tooth Curriculum*, Harold Benjamin's (1939) parody that spotlights some of the absurdities of educational systems. The sabre-tooth curriculum dryly describes the activities of a fictional primitive tribe, in which some intelligent members decide that some of the more important learning activities required in children growing up in the tribe can be carried out more effectively if specific learning goals are set up and a curriculum constructed. Accordingly, a curriculum is devised to teach some of the basic skills necessary for staying alive, such as "fish-grabbing-with-the-bare-hands," essential for obtaining food to eat; "clubbing-little-woolly-horses," required for obtaining skins to keep warm; and "driving-away-sabre-tooth-tigers-with-fire," necessary for safety at night. The children learn well from the three-subject curriculum, and the education system is a success. After certain conservative opposition to the new system of schooling subsides, everybody in the community begins to realize its value. All might have gone well forever, but the living conditions of the community change. A new ice age causes the approach of a glacier, bringing dirt and gravel into what had been crystal-clear streams, so it is no longer possible to catch fish with the bare hands because the fish can not be seen in the muddy water. Also, selective breeding produces more agile fish, since the clumsy ones have been caught by the bare hands method, leaving only the more agile fish to propagate. As a result of these two changes, no matter how good a man's fish-grabbing education had been, he can no longer grab fish.

The approaching glacier also affects the stupid woolly horses. Not liking the wet marshy country produced by the approaching glacier, they go elsewhere, far from our community. Thus, however well educated the horse-clubbers, they have little success. The sabre-tooth tigers are also affected by the glacial changes. The dampness in the air gives them pneumonia which causes them to die off. Without any tigers left to scare, the practical value of tiger-scaring techniques becomes somewhat limited.

However, there are new and adaptable men in the community, and they eventually develop methods of surviving in the new-changed environment so that they were able to satisfy their needs for food, clothing, and safety.

One or two radicals ask why the new activities that have been developed to cope with the changes in the environment cannot be taught in the educational system; could not the curriculum be altered to deal with the changes in society? Such foolish and naive questions are soon shot down by the safe and sober majority. The radicals persist a little, pointing out that the new activities required intelligence and skills which the schools were surely intended to develop. Why, they ask, could the schools not teach them?

"But" . . . *the wise old men who controlled the school, smiled indulgently at this suggestion, "that wouldn't be education," they said gently. "But why wouldn't it be?" asked the radicals. "Because it would be mere training," explained the old men patiently. "The school curriculum is too crowded now. We can't add these fads and frills of net-making, antelope-snaring, and of all things—bear-killing . . . what we need to do is to give our young people a more thorough grounding in the fundamentals. . . ." "But, damn it," exploded one of the radicals, "how can any person with good sense be interested in such useless activities? . . . how can a boy learn to club horses when there are no horses left to club? And why in hell should children try to scare tigers with fire when the tigers are dead and gone?" "Don't be foolish," said the wise old men, smiling most kindly smiles. "We don't teach fish-grabbing to grab fish; we teach it to develop a generalized ability which can never be developed by mere training. . . ." ". . . you must know that there are some external verities, and the sabre-tooth curriculum is one of them!"*

(Benjamin, 1939, pages 41–44.)

This parody, written in 1939, gives an uncomfortably accurate picture of the reality of much thinking that determines education in the 1970s. Consider the following quotation, written by a relatively progressive modern educator.

> *The elementary logic of Latin is the best foundation for learning to think and how to learn, its straightforward discipline, simple and yet rigid, is the best training in clear thinking and accurate expression that has so far been discovered. But if anyone doubts its value altogether, let him teach for some years in a school where Latin is done by all, and let him then transfer to a school (of the same age) where no Latin is done. He will find himself dealing with boys who speak a different (and largely unknown) language, who are to some extent incapable of clear thinking or precise expression, and with whom he can only communicate freely by limiting his words to comparatively simple forms.*
>
> *(Snow, 1959, page 90.)*

It is sufficient to state (in comparatively simple forms) that there is absolutely *no* objective evidence that Latin develops clear thinking and accurate thinking any more than does learning other subjects. The implicit assumption that Latin is some sort of "eternal verity," essential for clear thinking, is as erroneous as the notions about training "faculties" of the mind, discussed in Chapter 4.

Benjamin's parody provides an amusing, if alarming, illustration of the sorts of things that can and do happen when learning is institutionalized in an educational system, with the consequent necessity for schools and set curricula. As Bruner and others have pointed out, by institutionalizing learning and removing it from the immediate needs of production in order to survive, the potentialities are enormously increased. Away from the pressure of material necessity there is time for reflection, for looking back, and the opportunity for thought removed from action. This has made possible the enormous cultural advances of modern civilization. But separating learning from material action can also create opportunities for sterility and irrelevance. What is taught in the school may become more and more removed from the society outside; society may change, while the school stultifies. Separation of school and society can lead to artificialism and to a purposeless round of school activities in which the participants become unable to think outside their now pointless curriculum.

Differences in Needs

We have already discussed some reasons for the necessity of relevance in learning, and we have briefly noted some necessary conditions. School activities must be related to the student's needs. Students are not likely to engage wholeheartedly or become cognitively involved in situations where there seems to be no purpose, where learning does not appear in any way to be related to their needs, and where the contents of learning do not "make sense," or relate in any manner to what the individual knows or has experienced. To say that some knowledge is "relevant" to an individual means that it does relate to his experience.

There is no way of telling any teacher how to produce relevance. Relevance cannot be prescribed. It partly depends on the particular students who are learning. What is relevant to a group of children in Harlem may not be relevant to middle-class suburban children, and vice versa. The teacher as well as the children has to be rather closely involved in what is going on in the classroom. However interesting the subject matter, a teacher who finds it boring is unlikely to generate sufficient enthusiasm to effectively facilitate genuine learning.

Although relevance cannot be prescribed, it is possible to learn a good deal from what others have done. Perhaps one of the best ways is to read some of the accounts that a number of teachers have given about their own classrooms. Some good examples are Herbert Kohl's (1967) *Thirty-Six Children*, E. S. Richardson's (1964) *In the Early World*, and Sylvia

Marshall's (1963) *An Experiment in Education*. From reading books like these, it is clear that there are huge differences between what the various teachers did, although all the learning situations seem to have been highly relevant for the children.

Herbert Kohl taught a sixth grade class in Harlem. On one occasion some of his "problem" students spent a lot of time examining the architecture of Chartres Cathedral. The children studied Greek and Roman civilizations, and found out about the myths of Egypt and Mesopotamia. Kohl asked himself:

> *How we became modern America, how we became modern man—that was our problem, my problem is to teach, but where to start, what moment in history does one say, "Ah, here's where it all began."? How could the children get some saving perspective on the mad chaotic world they existed in, some sense of the universality of struggle, the possibility of revolution and change, and the strength to persist? That, if anything, was my challenge as a teacher— it was spelled out before me unambiguously. Could I find anything in human history and the human soul that would strengthen the children and save them from despair?*
>
> (Kohl, 1967, page 52.)

In searching for an answer, Kohl and the children looked back into prehistory. They traced Greek myth to earlier African and Asiatic sources, exploring the earliest civilizations and dynasties, Sumer, Akkad, and their successors. Their history was less smooth, less bland, less blithely optimistic than that of the textbooks. They discovered misery and oppression in the past of mankind, they saw hyprocisy where it existed, they noted that one man's "barbarian" was another's "civilized ideal," and how one nation's hero was another's villain. They learned about morals and violence, love and hate, how all these things went into the world they live in.

The school where E. S. Richardson taught—a small square

wooden building in a remote rural area in northern New Zealand—was about as different from Kohl's classroom in the crowded urban ghetto as any could possible be. The activities that went on in school were correspondingly different. The children learned from their rural environment; they collected the various clays in the area and discovered which were most suitable for the various types of pottery. They made designs with lino and used these in conjunction with silk-screen printing methods. They made all sorts of things. They read a great deal and expressed themselves in writing, in drawing, and in various sorts of visual art. They learned to look and to see, and to go beyond the clichés which hinder perception and thinking in everyday life. They learned mathematics because it was necessary for calculating the most effective mixtures of clay, for working out how much the clay would shrink, and for knowing how to fire their wares in the kiln most effectively without damage. It was also necessary when children had to design and construct a workshed for some of their crafts. They had to work out the correct dimensions so there would be space for all the desks, tables, chairs, and cupboards. The children learned to evaluate their own work, to see what was genuinely fresh and insightful.

Sybil Marshall was the only teacher in a small country school in England. As in Richardson's school, there was much emphasis on expression through the visual arts and in writing, both prose and poetry. The children explored their environment, they found out about the present and the past of the area in which they lived, and visual and written expression were combined in learning. They made maps of their region. They did a great deal of discovering about themselves. They looked at themselves and the world, they expressed nature in their art, and they performed, enthusiastically, a great number of activities that could not be placed into any subject matter category.

It is, of course, impossible in a few brief sentences to give any real idea of the types of learning that occurred in the children taught by these three very different people. The reader is urged to read their books. In any case, just to describe what the teachers did, at whatever length, does not tell us what was actually learned. Accordingly, the major part of each of the three books consists not of the teacher's account, but of the works produced by the children. They are exciting, full of freshness and vigor and passion and feeling, and of open-eyed wonder about what was being discovered in ways which contrast sharply with the blandness of so many of the things that children produce in school.

The three teachers were different in many ways because they had to be. The areas in which they taught were different, the children were different, the resources were different, and their own interests and abilities were different. They also had many things in common, such as imagination, sensitivity, interest in the needs of children, and an awareness of the difference between genuine insight and formalized cliché. They were all able to help their students become more self-reliant, better able to use their own perceptions, and to trust their own feelings. All three were imaginative in making use of the various amenities at their disposal, and in using their own skills, whether artistic, literary, or whatever. They were able to ensure that all learning had a definite meaning for the children. There was little of the usual separation among different subjects; in fact, avoiding the splitting of learning into discrete areas of subject matter was an important common element contributing to the liveliness of these three classrooms.

There is a lot of talk about the need for a "balanced" curriculum. The basic idea seems to be that the correct proportions of history, literature, social studies, mathematics, and so on, should be mixed together, as if the object was to produce cakes, rather than educated individuals. One can picture some educators throwing up their arms in horror when reading about the sort of things taught by Kohl, Richardson, and Marshall. Did the children get the right amount of spelling practice? Did they learn equations? The point is that this kind of balance hardly matters. By any realistic definition of the word, the curricula of these three teachers were probably more "balanced" than most. These teachers were able to look behind the subject matter labels that form a basis for curricula, and to go more directly into the sorts of experiences through which the children could really become able to think, to judge, and to live with inquiring minds in their own world.

The particular knowledge acquired by children is not all-important. Kohl made great use of ancient history in his class. Exploring and discovering early civilizations were exciting and valuable for his Harlem children. Other teachers have different interests. Postman and Weingartner (1969), for example, write scathingly about the use of ancient history in today's schools. They quote the question, "What sort of religion did the ancient Greeks have? How does this compare to that of the Egyptians?" as examples of what they call "pretentious trivia," failing to realize that although ancient history as presented at school is often trivial and irrelevant, it does not have to be. The children in Kohl's classroom, encouraged by their teacher's obvious enthusiasm, might have enjoyed exploring problems like these as part of their search for understanding the modern world. To insist that all children learn about the ancient Greeks is absurd, but some children may be genuinely affected by such learning.

Relevance and Everyday Life

In discussing relevance, we can underestimate the extent of children's imaginations. The assumption that everything has to be related in a very direct, immediate, practical way to the here and now of a child's everyday world is incorrect. Some of the things that interest children, the cartoons they see on television, the fantasy stories they read, and their interest in space exploration, are not in any obvious sense relevant to daily life. The events and the people in them are often strange and far removed from direct experience, and yet they hold children's attention and curiosity. Children are often interested in things that are by no means relevant in this immediate sense.

Too much emphasis on relevance in a narrow sense can be stultifying and harmful. There have been some tendencies in what has been called the "progressive education movement" towards bringing everything in learning very close to the child's world. Often the result is trivia, with too much emphasis on adjustment and too little on imagination and growth. It is one thing to *start* with the familiar, bringing the content of learning close to the child's understanding, but learning does not have to remain there. If this appears to contradict what we have been saying about meaningful learning, it might be useful to make a distinction between some of the ways in which learning can be relevant. Relevance is related to understanding. Attempts to be relevant in education too often take the form of matching superficial subject matter to a child's experience. Thus, we have mommies and daddies, and the friendly postman in the friendly neighborhood, on the assumption that familiar characters of this kind help students relate lesson contents to their own lives. Bruner (1959) provides an example of this sort of material at its worst in a textbook presentation of Christopher Columbus.

> *Young Chris is walking along the water front in his home town and gets to wondering where all those ships go. Eventually, he comes back to his brother's cobbler shop and exclaims, "Gee, Bart, I wonder where all those ships go. . . ." Bart replies with pleasant brotherly encouragement. Chris is a well adjusted kid. Bart is a nice big brother.*

> *(Bruner, 1959, page 188.)*

There are better ways to make learning relevant. Materials can relate to children not only on the basis of subject matter familiarity, but on the basis of emotions, feelings, fears, excitement, and so on. To be relevant, what is being learned has to make some sort of contact with the learner, but that contact can equally well involve feelings, passions, and imagination. Young students are enthusiastic about things that have vigor and color, and are full of excitement, even when the subject, time, and place are very far removed from the familiar world. In short, although we need to be concerned with relevance, we should realize that relevance can exist in the absence of frequent references to everyday life.

Indeed, much of the value of learning in schools revolves around learners being able to escape temporarily from everyday realities, to look around and reflect. We learn by gaining new perspectives on the familiar. One might say that a function of education is akin to letting the goldfish see what is outside the bowl. If we are concerned all of the time with what is most obviously relevant in a narrow sense, some important results of education are lost, such as opening individuals to new experiences, making them aware of different perspectives, and creating an awareness of the relativeness of various aspects of a particular culture. The resulting output of narrow, myopic adults might have been thought quite desirable in ancient Sparta, but we do not want it now.

It is not likely that many students will become involved in ways which bring into full action the constructive learner processes that result in efficient learning if the content of education is stripped of the passion, controversy, and heat-producing issues that are inevitable in the important questions of mankind. As Bruner says,

> Education must no longer strike an exclusive posture of neutrality and objectivity. Knowledge, we know now as never before, is power. Rather, let knowledge as it appears in our schooling be put into the context of action and commitment. The lawyer's brief, a parliamentary strategy, or a town planner's subtle balancing, are as humanly important a way of knowing as a physicist's theorem. Gathering together the data for the indictment of a society that tolerates in the United States, the ninth rank in infant

mortality when it ranks first in gross national product—
this is not an exercise in radical inventive but in the mobil-
izing of knowledge in the interests of conviction that
change is imperative. Let the skills of problem solving be
given a chance to develop on problems that have an inher-
ent passion—whether racism, crimes on the street, pollu-
tion, war and aggression, or marriage and the family.

(Bruner, 1970, page 78.)

Emotions and Learning

The "inherent passion" of which Bruner speaks is an ingredient of learning. A contemporary problem is that current
knowledge that we now possess about the relationship between emotions and feelings and our more "cold-blooded"
cognitive functions is inadequate. The importance and cen-
trality of emotions and passions are realized, but very little
is known about how they operate in connection with the
other aspects of functioning. A symptom of this fact is the
very restricted vocabulary available for dealing with things
to do with feelings and emotions. It has been argued by one
writer (Koestler, 1967) that the very limited understanding
of how human emotions operate, and the lack of success in
integrating the operations of emotions and passions with
human cognitive processes, is evidence of a "fault" in the
development of the human species. The emotions and the
higher thinking processes are governed by different parts of
the brain which evolved at different times in the development
of man. According to Koestler, the integration between that
part of the human brain governing emotions and the parts
responsible for higher cognitive process, is seriously deficient,
and the consequent lack of integration between emotions and
higher reasoning constitutes a dangerous flaw in the human
species, which may adversely affect the chances for human
survival in the future.

The topic of *anxiety* has generated considerable amount of
research. The relationship between anxiety and learning de-

pends on a number of attributes in the learner (for example, IQ, personality) and in the type of material being learned. In some learning tasks, it has been observed that subjects with a medium level of anxiety perform better than low-anxiety subjects. However, this is generally true only for tasks requiring rote learning, and anxiety normally impedes learning in situations where the content is complex or unfamiliar (Ausubel, 1968). Even in the case of rote-learning situations, it seems doubtful whether the findings that relatively high anxiety levels may benefit learning in situations that last for short periods of time is sufficient evidence for favoring the deliberate raising of anxiety levels on an extended basis. Whatever slight and temporary advantages may acrue are very small in relation to the powerful detrimental effects (Sarason, et al., 1960; Holt, 1964). One needs to be very cautious in following suggestions, such as "On occasion the teacher should deliberately increase anxiety, particularly for students with high IQs" (DeCecco, 1968).

One cannot "teach" feelings and emotions. They are not teachable in any simple sense, and problems of understanding and dealing with feelings and emotions arise in response to various situations, the emotions being part of the student's response, and not of the situation. There have been some attempts to devise circumstances in which students are able to develop an increased awareness and understanding of the place of emotions in their lives. Jones (1968) describes a particularly interesting attempt to devise a program which gives experiences whereby children can become aware of, learn about, and in some ways learn to control and integrate their emotions and feelings with their cognitive functions. His book, *Fantasy and Feeling in Education*, describes a course based on Bruner's *Man: A Course of Study*. The latter attempts to examine the nature of man as a species, and observes the forces that have shaped his humanity. It asks what is human about human beings, how they have become the way they are, and it explores certain great humanizing factors, tool-making, language, social organization, the management of man's prolonged childhood, and his urge to explain his world (see Bruner, 1966, pages 74–75).

The program used by Jones involves a very considerable amount of participation by the children, and the source materials include films, slides, and tape recordings that attempt to provide ways of looking at the human species. Some of the films give a detailed account of the lives of Eskimo peoples, showing how they attempt to cope with the problems involved in staying alive in their environment, which is very different from that of modern North America. The children become aware of the harsh lives of the Eskimo people, and learn how life depends on animals, such as caribou, seal, and salmon. They learn about Eskimo customs, such as female infanticide and senilicide, which appear senseless from the perspective of Western man, but have vital functions in Eskimo society. In the course of this learning, the children inevitably experience very strong emotions and feelings. Jones considers that teachers are generally unprepared for helping children come to grips with their emotions in learning. He writes:

> There are times for dispassion in school rooms; but teachers need no reminding of this. They do, however, need reminding that there are also times for passion in school rooms. . . . It is true that emotions and fantasies can obstruct learning when they are controlled. Uncontrolled emotions and fantasies obstruct almost all aspects of learning. The other half of this truth is that the control of emotion and fantasy is substantive in one kind of learning (the attainment of discovery of knowledge) and preparatory to another kind of learning (the formation or invention of knowledge).
>
> (Jones, 1968, page 25.)

Jones is critical of those who assume that the material will automatically suggest to the teachers how emotions and images that are aroused can be made pedagogically relevant. He feels it important for teachers and teachers of teachers to think hard about how emotions and feelings can contribute to learning and can be made useful and positively effective through learning. He puts a lot of emphasis on discussion of emotions in order to gain more self-awareness about them. The children talk about their fears and beliefs. As in the case of the three books by teachers mentioned earlier in this chapter, it is impossible, without quoting at great length, to communicate the real flavor of the Jones' program, but the following short quotations convey some of his ideas.

> The co-ordination of cognitive, emotional and imaginal skills may be left untutored in exceptionally healthy children. For the rest, if exclusive evidence is placed upon cultivating cognitive skills, and development of emotional and imaginal skills is left to random encounters, we run the risk with the child who tends to lead with his head of encouraging pedantry; with the child who tends to lead with his heart supposing anti-intellectualism; with the child who tends to lead with his fantasies of inviting estrangement.
>
> (Jones, 1968, page 198.)

> Relevant confrontations of emotional issues centering around initiative and guilt, and relevant employment of discovery, exploration, and origination fantasies, must automatically work to humanize the child's growing ability to think critically. Relevant concentrations of emotional issues centering around competence and inferiority, and relevant employment of achievement fantasies, must automatically work to broaden the child's development of representational skills. Relevant concentrations of emotional issues centering around identity and diffusion, and relevant employment of Utopian images, must automatically work to inspire creative thinking.
>
> (Jones, 1968, page 199.)

Certainly, there are no easy ways of arranging educational experiences to encourage the maximum growth in ability to live with emotions, but we must at least be willing to face some of the problems that arise. The imbalance between human emotions and other human functions seems to be a central fact in the dark forces which threaten the existence of the human race. Emphasizing the importance of the emotions in education follows from the knowledge that emotions are crucial in learning, that feelings are important in everything a person does, and that humans as a whole, especially in Western civilization, need greater ability than they now possess to integrate those aspects of their experience which are dominated by their emotions with the largely cognitive aspects of experience. Present knowledge and awareness about the place of emotions in life falls short of what we need to know. It is not a simple matter of controlling one's emotions nor of having a cognitive understanding of the "role of emotions in experience." That would be a contradiction in terms.

A final point for this chapter is one which might seem obvious but which is often ignored. All students, young and old, sometimes need to be made aware of the relevance of things they learn, in that certain things are connected and related to other things. They need opportunities to discover how things learned in one context, on a particular occasion or in connection with particular bodies of knowledge or skills, have meaning and utility in other contexts, on other occasions, and in conjunction with other areas of knowledge. Adults are liable to assume that if they can see the relevance of something, the relevance will also be apparent to children. Sometimes it is necessary to draw connections, to make the lines of contact explicit. How this can be done in specific situations will depend on what is being learned and on how it is being learned.

The need to make things explicit exists even at higher levels of education. Many college professors have had the experience of finding their students treating bodies of knowledge as entirely separate and fragmented, although the professor is aware, and assumes that the students are aware, of connections and relationships that are clear and obvious to him. It is a mark of an educated person to be able to integrate and tie together experiences and things learned in diverse situations, times, and contexts, and one cannot expect all students to do this sort of integration automatically. There has to be some explicit demonstration of connections and deliberate encouragement to look for them, if what is taught in school is to become as relevant as it can be.

Chapter 9

Questions and Answers in School Learning

Questions present something of a paradox in education. On the one hand, questions—asking them, answering them, sharpening them, inquiring, and trying to solve problems—are the very meat of learning. On the other hand, questions can cause some of the strongest barriers to learning in the schools.

Questions and "Right Answers"

We have already mentioned some of John Holt's observations about the effects of situations in which emphasis is placed on getting the "right answer" to questions at the expense of real learning. If a teacher makes it clear that it is the right answer that she is most concerned about, then the students are likely to become equally concerned about it. The result is the child who is a "producer" rather than a thinker, and who is anxious and frightened of being wrong. Children adopt various rote-learning strategies designed to convince the teacher that they know the right answer, even when they do not, and the effort that should be going into meaningful learning goes into getting the answer. There are good reasons for having some questions designed simply to find out if children know the correct answer, and they sometimes help children pay attention. The detrimental effects of such questions can be serious when children adopt strategies that are destructive to meaningful learning.

Sometimes the actions of a teacher can make such strategies inevitable. Leacock (1969) gives a horrifying example:

"I ask the leading question to get the answer I want," said a teacher when discussing "experience charts." "As we are discussing, I will put down the main thoughts of what I want to go down on the chart. They enjoy that. They like to talk. They enjoy a discussion. . . ."

(Leacock, 1969, page 51.)

Glasser (1969) makes a similar observation:

*While talking to elementary school teachers and asking them whether they allow free discussion in their classes, I have been told hotly by several teachers that they do encourage free discussion. They say, "We discuss everything until we arrive at the right answer."**

This sort of teaching has results:

Some pupils learn how to daydream; others, how to take tests. Some learn the petty deceptions involved in cheating; others, the larger deceptions of playing the school game absolutely straight (the well-kept notebook, the right answer, the senior who majored in good grades).

(Leonard, 1968, page 10.)

Perhaps half of all learning ability was squelched in the earliest elementary grades, where children found out that there exists pre-determined and unyielding "right answers" for everything, that following instructions is what really counts, and most surprisingly, that the whole business of education is mostly dull and painful.

(Leonard, 1968, page 120.)

In attempting to explain the overemphasis on right answers, Glasser (1969) draws attention to what he calls the

* From *Schools Without Failure* by William Glasser, M.D. Copyright © 1969 by William Glasser. Reprinted by permission of Harper & Row, Publishers, Inc. P. 37.

certainty principle in education, according to which "there is a right and a wrong answer to every question; the function of education is then to ensure that each student knows the right answers to a series of questions that educators have decided are important" (Glasser, 1969, page 37).

Some of the criticism of those who place emphasis on right answers may be a little unfair. After all, there are important questions for which it is necessary to know the answers. Two plus two makes four, and anyone who thinks that it is three or five will clearly be handicapped in life. The teacher requires some feedback to give an indication about how well the students are learning. Often, asking questions which have definite answers is the most convenient method for the teacher to get information about learning in the pupils. Since questions are so often used it is not very surprising that they may sometimes be misused, that right answers will be confused with understanding, and that sometimes people will forget that there are no simple right answers for many important questions. The examples given by Holt and others make it clear that such misuse of questions does have disastrous results for many children, so the problem requires close attention.

The emphasis on producing right answers where none really exist is found not only in education, although its effect on school learning is particularly destructive. We might call it a cultural malaise. The smart politician is the one who knows all the answers; a politician who frankly admits, "I don't know," is something of a rarity. Ours is not a culture in which it is easy for any individual to admit ignorance. It is not entirely clear why this is so. Certainly, there are some individuals who have to have an answer for everything, and who feel threatened by feelings of uncertainty and complexity. Research into the psychology of personality has shown large differences in the extent to which people can tolerate such uncertainty and ambiguity. Perhaps intolerance of ambiguity provides some individuals with the appearance of stability and regularity in their world. Glasser's (1969) "certainty principle" might be seen as one manifestation of people's need to eliminate ambiguity from their lives.

Three suggestions may help explain the apparent over-emphasis on correct answers in much school learning. First, there are valid and important right answers in much of the content that children learn early in school, especially in reading and elementary mathematics. Thus, learning habits emphasizing correct answers may be quite appropriate in much of what is learned in the first year or two at school. The trouble is that such habits are extended to situations in which they are no longer apt. Even in subjects such as arithmetic, however, where right answers are important, having the answer is no guarantee of understanding. In fact, most of Holt's (1964) examples are from mathematics teaching.

Another possible reason for overemphasis on right answers in school learning lies in the legitimate needs of teachers themselves, and is related to the requirement for feedback about learning, mentioned above. A teacher has to know if she is communicating to the pupils successfully, and if they are learning. A straightforward, if sometimes misleading and inaccurate, indication is the extent to which children get the right answers to questions. It is encouraging when a student gets the right answer, or the answer that the teacher is "looking for," and as a result her eyes may light up, and she smiles, spontaneously, and the student in turn is encouraged by this sign of approval. Hence, unless one is cautious, the legitimate needs of both teachers and students may help perpetuate another vicious circle.

Thirdly, and contributing to the fear of admitting ignorance in our culture, is the knowledge that to be correct is to be regarded as successful, and to be incorrect is to be a failure. Evaluation is necessary in education and has the function of providing information about degrees of learning to both students and teachers, making it clear what has been learned and what has not. Too often, however, a student's success, or lack of it, in a question-answering situation is seen as an indication of his worthiness. In addition to being successful, the individual with the right answer is seen as good, virtuous, and diligent, while the student who is wrong is shiftless, lazy, and inattentive. Consequently, children learn early to make great efforts to avoid getting wrong answers.

The Need to Ask Questions

Despite the difficulties we have mentioned, questions are at the heart of meaningful learning. We have to ask questions and try to answer them, if we are to learn anything worthwhile. Scientific activity is, basically, the asking of questions.

The active learner has to be concerned not only with answering questions, but with asking them. Individuals whose school education consists mainly of situations where the emphasis is on their knowing the correct answers for particular questions get out of the habit of asking questions themselves. If teachers do all the asking, and if there are always right answers, then question-asking does not come to appear as a very interesting, or purposeful activity. Even when there is the semblance of discussion, of asking and inquiring about important questions, the reality is often different. Sometimes discussion is just a means for arriving at a predetermined answer. Leacock (1969), after observing a number of schools, noted that all too frequently,

> *Instead of inquiry, questioning, exploring the significance of various happenings, teaching, by and large, involved a repetition of events and a search for predetermined interpretation of these events, drawn from the children through the medium of a question-answer interchange or "discussion". . . . In "discussions" honest, eager questions of significance—such as questions or comments about slavery, some aspects of our economy, the Soviet Union, or a current political event—were either ignored, said to be beside the point, or otherwise cursorily disposed of.*
>
> *(Leacock, 1969, page 47.)*

Such situations do not encourage genuine inquiring. It is not surprising that, as George Wald has said, "The great questions are those which an intelligent child asks, and, getting no answers, stops asking," or that Richard Suchman (Taylor, 1967, page 43) found high school students to have a greater need than second graders for training and inquiring. The second graders were better than the older students at asking questions, a sad reflection on some effects of schooling.

Although the school should do all it can to encourage and help develop inquiry skills, there is room for differences in the degree of emphasis on inquiring in education. For some (for instance, Postman and Weingartner, 1969), education *is* inquiry. They would stress inquiry not as a means to any goal, but as an end in itself.

> The inquiry method is very much a product of our electric age. It makes the syllabus obsolete; students generate their own stories by becoming involved in the methods of learning. Where the older school environment has asked "Who discovered America?" the inquiry method asks, "How do you discover who discovered America?" The older school environment stressed that learning is being taught what happened. The inquiry environment stresses that learning is a happening in itself.*

Other educators, while agreeing with Postman and Weingartner that inquiring is extremely important both for gaining knowledge about the world and for developing the skills of asking and answering questions, would stop short of completely equating inquiry and education. Many would insist that knowledge also has an important place in education without denying the value of the skills and processes gained in inquiry. However, whatever one's point of view about the

---

* From *Teaching as a Subversive Activity* by Neil Postman and Charles Weingartner. Copyright © 1969 by Neil Postman and Charles Weingartner. Reprinted by permission of the publisher, Delacorte Press. P. 29.

relative value of product (for example, knowledge) against process (for example, inquiry) in learning, there is no doubt that the product, in the form of knowledge and information, tends to become obsolete, whereas process does not. Any separation between product and process is to some extent artificial, but if education is to have lasting value to the individual, especially in a world changing at a fast rate, there must be sufficient emphasis on learning processes and skills to ensure that the adult can adapt to a modern world in which learning continues to be necessary long after he leaves school. A man who leaves school with no more than a body of knowledge would seem to be less well equipped for future learning than a person who has less knowledge but possesses attitudes, skills, and habits of mind that incline him to inquire and to gain understanding through learning. The second person is in a better position to meet the changing demands of his life. However, we must avoid thinking of this as a simple either-or issue, since learning processes and products are closely related.

Encouraging Inquiry

What can a teacher do to encourage students to develop skills for inquiring and finding out about the world? One gains inquiry skills by inquiring. People learn when they are actively involved (Chapter Three), and this is especially true in learning how to ask questions. Inquiring can occur in many contexts, including projects and discussions, and the teacher can play a fairly active role in discussions, at least in the initial stages. It is a mistake to think that when the teacher's role ceases to be one of providing knowledge it should be entirely passive.

Some advice about procedures to help bring about valuable discussions is given in W. Glasser's (1969) book, Schools Without Failure. He notes that exciting classroom discussions do not develop on every occasion, right from the outset. It is quite possible that a teacher may develop what seems to be a good and exciting question, only to find that the children seem to be completely uninterested. At such times, teachers, being mortal, can easily get discouraged. Assistance and optimism are needed, especially at first. It can be surprisingly difficult to think of questions that will really interest the class. As Glasser says,

> For every teacher who gets a class discussion going, there is at least one other teacher who believes in the method, who has tried it and would like to continue, but who falters because she cannot think of·enough questions that lead to interesting meetings.*

Glasser feels that general questions often fail to arouse enthusiasm, and students react much better to questions that are relatively specific. Glasser gives "Why do we go to school?" as an example of a general question, and he suggests that instead of being stimulated the students usually answer with clichés. The discussion can become an impersonal, rote exercise in which the students mouth the answers which they think the teacher wants to hear, such as: "A good education leads to a good job." "Education is important for college." "Education is important for life."

In order to get real involvement, at least at first, questions have to be more pointed, and rather specific. Glasser suggests one should try to develop series of questions in which the answers lead in turn to more questions. To give an illustration of the way ideas and questions might develop, here are some of the alternatives to the general question, "Why do we go to school?"

> If each of you could have a million dollars right now, a sum that would be ample for the rest of your life, would you continue to go to school?

---

* From *Schools Without Failure* by William Glasser, M.D. Copyright © 1969 by William Glasser. Reprinted by permission of Harper & Row, Publishers, Inc. P. 163.

Why would you go to school? Just a few minutes ago you said that the purpose of education was to get a good job. Now you say you would continue to go to school even if you didn't need the money from a job.

If you still want to go to school to get a good job, even though you would have enough money, work must be important? Why is work important? And if work is important, how does education relate to work?

Do all rich men's sons avoid work? Why, in many cases, do rich men work harder than people who are poor? Do some poor people work as hard or even harder than rich people?*

Both students and teachers need to develop skills of asking questions and inquiring. An interesting classroom approach developed by Frank Miceli is described by Postman and Weingartner (1969). The instructor brings a black attaché case into the class. He informs the students that inside the case is a small computer capable of producing the answer to any question that anybody can ask. He then asks the students for questions, and many are produced. For example:

When was I born?
What is my mother's maiden name?
What should we do about Viet Nam?
Why can't we grade ourselves in school?
Why are grown-ups always angry at teenagers?
If love is dead, why do I feel so great with my boyfriend?
How many miles is it to San Francisco?**

---

* From *Schools Without Failure* by William Glasser, M.D. Copyright © 1969 by William Glasser. Reprinted by permission of Harper & Row, Publishers, Inc. Pp. 166–167.

** From *Teaching as a Subversive Activity* by Neil Postman and Charles Weingartner. Copyright © 1969 by Neil Postman and Charles Weingartner. Reprinted by permission of the publisher, Delacorte Press. P. 172.

The instructor goes on to give the class some more information about what the computer can and cannot do. He explains that the computer is very expensive to operate, so it is wasteful to use it on questions to which the answers are already known. The students are told to look at their list of questions and eliminate those to which known answers already exist. In the above list questions like "When was I born?" or, "What is my mother's maiden name?" come under this category. Next, the students are told that the computer cannot cope with questions that are vaguely phrased. It has to know exactly what is meant by the words in each question. For instance, in the question, "What should we do about Viet Nam?" the computer needs to know precisely what is meant by "we" and by "should," and whether it is a "moral should" or a "political should."

Postman and Weingartner describe a project in which this game was continued over three weeks during which the students developed numerous questions to ask about their initial questions. They came to realize that certain questions are more useful than others, and that one has to think rather carefully about the sorts of questions that are asked. They also came to appreciate that questions, more often than leading to clear answers, lead to other questions, and to understand that the progress of science commonly takes the form not so much of finding simple answers to questions, but in developing new questions which have greater power and lead towards further understanding. The students learned much about clarity of communication, and about the ways value judgements are often expressed unawares in statements and questions. The resharpening and reformulating of questions, the careful emphasis on defining and redefining, are all essential components of the skills necessary in scientific understanding and discovery. The students in this project,

> . . . came to believe that their question list was a powerful instrument in helping someone to know a) what he is talking about; b) what sort of information he wants; c)

*whether or not a question can be answered; and, d) what he must do to find an answer if one can be found. . . . If we can say that all human discovery, regardless of discipline, starts with an answerable question, then we ought to look at the curriculum as a series of questions from students that the school helps them to explore—regardless of how indelicate these questions might be.**

This particular program produced more than skills of inquiry. It allowed the students to bring themselves more and more into their learning, so that education became a highly personal, individual thing. Questions were related to things that the students felt strongly about, that were important to them. They asked many questions about language, sex, friendship, parental control, and social rejection. It is clear that there was a high degree of cognitive (and emotional) involvement. The curriculum did not follow a logical sequence of predetermined material. It was:

*. . . a flow of ideas, one idea leading to the next because that was the order in which the students thought of them. The instructor never had occasion to say, "Today we will discuss. . . ." The students always knew what they were to discuss because, in a sense, the discussion of the previous lesson had not ended.***

The students tried to answer questions, such as "Why do we have such a thing as a 'dirty word'?" "Why do I fear certain words?" "Do people kill each other over words?" and, "Should people kill each other over words?" (Postman and Weingartner, 1969, page 179.)

---

* From *Teaching as a Subversive Activity* by Neil Postman and Charles Weingartner. Copyright © 1969 by Neil Postman and Charles Weingartner. Reprinted by permission of the publisher, Delacorte Press. Pp. 173–180.

** From *Teaching as a Subversive Activity* by Neil Postman and Charles Weingartner. Copyright © 1969 by Neil Postman and Charles Weingartner. Reprinted by permission of the publisher, Delacorte Press. P. 178.

The contents of these questions do not belong to any particular curriculum "subject," and it would be difficult if not impossible to specify the appropriate field of knowledge for questions like, "Is there any moral or legal relationship between fooling around with marijuana, fooling around with someone's else's wife or husband, and fooling around with an income tax return?" (Postman and Weingartner, 1969, page 179.)

Postman and Weingartner point out that children are usually interested in questions about the future, whereas school curricula are more concerned with the past. The world is changing so rapidly that ability to deal with the future is important for all. After all, they argue, by the time children in school now have finished, the future you will have asked them to think about will be the present. These authors also suggest that teachers be prohibited from asking any question to which they already know the answer. It could be very wasteful to follow slavishly such a suggestion, but there might be advantages. A teacher avoiding these questions would not only eliminate the dangers of too much emphasis on right answers, but would be encouraged to ask questions which raise real problems. Although it may be an exaggeration to state that *all* important questions do not at present have right answers, it is certain that many do not. Such a prohibition might also encourage teachers to see the enterprise of learning from the perspective of a learner, and thus help avoid the artificial situation whereby the teacher is expected to have all answers and knowledge which he imparts to the students who have none. Students may gain when their teacher is involved as a learner and is learning himself. Apprentice-artists profit from their masters' involvement in creative work, and, similarly, students may gain from the involvement of their teachers (as "master-learners" perhaps) in using their learning skills to gain increased understanding. Another suggestion, which if followed, would help teachers to see their task from the perspective of learners is that all teachers be required to take a test prepared by students on what the students know.

Getting Out of Blind Alleys

Popular knowledge has it that people sometimes solve problems better if they first "sleep on" them, and we have already said that efficient abstract reasoning tends to flourish when one is somewhat removed from situations where activities are determined by immediate survival needs. In separating thought and learning from action, a movement that is accentuated when learning is institutionalized in an educational system, there arises a risk of developments that result in artificial and irrelevant learning environments, and yet such separation appears 'necessary for the growth of man as an animal who thinks and reasons. We thus encourage the reflective thinking on which progress feeds, and enables man's self-awareness to develop.

Dependent on this separation is a phenomenon that often accompanies advances in learning. Koestler (1964, 1967) points out that in order to progress we sometimes first have to undo; to escape from "blind alleys" we have to withdraw in order to advance, and old assumptions need to be jettisoned before we can create new forms and make new discoveries. The value of being able to "retreat from the front," moving toward the rear in order to get a better vantage and time to reorganize, indicates that a willingness at times to "move backwards, both in thought and action, can have great rewards." As Koestler says:

> The point to retain is that the creative act in mental evolution again reflects the pattern of reculer pour mieux sauter, of a temporary regression, followed by a forward leap. We can carry the analogy further and interpret the Eureka cry as the signal of the happy escape from a blind alley—an act of mental self-repair.
>
> (Koestler, 1967, page 181.)

Koestler suggests that in both scientific and artistic fields, this pattern of retreating before advancing, undoing and redoing, and making forms by a kind of zig-zag course, paral-

lels certain forms of adaptation in biology. Escapes from blind
alleys are important in phylogeny, he claims:

> *Indeed the main line of development which led to our
> species could be described as a series of operations of
> phylogenetic self-repair: of escapes from blind alleys by
> the undoing and remolding of maladapted structures.*
>
> (Koestler, 1967, pages 203–204.)

Some questions are especially well designed to carry out
the function of helping people escape from blind alleys in
learning and thinking, moving away from the fixed reality of
a situation and the aspects of it that are most familiar. A good
instance is a question provided by De Mille (1967). He says:

> *To take an example from the field of history of social
> studies, Matthew Perry's visits to Japan in the 1850's are
> said to have brought Japan into the modern world. In less
> than a century, Japan changed from a predominantly feudal
> agricultural society into an industrial power that could chal-
> lenge the most powerful nation on earth, both in commer-
> cial trade and in land, sea, and air warfare. The student
> may be aware of the events of World War II and may
> understand that Japan was not one of the very first indus-
> trial nations, but will he grasp the significance of Perry's
> mission?*
>
> *The teacher has a choice. He can, on the one hand, tell
> his students that Perry's insistence on negotiating a treaty
> changed the history of Japan and the United States. The
> students may remember that or they may forget it, but
> either way they will not have had much practice in think-
> ing. On the other hand, suppose the teacher said: "What
> would have happened if, in 1808, Perry had joined the
> army instead of the navy?"*
>
> *A panorama of historical possibilities opens up. Each
> student can now imagine a new history of Japan or the
> United States. Perhaps President Fillmore would have sent*

another man who would have done the same things Perry did. But if not, Japan still might be feudal today. Or Japan might now be part of the safe Soviet Union. Since there would have been no Pearl Harbor attack, the United States would have stayed out of World War II. On the contrary, we would have entered the War sooner because there would have been no worries about what Japan was going to do. And so on.

(De Mille, 1967, page 10.)

It is not difficult to see that a question like this makes for inquiry which escapes from the immediate present and from the bounds of reality, in the manner indicated by Koestler. From the more distant vantage point, it may be possible to think more freely than before, and discard inhibiting pre-suppositions.

Something of the same effect is provided by what Glasser (1969) calls "reversal questions." The examples he gives include:

If you woke up tomorrow as a girl instead of a boy, how would you behave?

If you woke up tomorrow as a Negro instead of white, what differences would it make in your life?

What do you, as the class, think would happen suddenly if all the white people became Negroes or all the Negroes became white? How would it affect you? What do you think you would do? What do you think your parents would do? What would happen in your neighborhood?*

Again, by moving away from everyday reality, in this case by a simple type of reversion, we can gain a new and different perspective, which facilitates thinking in less limited and con-stricted ways about some important questions.

* From *Schools Without Failure* by William Glasser, M.D. Copyright 1969 by William Glasser. Reprinted by permission of Harper & Row, Publishers, Inc. P. 177.

Another variety of problems which seem to help fulfill this function is the future-oriented question, advocated by Postman and Weingartner (1969). Among the examples they give are:

> *What effects on our society do you think the following technological inventions will have?*
> *a. the electric car*
> *b. television telephone*
> *c. the laser beam*
> *Can you identify two or three ideas, beliefs and practices that human beings will need to give up for their future well-being?**

Yet another method of gaining the perspective and the various sorts of freedom in reasoning that becomes possible when we withdraw from immediate reality is described by Sybil Marshall (1963). Notice that the present example, which is more appropriate for younger students than the previous ones, includes discussion, but concrete physical activities are also incorporated.

> *I had been struggling to impart some knowledge of contour lines, without much success . . . the trouble was that we lived in such a flat country that it was really very difficult to relate the lines on the map to the actual countryside. Somehow I had to demonstrate the meaning of all the curious squiggles on our map. We used [clay] to create an island. We pinned white paper carefully to a table and then emptied the clay-bin bit by bit onto the paper, moulding the wet, sticky clay into hills and valleys and cliffs and beaches and promontories and harbours and peaks and estuaries . . . when he had finished, we coloured the paper*

---

* From *Teaching as a Subversive Activity* by Neil Postman and Charles Weingartner. Copright © 1969 by Neil Postman and Charles Weingarten. Reprinted by permission of the publisher, Delacorte Press. P. 203.

*all round blue, to represent the sea. Then with a mighty
concerted effort, we heaved the whole island up just far
enough for someone to pull out the paper from beneath it.
. . . The paper showed very clearly the outline of the island
at sea level; for the first time many children understood an
outline map properly. We then made a wire cutter, . . . and
proceeded to cut off layers of our clay island. Each time as
we cut it, we placed the lump we had cut off onto the original outline map and drew round it. When we had finished
we had a complete contour map of our island which everyone understood. We then used our contour map to construct sections . . . we created the storms by raining on the
island with a watering can with a rose on the end of the
spout. We watched where the water ran between the hills,
and marked out the course of the rivers. . . . Now rivers and
peaks began to be claimed by the children and when at last
one of the more romantically minded boys invented a cove
full of buried treasure, geography gave way at last to English and story-writing in particular.*

(Marshall, 1963, pages 56–57.)

At first sight this exercise is a very useful way of teaching
about contours, but it does not take too much imagination to
see that activities like this can have many other functions. We
might ask questions such as where towns and ports could be
situated, where would rivers flow, where would trees grow,
where would the climate be the coldest or hottest, where
would the people live, what sort of government might develop,
where would roads be made, what sorts of transportation systems would develop, what would the people eat, and so on?
In this way, we could study what are called geography, history, politics, transportation, or whatever. A difference would
be that instead of starting with the result, we would be starting at the beginning. Again, away from the inevitability of
the present, reasoning and learning would be possible in an
atmosphere wherein imagination can flourish without normal
restrictions.

Similar, but not identical conditions are mentioned by Wallach and Kogan (1965) as contributing to human creativity. They use terms like "letting things happen" and "combinatory play" in describing the conditions in which creative thinking takes place. Suggesting that in these situations critical faculties or censors are to some extent stilled, they quote Rogers' remark that "In the person who is functioning well, awareness tends to be reflexive, rather than the sharp spotlight of focussed attention" (Rogers, 1963, page 17).

The Cognitive Processes Underlying Answers

There are, as we have said, many questions to which there are right answers, or to which there are answers which are more or less appropriate, and these have a very important and necessary role in education. It would be useful to classify questions according to the sorts of cognitive processes that are required in answering them, and Sanders (1966) has attempted to do just this. He bases his classification on Bloom's taxonomy of educational objectives (described in Chapter 4) and suggests that it is possible to develop the various levels of reasoning by carefully devising appropriate questions so that answering necessitates the various types of cognitive processes described in the taxonomy. For example, Sanders gives this instance of a question requiring Bloom's first category, *memory*. "What is meant by 'Gerrymandering'?" Here the student is required only to recall a definition presented to him earlier. An example of a question requiring the *translation* category in Bloom's taxonomy would be one in which the student was asked to restate a definition in his own words. Sanders gives the following question to illustrate *application*:

> *The mayor recently appointed a committee to study the fairness of the boundaries of the election districts in our community. Gather information about the present districts and the population in each. Determine whether the present city election districts are adequate.*
>
> *(Sanders, 1966, page 4.)*

As Sanders points out, the student is expected to apply to this new problem principles of democracy that were previously discussed in class. A question based requiring the use of the *evaluation* category in Bloom's taxonomy is this one. "Would you favor having your political party engaged in 'Gerrymandering' if it had the opportunity?" Sanders' book provides numerous useful examples of questions supplementing the illustrations provided by Bloom (1965), mentioned in Chapter 4.

In practice, it is often difficult to formulate questions whereby the cognitive processes underlying the answers can be entirely determined by the question. It is relatively easy to classify a question in terms of the taxonomy, but it is difficult to say what processes will be used by the student when he goes about trying to answer it. As Sanders admits,

> For example, suppose a teacher presents general differences between the beliefs of the Republican and Democratic parties and then asked students to study quotations from political speeches to determine which party's philosophy is illustrated. A student who reads the newspaper with more than ordinary devotion might remember a quotation as being part of a speech by a well-known member of one of the parties. For this student the question on the quotation requires only memory. . . . Other students who had not read the speech might reach the same answer legitimately by using only the category of interpretation.
>
> (Sanders, 1966, page 8.)

A related observation is that the thinking that goes into answering a question might depend on the recent instruction given by the teacher. In the case of a question, such as "Why is Canada wealthier than Portugal?" students who had just listened to a lecture or read a chapter devoted to that particular topic would need only to depend on memory in order to answer appropriately. Students who had not gained this specific information might be more inclined to make use of application, analysis, and the like. Sanders points out that it is

fallacious to assume, as we sometimes do, that when questions
are ones of "why?" or "how?" the answer necessarily demands
more than memory. Quite often "why" and "how" questions
require no more thought than do "what," "where," and
"when" depending on how they are presented.

> The question: Why did the United States enter a depres-
> sion in 1929? is only a memory question if the student is
> expected to give back the same little neat package of an-
> swers provided in the text or in the teacher's lecture.
> "Why" and "how" questions are excellent when they are
> presented in a way that leads students to figure out the
> answers—not simply to remember them.
>
> (Sanders, 1966, page 9.)

Analysis of Errors

One effect of an emphasis on right answers is to place too
little emphasis on learners' incorrect answers. Klinchy and
Rosenthal (1971) consider that errors can have some very
valuable functions which are lost when errors are ignored.
Making the assumption that teachers need to know as much
as possible about how their students' minds work, Klinchy
and Rosenthal suggest that one of the best sources of information is the students themselves. They focus on students' failures, on their errors, rather than their successes, simply because they feel that failures are much more informative than
right answers. Success, state Klinchy and Rosenthal, is often
ambiguous and hard to interpret. A child may solve a problem
correctly by using principles other than the appropriate ones.
As John Holt (1964) illustrates, this very often happens, and
it is hardly surprising when we overvalue correct answers,
thereby encouraging children to be producers rather than
thinkers.

Klinchy and Rosenthal think that teachers often fail to
profit by their students' mistakes, since in classroom situations, errors are very often simply ignored. The teacher may
ask a question and if she receives an incorrect answer from
one child she passes to the next child, and the next, until

someone gets the answer which is sought. Sometimes errors are punished or reprimanded as constituting some sort of sin. Perhaps one of the reasons for this is to repress any suspicion that the error provides an indication that something has gone wrong with the teaching.

At the very least, a child's failure tells the teacher that further instruction is necessary. However, the mere fact that the answer is incorrect does not tell us much about what sort of instruction is required. The number of errors may give some indication about ability, but the sheer quantity of errors that a child makes in, say, reading, does not provide any suggestion about how to teach him to read. Yet, it may be possible to find out something about what prevents a child from reading if we examine the precise nature of the errors.

Klinchy and Rosenthal make the assumption—it is one which runs through Holt's book *How Children Fail,* and which is central in Piaget's thinking on intellectual development—that the particular errors a child makes can tell us much about how he is thinking. They attempt to look rather systematically into the problem of trying to deduce the nature of the errors in children's reasoning processes from the particular mistakes or errors that appear in the outcome. They discuss three categories of errors, using the word "error" to refer to incorrect reasoning, rather than an incorrect outcome (that is, a wrong answer). The categories are *intake errors, organizational errors,* and *executive errors.*

Intake errors refer to the child's conception of the goals and data of the task. The child might ask what he has to do, or what knowledge does he have to work with? There is an intake error if the child's answer to this question is different from the teacher's answer. Bruner makes a similar point when he quotes David Page as saying,

> *When children give wrong answers it is not so often that they are wrong as that they are answering another question, and the job is to find out what question they are in fact answering.*

> *(Bruner, 1966, page 4.)*

Klinchy and Rosenthal refer to this specific type of intake error as an error in perceiving the goal, indicating a discrepancy between the purpose of given instruction as conceived by the teacher and the purposes as seen by the child. An example is provided by Holt (1964) who describes children playing the game of Twenty Questions. The most effective questions are those that systematically narrow the range of possible solutions, but as Holt points out, for many children the aim is simply to ask *any* question since this at least results in letting them "off the hook." The outcome may be the sort of question that looks like a wild guess, or a "safe" question, meaning one which the other kids will not laugh at. An example is the intriguing disguised guess "Was he killed by Brutus?"

There are a number of reasons for discrepancies between the goals of teachers and those of children. Sometimes the teacher fails to make clear her own version of the goal. This is preventible if the teacher is careful and explicit in stating intentions. However, even where the teacher makes her version of the goal clear, the child may substitute a different goal. For instance, in the Twenty Questions situation, however clearly the teacher states the objectives and intentions of the game, the student may have a stronger need to maintain the approval of classmates or status within a group, so his goal impedes effective functioning towards the objectives stated by the teacher. An effective way of presenting problems arising from such discrepancies between teachers' and learners' goals is to allow students to generate their own goals. Such a strategy has the added recommendation of happening to coincide with the suggestions we have made earlier on the basis of what is known about the role of cognitive involvement in meaningful human learning.

There are other forms of intake errors in addition to errors in perceiving the goals. Students may misperceive information as a result of some informational overload, and it is well known that young children are more hampered by occasional omissions in data than are adults (psychologists would say they need more "redundancy"). Hence, slight errors in perceiving content to be learned may have large effects on learning. The older a child is, the easier it is for him to recognize information on the basis of insufficient cues. Errors in perceiving the data may also occur because of ambiguity. Again, this is more likely to occur in children than in adults, since, as we saw in Chapter Three, the more restricted the perceiver's frame of reference, or cognitive structure, relevant to the information perceived, the more effectively ambiguous is the information for the individual learner, and the more it is subject to distortion. This was clearly apparent in Allport and Postman's (1947) research on the mechanisms by which rumors are communicated.

The second category of errors, *organizational errors,* are more closely related to the actual thinking process in solving the particular problem, and consequently one cannot make any simple generalizations about them. The precise nature of these errors will be related to the nature of the problem. *Executive errors* form the third category and are those which arise not from any failure to understand either the nature of the question or how the problem should be solved, but simply from detailed failures in the actual carrying out of the required manipulations. We can make this clearer by observing that the difference between organizational and executive errors is the difference between the child who does not know how to add and the child who forgets to carry the two. It is generally easy to observe when errors are of this type, and generally they do not merit much loss of sleep on the part of the teacher or the student. Teachers often refer to these as "careless" errors, and some individuals become incensed about errors of this kind for reasons which are not entirely clear. On some occasions they can be important. A bank clerk who "forgets" the occasional zero will soon find himself unemployed however good his understanding of principles of banking.

Klinchy and Rosenthal's analysis leaves no doubt that the examination of errors can provide the teacher with a number of very useful clues for examining thinking and learning in children. Of course, the everyday use made of such clues is subject to constraints imposed by the rush and bustle of the classroom. It would be fine if every teacher had time to sit back and analyze each error a child makes, and gain insight thereby, but the realities of the classroom situation by no means leave sufficient time and energy for this to be possible. However, the basic ideas are valuable.

Questions then are right at the center of the enterprise of learning. If we expect students to learn, we have to pay a lot of attention to the questions we ask them and to their own developing abilities to ask and answer questions for themselves. Above all, we need to be very sensitive to the nuances of any learning situation wherein questions are posed and answered.

Chapter 10

Some Aspects of Simple Learning and Memory

Introduction

In most of this book we have been concerned with learning that is highly meaningful and structured. We have suggested that most of the things that are worth learning are potentially meaningful, by which is meant that new material can be related to and integrated with the contents of the learner's existing cognitive structure, and structured, in that there are nonarbitrary connections between the different parts of the new material. We suggested that in the case of situations where potentially meaningful material is not currently meaningful to the learner because of gaps between the new content and the learner's existing knowledge, the appropriate procedure is to enable the learner to obtain appropriate preliminary learning, to "bridge the gap," for instance, by an "advance organizer" or by supplying the intervening steps in a hierarchy of skills.

In the present chapter we are concerned with types of necessary learning in which there is not a high degree of structure within the material, and where there is little probability of closely relating and integrating the new content with the learner's existing cognitive structure. In such situations the learner commonly adopts, for lack of better alternatives, a strategy of "memorization" or "rote learning." We have to remember that although the distinctions between "rote" and "meaningful" and between "structured" and "unstructured" are useful, there is some arbitrariness in such distinctions. In fact, there are degrees of structure just as there are degrees of meaningfulness.

The emphasis of the present text, apart from this chapter, on structured and meaningful types of learning, follows the author's conviction that the majority of learning situations likely to produce changes leading to a person becoming "educated" are structured and highly meaningful. Yet there are some instances in which learning strategies approximating rote memorization are inevitable or desirable, and such learning therefore merits at least brief attention.

As has been shown, the factors influencing simple unstructured learning, and hence the situations and conditions in which such learning occurs, are different from those that hold for learning which is meaningful and structured. Psychologists have carried out a considerable amount of research on simple verbal learning, and good accounts of much of this can be found in a number of sources (for example, Hill, 1971; Travers, 1967). Typical of the products of the extensive research carried out on simple verbal learning are the curves of forgetting and learning, showing that forgetting of nonsense syllables is considerable over the few seconds immediately succeeding learning, after which the curve levels out, the exact shape of the forgetting curve being affected by such factors as overlearning of the verbal items.

Some instances of school-learning situations which are inevitably to some extent rote and unstructured occur in the area of foreign language acquisition. Vocabulary skills and the learning of grammatical rules and exceptions have to be learned largely in a rote manner. The reason why meaningful learning is not always possible in foreign language learning is that, although there are some general rules and principles, many of the items to be learned are relatively discrete. For most learners there will be no structured connection between many words in the native language and the foreign language equivalents that have to be acquired. In addition, with certain basic learned skills, for example, reading, there are some aspects of the learning process where meaningfulness, in terms of relatability to existing skills and knowledge, is relatively limited, and where there is little structure in what is to be learned. There are further situations in education where memorization, although contributing little or nothing to basic understanding, may have the useful function of providing the learner with a repertoire of facts or skills that can be produced automatically, resulting in the saving of time required in useful functions. An example is multiplication in arithmetic. Certainly "learning tables" is no substitute for a basic understanding of the principles of multiplication, but, as Ausubel (1968) points out, when these principles have been established, it may be desirable to produce rather quickly, say, the product of six times four, and memorization may make this possible. Rote learning is necessary also in acquiring the ability to alphabetize. Without this ability a person will be quite unable to use a telephone book. Such memorization is justified only if the skill or skills attained thereby are frequently in demand, and if there is no meaningful way of obtaining them. In short, although meaningful acquisition is possible in most school learning situations, there are some circumstances where rote learning is inevitable. However, the need for memorization on some occasions need not blind us to the fact its place in education is small. The major part of learning in school has to be highly meaningful if it is to have lasting value for the learner.

Interference in Simple Learning

Structured and unstructured verbal learning differ in their vulnerability to certain types of interfering events. Experimental research on the learning of unstructured verbal materials has shown that when highly similar tasks are presented for learning in close temporal contiguity, the learning of one task has the result of making more difficult the acquisition of the other. The closer the degree of similarity between the materials, the greater the degree of "interference" between them. Interference can occur when previously presented content is highly similar to what is to be learned; this is called "proactive interference." Alternatively, similar materials presented after the materials to be learned can cause interference, in which case the term "retroactive interference" is used.

The exact nature and degree of interference will depend on a number of factors, for instance, the particular materials being learned, the degree of similarity, the temporal intervals between presentation of them, and on whether the similarity occurs in the "stimulus" or the "response" items.

These experimental findings have some implications for classroom situations in which simple unstructured learning occurs. For instance, the results indicate that it might be unwise to follow a class devoted to translation between French and English by one requiring translation between Spanish and English. In such a situation it would seem quite likely that interference would occur. Similarly, in those aspects of arithmetic where there is clear justification for types of learning which approach rote memorization, it would be sensible to avoid situations in which learning of similar sorts of content occurs in close succession.

A number of writers have assumed that the findings about interference effects in simple and unstructured verbal learning indicate that retroactive and proactive interference can also occur in highly meaningful learning situations. The authors of a number of textbooks in educational psychology have referred to interference phenomena with implicit or explicit suggestions that interference is an influential variable in a wide variety of situations in classroom learning. One writer, for instance, states that: "In general, the teacher should expect students to have difficulty retaining highly similar materials which are learned in close proximity to each other" (McDonald, 1965), and he suggests that teachers should take precautions to avoid such situations.

As it happens, there is considerable doubt whether either proactive or retroactive interference occurs to any great extent in situations where learning is structured and meaningful. A number of studies by Ausubel and his colleagues (for example, Ausubel, Robbins, and Blake, 1957; Ausubel, Stager, and Gaite, 1968) have failed to produce any evidence of retroactive or proactive interference in meaningful human learning. It would appear that only in learning situations approaching rote memorization does interference related to similarity of materials exert a noticeable influence on learning. This conclusion is supported by the findings of a study by Howe and Cavicchio (1971), in which there was no evidence of interference effects although subjects had to learn highly similar meaningful passages in close proximity. Jensen and Anderson (1970), however, found some interference using learning materials that were "extremely obscure and unfamiliar to the subjects," and Crouse (1971) provides more evidence that retroactive interference can occur in meaningful learning. Wong (1970) failed to find statistically significant differences although a number of small differences were consistent in showing slight interference effects. In short, the findings are conflicting. On the one hand, it is clearly wrong to assume that interference always or commonly occurs when similar materials are meaningfully learned. On the other hand, it is not true to say that interference never occurs. However, the fact that effects have been hard to detect, and are small when found, even in carefully controlled research, suggests that what interference effects there may be are not large enough to be very important in school learning.

Motivation in Acquiring Foreign Languages

Rote or unstructured learning and meaningful learning differ in the extent to which they are influenced by extrinsic motivational variables. It can be reasonably assumed that much meaningful learning itself generates intrinsic motivation; it may "fill a gap" in the learner's knowledge, and the relating of new to previously established skills and bodies of knowledge in itself provides interest and relevance. This cannot be said for much rote learning. There may be little or no inherent interest generated by the learning task. It follows that motivation produced by factors other than those involved in the actual learning is more likely to be important in the case of rote learning situations than in meaningful learning. That this is so is very clear in the example of language acquisition. Success in learning is very closely related to the extent of one's need to know the language. Such factors as the interest, attitude, and degree of involvement felt by students in the experience of learning the foreign language are extremely important, and consequently teachers frequently attempt to "bring to life" the foreign language, for instance, by talking about the country in which the language is spoken and about the people who speak it, and by introducing students to traditions, songs, and other aspects of the culture.

In a study carried out in Montreal, Gardner and Lambert (1959) found that success by English-speaking high school students in learning French could be just as accurately predicted on the basis of motivational measures as on the basis of scores of intelligence and aptitude for foreign language acquisition. In other words, the study showed attitudinal and motivational considerations to be as important as those of mental ability in determining success at learning. It was found that motivational factors were *more* important than ability in determining the learning of those skills required for the active use of language in settings where meaningful communication has to occur. Thus, the extent to which the learner feels a need to acquire the foreign language is a very important determiner of success. In foreign language learning, lacking the learning-generated interest that is found where there is a high degree of structure and relatability in the material,

> *It is essential to ensure that everything possible is done to increase student's interest in and enjoyment of the language being learned, to encourage favourable attitudes towards the culture, and generally to help bring about in students a desire to identify with and become involved in the whole civilization which surrounds the language.*
>
> (Howe, Gordon, and Wilman, 1969, page 29.)

The high degree of importance for language acquisition of motivational factors extrinsic to the actual learning task may explain one phenomenon to which attention is often drawn. People who have observed language learning among individuals of different ages have often suggested that young children seem to be more efficient at acquiring foreign languages than are adults. Assuming this observation to be correct, it may well be due not to any superior learning ability per se, but to motivational and attitudinal factors. For instance, children may be less self-conscious than adults about their attempts to speak in a foreign language. Since it is true that success in learning a language is highly related to its value for the individual, it may well be that such value is higher for children than adults, if the former are placed in a position, as in school, where there is a very strong need for communicating with others, and acquiring the foreign language is necessary for meeting this need.

Mnemonics and Imagery in Learning

Various devices and systems can facilitate the learning and retention of materials that are not highly structured or meaningful to the learner. Generally, these are called mnemonics. There is a variety of types of mnemonics, some being very simple and others extremely complex. Examples of simple mnemonics are rhymes, such as the one beginning "Thirty days hath September," which helps people remember the number of days in each month. Similar rhymes can be used in foreign language learning, for instance, in remembering plural forms or exceptions to grammatical rules. Then there are phrases and sentences such as "On old Olympus' towering top," which is used to aid recall of the names for cranial nerves (olfactory, optic, oculomotor, trochlear, trigeminal). Other verses and phrases have been devised to aid retention of names of United States presidents, kings and queens of England, planets, colors in the rainbow, and so on.

Such simple mnemonic devices have been extensively used, and many learners have found them useful. The precise ways in which they work vary greatly, but in general it is reasonable to say that all such devices provide some way of relating to what is already meaningful to the learner, however imperfectly, material which is currently lacking structure and unrelated to existing cognitive structure. An additional function of a number of the mnemonic examples is to provide some sort of organization *within* unstructured lists of items which otherwise would have only arbitrary inter-item relationships. For instance, in the "Thirty days hath September" rhyme, unconnected information about the various lengths of twelve months, which would otherwise be somewhat difficult to memorize, are brought together in a poem which obeys the constraints of meaningful English and is consequently easy to recall.

Some mnemonic systems are quite complicated. These often underly the apparently wonderful and impressive feats of "memory experts" and others who use their knowledge of mnemonic principles either to display their powers on the stage or to persuade gullible consumers to purchase courses of instruction apparently designed to develop "a superpower memory."

Readable accounts of some complex mnemonic systems are provided in the books by Hunter (1964) and Norman (1969). As in the case of the simpler systems, they have in common means of enabling the learner to impose some organization on initially unstructured material and of relating the material to what is already familiar and organized. An additional characteristic of many mnemonic systems is that they make a great deal of use of imagery, usually visual. That this makes good sense has been shown in a number of studies (see Paivio, 1969; Bugelski, 1970) showing that simple learning of unrelated concrete word pairs is improved when the learner can produce appropriate visual images. These can both give concrete form to the items and can provide a vehicle for relating the word referents. In general, visual imagery can have value in facilitating the learning of words, and mnemonic systems that encourage learners to use imagery in such learning are often successful.

The proposal that visual imagery may be useful in rote learning is indirectly supported by the results of an experiment which compared different methods for learning vocabulary words in a foreign language (Kellogg and Howe, 1971). Children aged between 9 and 11 years learned words in the Spanish language. During the learning sessions, the Spanish words were spoken by a teacher, and the English equivalents were shown, either by displaying the written word, or by showing a picture of the object. It was found that learning the Spanish words took place more easily with the pictures than with the written English equivalents. The finding that pictures can be more effective than words for young students who are learning oral vocabularly in a novel language has a clear implication for teachers. In addition, it provides a further indication that visual considerations can be important in learning words.

A Mnemonic System

We have already mentioned some mnemonic devices, but it is worth describing one system in more detail. In the following example (described by Hunter, 1964), visual imagery is used to great advantage. This mnemonic system can be used to aid retention of lists of words. The method is first to write down the numbers one to ten and learn a rhyme based on the numbers; for example, "one is a bun, two is a shoe, three is a tree, four is a door," and so on. The person using this system has to visualize the items while learning the rhyme so that each of the words takes on a clear and concrete form. Then he reads the lists of word items, and for each word he makes a strong visual image which firmly relates the word to the object corresponding to the number. For instance, if word number one is sugar, a person trying to memorize the list might form an image of a huge soft brown currant bun ("one is a bun") upon which there is a vast heap of glistening white sugar. The stronger, more striking, and even bizarre the image, the better. For each word, a new visual image is used, making a connection between the striking concrete representation of the word to be learned with that for the word corresponding to the number. This proceeds until the list is finished. In one experiment (Hunter, 1964), this method was used by subjects for learning lists of ten words. Half the subjects were instructed to use the mnemonic system, and the other subjects were not. Among the subjects who were not informed about the system, only 2 out of 30 were able to reproduce all the words after one presentation. However, 17 out of 35 people who were instructed in using the mnemonic system were able to recall the words correctly, and most of the others made no more than one or two errors. The present author has repeated this experiment informally with students on a number of occasions, usually with similar results.

There is no doubt that mnemonic systems, such as the one just described, can be remarkably effective in enabling people to learn much longer lists of words and other unrelated verbal materials than would otherwise be possible. Hence, it is not surprising that mnemonists and other "memory experts" can produce such striking results, and ones which apparently vindicate their claims to enable people to develop a better memory. The snag, of course, is that striking as these methods may be, their utility is limited to situations in which memorization is necessary, for lack of a more meaningful way of learning what has to be acquired. We have already pointed out that for the majority of the learning that has value in education, meaningful methods of acquisition are possible. The integration and relating of new to previous knowledge that occurs in such meaningful learning is clearly superior to the somewhat precarious connections that are made possible by mnemonic systems based largely on imagery. When the learner is in a situation where knowledge which has to be acquired cannot be structured or related to existing knowledge, some type of mnemonic device or system may be helpful, but outside the restricted range of such relatively unstructured and nonmeaningful situations, mnemonic methods have limited value.

Very strong visual imagery exists for some children in the form of accurate visual records of a perceived stimulus. Such children are said to have "eidetic imagery," and it appears that it is sometimes possible to "read off" the content to be reported rather than deliberately attempting retrieval and recall. The term "photographic memory" is sometimes used to describe this ability. However, there are serious problems that make it difficult to conduct reliable research in this area, and it appears likely (Leask, Haber, and Haber, 1968) that although eidetic imagery exists in some children, in varying degrees, few if any of them are able to make use of their eidetic images to improve long-term remembering.

Learning and Remembering

Some of the questions that are asked about remembering presuppose that humans possess a memory system which is independent of learning mechanisms. "How can I improve my memory?" is a common example. As it happens, the likelihood of a person remembering something depends on largely the same factors as those that determine learning. It follows that "If we want to remember something, we should be sure we understand it" (Howe, 1970a, page 95). It is certainly useful to distinguish between the concepts of learning and memory, but the phenomena they describe are by no means entirely separate. Research on learning usually emphasizes the acquisition of skills and knowledge, whereas memory research is largely concerned with retention (Howe, 1965, 1966) and retrieval (Howe, 1969). Clearly these are interdependent; considerations like structure and meaningfulness in information are largely defined in terms of existing (retained) knowledge, and influence both the acquisition of the information by a learner and the manner in which it will be organized for subsequent retention and retrieval.

Some of the remarks made in Chapter 6 about the concept of intelligence and its misuse apply equally to the concept of memory. A person who hears a message and later is able to repeat it can be said to have remembered the information over the intervening period, but this is simply a description, and not an explanation. Consequently, to suggest that the reason why a man remembers something is that he has a good memory is conceptually on a par with the statement that he is happy because he has happiness, which is true but somewhat trivial.

Life constantly demands the ability to retain information. Lacking such retention, some of the most basic human activities would be inconceivable. For instance, a person who hears a single sentence, such as "The man bit the dog," must be able to retain something about the early words until the time when the passage ends. In the absence of such temporary retention, the meaning would not be communicated, and, in fact, all language would be incomprehensible. Very often, the "difficulty" of a task is closely related to the amount of remembering that is necessary. Compare the following two problems of mental arithmetic. The first is to multiply 22×22, a task that is not particularly difficult. The second is 2222×2222, and it is much more difficult. However, when we ask why the second is so much harder than the first, and examine the different mental capacities required in the problems, they appear to be remarkably similar. Both demand only the skills of multiplying 2×2 and adding by 2's. However, the second problem is made difficult by the large amount of information that has to be stored. The task becomes much easier if it is possible to reduce the amount of information that has to be stored in human memory, and using pencil and paper is a convenient means of accomplishing this.

Memory is generally regarded as having the function of storing information. Storage is clearly important, but certain additional processes are necessary for remembering. In order for material to be stored, it has first to be perceived and somehow placed in the storage system. When the time comes for using it, retrieval is necessary. In any system wherein a large number of items are retained, it is essential to have careful organization, otherwise it would not be possible to locate and retrieve items on demand. Hence, human memory must make provisions not only for retention, but for effective organization, otherwise many items, once stored, might be extremely difficult to locate.

Some Memory Processes

In research on remembering, it is customary to make a distinction between "short-term" memory and retention over longer periods. There are numerous occasions in which it is necessary to retain information for brief periods, typically several seconds. For this purpose, it is economical for the brain to have a system in which such items can be temporarily stored without using the limited capacity available for the complex processes required in retaining vast quantities of information in a relatively permanent store, in an organized manner, that makes it possible to locate and retrieve the contents when required. Such short-term retention is required, for instance, in dialing a telephone number, in "holding" digits in mental arithmetic, and in retaining the early words of a sentence (or a coded version of them) until the whole sentence is complete. It is likely that there is considerable two-way flow of information between the short-term store and the permanent system, the former functioning as a sort of brief holding mechanism which obtains some of its items from and transmits some items to a system underlying retention over long periods (See Howe, 1970a, 1970e).

Research in the past few years has resulted in progress towards an understanding of what is stored in memory. This may appear to be an odd problem. Surely, it seems, if I store some sugar, I store sugar, period; and the same must be true when a word is stored in memory. However, there are a number of different ways of storing a word. Writing the word provides a visual record, and so does typing. A tape recorder can be used to store the word on magnetic tape; in this event, it is a representation of the sound of the word that is stored. In each case, it is true to say that the word is stored, but there are large differences in the ways of accomplishing this retention. The stored representations are based on entirely different aspects of the information.

A great deal remains to be discovered about storage in human memory, and it is likely that each of several characteristics of perceived materials can be used as a basis for storage. However, it is reasonably certain that short-term memory makes use of the auditory aspects of items in storing them. Some research evidence for this assertion comes from experiments comparing short-term memory for sequences of letters that sound alike (for example, b, t, d, e) with sequences that sound different (for example, c, f, a, r). When other factors (such as letter frequency and pronunciability) are controlled and precautions taken to ensure that all the letters are perceived correctly, it is found that retention of sequences of dissimilar-sounding items is considerably superior to that for like-sounding sequences. Note that this occurs even when the items are presented visually. This suggests that auditory or articulatory aspects of the letters are critical at some stage in the processes underlying remembering. Perhaps at some point there is a process that can retain one separate representation of each discriminable sound. Two letters which have a sound in common may make use of the same "storage space." Hence, when letters that sound alike are retained in the temporary store, they may interfere with retrieval of each other.

Much research into memory is directed at examining the physiological brain processes involved. Pribram (1969) claims that the brain may use holographic representation. Holograms have an unusual property in that each part of the hologram contains all the information needed to reconstruct the whole, and thus can be extremely effective for storage purposes.

Differences between individuals in capacity to remember largely depend not on characteristics of the memory system as such, but on how the system is used. For an analogy, consider two computers of the same make and model. Clearly their performance is limited by factors such as size, but what the computers actually *do* depends largely on how they are programmed, that is, upon the use made of their capacity. Similarly in human memory, what a person can recall depends on what is stored, and the efficiency of storage in turn relies on the manner in which information has been arranged and organized. Cognitive structure in humans is related to the manner in which stored processes are organized.

Chapter 11

Programmed Instruction and
the Role of Technology in Learning

In the late 1950s and the early 1960s many people involved in education became excited about what have been
variously termed "teaching machines," "programmed learning," and "programmed instruction." The innovations that
were so described were hailed, on one hand, as a great new
development that was going to revolutionize teaching, to make
school learning vastly more efficient, to relieve teachers of
much drudgery, and generally to lead to learning which was
more efficient, more pleasant, and more exciting than anything in the past. On the other hand, the apparent revolution
was regarded with dread by some teachers who saw in it a
threat to their jobs, a way of replacing the teacher and making
him redundant.

By 1970, it was clear that both the hopes and the apprehensions regarding the programmed instruction movement
were largely exaggerated. There is considerable agreement
that some forms of programmed instruction can have a useful
and constructive role, but it is clear that that role is a limited
one, and it certainly is not one which by itself constitutes a
revolution in the classroom. On the other hand, "computer-
assisted instruction," a later development which at least in
theory can considerably advance in sophistication, and hence
in effectiveness, some of the functions of teaching machines,
might, in the future, provide advances in the effectiveness of

instruction which could more realistically be called revolutionary.

Using Programmed Instruction

Programmed instruction, in its modern form, has many antecedents in educational methods used in the past, in particular, ideas developed by Sidney Pressey in the 1920s which anticipate more recent developments (Kay, Dodd, and Sime, 1968). A number of advances in instructional methods during World War II (for instance, simulators used in military training) are also important in this regard. It was not until the 1950s, however, that the possibilities of using teaching machines and programmed learning methods on a large scale began to be considered seriously, and the increasing attention was largely the result of the publicizing efforts of B. F. Skinner (for example, 1954). He not only drew attention to the limitations of current teaching methods, but also himself developed methods for automating instruction and was effective in producing and in encouraging others to produce appropriate learning materials in programmed form. At the same time Skinner's own distinction as a psychologist who had carried out considerable basic research on learning, and the parallels he demonstrated between techniques used in programmed instruction and methods successful in bringing about learning in nonhuman species, gave a persuasively effective impression of a scientific basis to the developments in instruction that he advocated for the schools.

There have been numerous varieties and subvarieties of programmed instruction. Correspondingly, numerous introductions and descriptions of programmed learning have been written. The book by Kay, Dodd, and Sime (1968) is strongly recommended, and a chapter by DeCecco (1968) provides a good introduction. In these pages, we shall merely attempt to give an idea of the original format developed by Skinner, and describe one major type of modification that has been rather extensively used.

As used by Skinner, a typical unit of instruction is broken

into a number of "frames," each typically consisting of a small amount of information, not usually more than a sentence or two, followed by or sometimes incorporating a question which the learner is required to answer, usually in not more than several words. The learner proceeds through a sequence of such frames. After each frame on which there is a question, the learner is provided with the correct answer. This might appear on the next instructional frame, or there might be a separate frame for the answer. Thus the material to be learned is broken up into very small steps (the frames), each step requiring an active response (answering the question) on the part of the student, and after each such response the student immediately learns whether he is correct or not. Compared with conventional instruction in the form of, say, books or lectures, there are the added features of gradual step-by-step progression, active student responses at each step, and provision for telling the student whether he is correct or not. Providing the correct answer is sometimes said to constitute "reinforcement" for the student, but there is some ambiguity in the use of the word in this context. As it happens, providing the correct answer could have any of a number of potentially beneficial effects. The learner might find it encouraging to know that he is right, and whether or not he needs or is rewarded by such encouragement, it might be useful to him to have feedback or "knowledge of results" to inform him whether learning is proceeding appropriately. Having to answer questions helps many learners pay attention to the material by giving them something to do, and it may make some students feel more involved in the learning situation than they would be otherwise. In addition, by requiring a regular and frequent response, it probably decreases the danger of the learner's understanding being "left behind" as can happen, for instance, when a person reading some prose material gradually becomes aware that not only is he failing to understand what he is reading, but that he has not really comprehended the preceding few paragraphs.

Skinner suggests that programs should proceed gradually,

in the small steps, so that the average student going through a program finds the questions fairly easy, and will not be incorrect on more than about one item in ten. This can be defended on the grounds that the encouragement given to the student favorably disposes him to the learning situation, adding to his enjoyment and self-confidence, and hence helps to develop positive attitudes to the material. It can also be defended on the grounds that when learners make incorrect answers, they are likely to learn such incorrect responses, and hence the less this occurs the better. The results of experiments discussed in Chapter 3, whereby it was found that when learners in meaningful learning situations make errors they are very liable to repeat them, give some support to Skinner's belief in the importance of avoiding errors. However, a strategy of avoiding errors has some strong disadvantages, and readers should refer to Chapter 3 for the various points and arguments involved in this issue. One additional point, made in Chapter 9, is that students' errors can provide valuable information about the adequacy of their reasoning skills.

Some Advantages and Limitations

The features of ("linear") programmed instruction as introduced by Skinner are clearly valuable in some circumstances, but there are occasions where they may provide a real handicap. Dividing materials to be learned into small steps may be useful for the learner who finds himself swamped by the same material in paragraph form, yet for other learners this division of content may provide only an irritating increase in the time required for learning. The effectiveness of breaking the content to be learned into gradual stages is likely to depend on the nature of the material itself; for some materials, with some learners, it may result in decreased continuity, and where such continuity is necessary learning will suffer. On the other hand, with some types of content, gradual step-by-step presentation may have real value for learners. Consequently, it is likely that presentation in programmed form will be more effective in teaching elementary statistics than in literary appreciation.

The provision of numerous questions and answers is another attribute of programmed instruction as used by Skinner which may have advantages or disadvantages, depending both on the nature of the learner and the nature of the material being communicated. A student who keeps having to answer questions which he considers very easy or trivial and who then is provided with the answers in spite of the fact that he already knows that he is correct, is likely to perceive the procedure as irritating, tiresome, and unnecessary. On the other hand, a learner with somewhat less confidence or ability may find that the questions make it easier for him to attend to the important aspects of the material and also provide feedback and encouragement which he finds valuable.

The value of providing both questions and answers is partly determined by an additional consideration which we have mentioned as being important in education. This concerns the extent to which the learning material is of such a nature that factual knowledge can be described as correct or incorrect. In arithmetic, for instance, it is clear that two plus two equals four and not five, and the knowledge that four is the correct answer may be essential in acquiring necessary arithmetic skills. Similar considerations apply in many important branches of knowledge, probably most frequently in science and technology, and less frequently in what can be broadly classified as the humanities. In English literature we might ask the question "Was the seventeenth century more productive than the eighteenth century?" Here it is immediately apparent that the question itself poses some important problems so that a simple "yes" or "no" answer is inappropriate. There may not be any simple answer to the question, and the answer may depend on certain undefined criteria of productivity. Even if it is possible to answer a question like this, answering may demand only a trivial aspect of the sorts of learning that are valuable in understanding English literature. In short, in certain areas of knowledge and understanding, even when it is possible to produce questions which do have unambiguously right or wrong answers, it is quite possible that a learning device, such as programmed learning, which by necessity concentrates on those matters to which such questions are applicable, communicates only the more trivial aspects of the subject. The learner is understandably liable to get the impression that the content of questions asked reflects important knowledge, and where this is not the case, his perception and understanding of the subject matter is likely to be restricted. So we can see that the necessary attention, when programmed methods of learning are used, to those aspects of the material to be learned for which questions that can be unambiguously answered are appropriate, results in programmed learning being ineffective or unsuitable for some areas of instruction.

· It follows that the effectiveness of a particular unit of programmed instruction will depend on how it was used, what it is used for, and on the various characteristics of the learner. We can ask whether the material is such that programmed instruction is an appropriate method for the learner. To the question of whether programmed learning is better or worse than other methods of instruction, the only reply is that it depends on factors such as these. There have been a large number of research studies designed to compare the effectiveness of programmed instruction and other methods, and it is not surprising that their results have not unambiguously favored one or the other. We would hardly expect them to. Programmed learning is a medium of instruction which is more suitable for some learning situations than others. One can no more say that to learn from programmed instruction is better or worse than getting the same material from books than one can state that lectures are more effective than books, or vice versa. It all depends how the various media are used, what they are used for, who is doing the learning, and so on. There is a tendency for people to make very firm commitments for or against recent developments, such as programmed instruction, on the basis of rather limited exposure to the medium. They tend to argue thus: "We used programmed instruction in this course, and it was good (bad). Therefore programmed instruction is good (bad)." This sort of reasoning is as absurd as deciding whether books are good or bad after one has read only a single novel.

As in the case of any other method of instruction, the effectiveness of a particular unit of programmed learning will depend largely on how it is written, in the presentation and organization of ideas, and the clarity with which the concepts are communicated. A unit presented by programmed instruction can be very effective or very ineffective, just as certain material in a book can be communicated very well or badly. The important point is that it is how the material is communicated, in the sense of organization and clarity of presentation, rather than whether the material is programmed or not, or what particular form of programming is used, that is most important in determining the effectiveness of learning. Again, just as in the case of alternative methods of instruction, the appropriateness of the particular material, in terms of difficulty, previous learning expected, and so on, largely determines what a particular learner will gain from a particular unit of instruction.

The organization and presentation of material seems to be more important than not only the precise method of programming, but also the type of machine or device used. Except in the case of computer-assisted instruction, the importance of machines and devices in programmed instruction has been exaggerated, and it would not be totally inaccurate to say that the role of the teaching machine is little more than that of a glorified page-turner. A machine may add to the convenience of instruction by providing quick access to the various units of material, but the machine in no way determines the course of learning nor provides any but mechanical aids to presentation. Thus it generally makes little difference to learning whether a teaching machine, a simpler device, or a programmed book is used. The convenience that teaching machines and devices may provide, compared with presentation in program book form may not compensate for the disadvantages—expense, lack of portability, and the tendency to break down. This probably accounts for the rather small number of teaching machines found in most classrooms in contrast with earlier predictions that they would become extremely numerous.

It seems now that the original excitement about the apparent promise of programmed instruction in education, and the corresponding apparent threats it posed, were based on somewhat naive estimates of the magnitude and variety of changes in education that it would make possible. In general, it appears that what is esssentially a new medium of instruction, with certain useful but well-defined and limited advantages over existing methods, was incorrectly seen as a fundamental educational innovation.

Programmed learning, when used in appropriate situations and with imaginative organization and presentation of materials, does have some very clear advantages over other methods of instruction. The gradual step-by-step presentation, the opportunities for active learner responses, the provision of feedback, can and have been effectively used in instruction, and in some ways these can provide learning situations which approximate those in which there is one teacher for each learner. The feedback and active response provisions of programmed instruction, limited though they are, can provide some of the features that would otherwise be possible only when a teacher has the opportunity to react to each learner's individual responses. In fact, plenty of programmed learning materials exist, and they are successfully used at many levels of education.

Evaluating Programs

The experience of actually writing a program can be very valuable for a teacher. In having a present material that proceeds step-by-step, with adequate questions and answers to test knowledge and provide feedback, the program writer is forced to think carefully about the organization and the sequencing of the material. With programmed learning, it is more readily apparent than with other methods of instruction if ideas are not being clearly presented or untenable assumptions are made about a student's previous knowledge. The reason is simple. A usual procedure is for a program to be written and then tested on a group of students. As the learners proceed through the program, answering the questions and receiving feedback, it becomes clear where deficiencies in presentation exist. For instance, a large number of wrong answers to a particular question would suggest that the knowledge tested by that question had not been transmitted very effectively. Since the question immediately succeeds the presentation of the material, it is much easier to see where the breakdown of effective communication has occurred than with other instructional methods, whereby testing for knowledge may succeed presentation only after an interval of some time. Also, whereas in conventional testing circumstances it is relatively easy for the instructor to shift the blame for wrong answers onto the student, in a programmed learning situation, as long as the student has been attending to the frames and successfully answering the questions therein, low achievement on a subsequent test strongly suggests that there are deficiencies existing in the program of instruction. Accordingly, the instructor is made more aware than he might otherwise be of the onus placed on the instructional material to effectively transmit what is to be learned. One cannot say that a student who uses a program fails to learn because of laziness or inattentiveness, if he carefully went through the program and correctly answered all the questions. In summary, the instructor who writes a program is forced to think rather carefully about the nature, structure, and organization of the materials, and the responses of the learners provide him with feedback about the effectveness of the program as a teaching device.

Thus developing and improving instructional materials is in some respects easier with programmed learning than with other modes of instruction. The instructor can write a program which he thinks satisfactory, and try it out on a group of suitable students. The presence of a large number of errors as responses to a particular frame usually indicates areas of weakness in the program, that is, steps at which it does not effectively communicate to the students. In developing the program, the instructor can modify or enlarge the program at such points, and then try out the revised program on another batch of students. Further modification can subsequently be carried out, if necesssary, until the writer is satisfied that the program is as effective as is reasonably possible. It is worth repeating, however, that no particular program is going to be suitable for all learners; considerations like age, intelligence, and previous knowledge determine whether a particular student will find a particular program right for him. The job of writing programs is itself arduous and lengthy, but a number of systems have been designed that facilitate effective presentation of information in this form.

Branching Programs

The "linear" programs advocated by Skinner suffer from a certain rigidity in format. It is true that each learner can proceed at his own pace, but the fact that each student has to proceed through an identical sequence of frames, progressing gradually in very small steps, can cause frustration and boredom. If one could devise a more adaptable type of program, in which it would not be necessary for all learners to proceed through exactly the same frame sequence, it is conceivable that programmed materials could be adaptive to the needs of a wider range of learners. Such an attempt at greater flexibility is provided by what are called "branching" programs. Figure 3 shows the main difference between linear and branching programs. In the latter, the basic sequence of frames generally proceeds in rather larger steps than is common with linear sequences, and if a learner makes an error he proceeds to a subsequence or "branch" of the program, which customarily reviews in more detail the material on which he erred. Thus

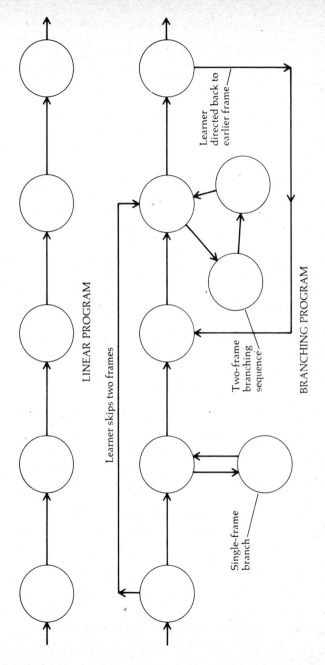

LINEAR PROGRAM

BRANCHING PROGRAM

Learner skips two frames

Single-frame branch

Two-frame branching sequence

Learner directed back to earlier frame

Figure 3. Linear and branching programs. The essential difference is that with the linear program all learners proceed in an identical sequence, whereas the branching program provides greater flexibility, so that the sequence of frames encountered varies considerably between individuals.

there is more effective provision for helping students when they have difficulties, and hence it is less necessary than in the case with linear programs to emphasize avoidance of errors. At least in theory, branching makes it possible to write programs which can be useful to a much wider range of students than are linear programs. There is no absolute limit on the number of branches, and it is possible to have sub-branches, that is branches within branches, if it is desired.

It is also possible to have what are called "skips" in the program. Skips are useful when the instructor thinks it likely that a fair proportion of the students using the program will already be knowledgeable about the material to be presented in the succeeding few frames of the main program. He can then ask a question which refers not to the material previously covered, but to the material in the subsequent frames. Students who already understand this material will make the correct response to this question, and accordingly they can be skipped to a later stage. Thus both branching and skipping increase the range of adaptability of the program. A given programmed sequence might contain 100 frames, made up of 30 frames in the main sequence plus 70 frames which form parts of branches. Typically there is considerable variation among students both in the number of frames they use, and in the particular sequence of frames they require. Branches can vary in length, from one frame up to four or more. In some instances, instead of providing a branch, the instructor might decide to direct the learner back to an earlier frame in the main program. It is quite easy to do this, just as one can skip frames.

Branching programs can be presented by teaching machine or in book form, and the term "scrambled book" is sometimes used for the latter. When branching programs are in the form of a book, it is necessary to do a great deal of page turning to reach the various frames in the branches and in the main sequence, and a mechanical teaching machine or device can be more convenient. Apart from this added convenience, the machine as such has no very great advantage over programmed books. Whereas with linear programs the learner usually writes in his responses, questions in branching programs are normally of a multiple-choice variety, the learner selecting the answer he thinks correct from four alternatives. Having chosen an answer, the learner is directed to an appropriate frame. With teaching machines, this is done automatically; the user of a programmed book is told to turn to a particular page.

Since the learner has to choose among four alternative answers, it is theoretically possible to direct him to a particular subsequent frame determined by the nature of his error. For instance, if the learner makes an incorrect response which is frequently made to that question, and indicates a slight miscalculation, he might be directed to a short extra branch. If he makes a response that indicates complete failure to understand the material, he might be directed back to an earlier section of the main program.

Just as there has been a great number of studies designed to find whether programmed learning is better than other modes of instruction, similarly there has been a large amount of experimental research to discover whether branched programs are better than linear programs or vice versa. Again, the multitude of studies has failed to produce a clear-cut answer, and for bascially the same reasons.

Some Comparisons

In some circumstances it would clearly be unwise to use programmed instruction. Pressey and Kinzer (1964) carried out an experiment in which they reproduced the content of part of a programmed unit on introductory psychology in the form of a much shorter prose summary. University students who read the summary performed just as well on a subsequent test as those students who had gone through the programmed version, although going through the programs took, on average, five times as long. This finding demonstrates that the program was an extremely inefficient method of instruction for those particular students. Similar results were obtained in a study by Roderick and Anderson (1968). They took a 3400 word segment of the same programmed introduction to psychology, Skinner's *Analysis of Behavior*, and made a summary of it, 1800 words in length. Again, undergraduate students who read the summary performed just as well on a subsequent test as did students who had been through the program, although the students who worked on the program took about four times as long as those who read the summary. However, high school students learned more from the programmed version than with the summary, according to some, but not all, of the tests that were used. We have to take a number of relevant factors into account in any attempt to compare the efficiency of programmed learning with other methods of instruction. A good suggestion by Roderick and Anderson is that "as a general quality control procedure, those who develop programs accept responsibility for demonstrating that their programs out-perform summaries" (Roderick and Anderson, 1968, page 170).

The learner who uses programmed instruction is typically required to make an overt response (answer) to the question on each frame. In a number of experimental studies, it has been found not to matter whether an overt response is required or not, and Cook (1963) holds that the requirement to make such responses reflects no more than "superstitious behavior" on the part of the people who write the programs. However, there are some other important considerations determining the utility or otherwise of overt responses. In research by Holland and Kemp (1965; Kemp and Holland, 1966), it was found that requiring students to make an overt response improved learning in some programs, but in others it did not. In addition, in some programs it was possible to "black out" quite a large amount of the material on each frame without seriously affecting the chance of making an error on the accompanying question. They use the term "black-out ratio" to indicate the proportion of the material that could be blacked-out without influencing error rate, and found that in some programs this can be as high as 60 or

70 percent. (A high black-out ratio does not necessarily indicate an inadequate program, but simply shows that the questions accompanying each frame can be correctly answered on the basis of less than total understanding of all the material in that frame.) Kemp and Holland found that in those programs where the black-out ratio was high, it generally made no difference whether overt responses were required or not. However, when the black-out ratio was low, that is where little of the material could be erased without affecting the number of errors made, learning was more effective when overt responses were required.

Computer-Assisted Instruction

Programmed instruction is a teaching medium which in some important but clearly restricted ways can be adaptive to the needs of individual students. Some of the restrictions can be overcome with the use of computer-assisted instruction. The presence of a computer coupled with complex electronic instruments can bring about certain important advantages. For instance, it is possible to present materials in various different modes; auditory and visual presentation are possible, using films, slides, and television, separately or together. The learner can respond in various different ways; by speech, by typewriter, or by light pen, and with the aid of a computer it is possible to make far more complete reactions to the learners' responses. With conventional programmed instruction the frame to which the learner is directed is determined solely on the basis of his performance on the previous frame, but when a computer is available it is possible to use other information in order to determine the sequence of instructional items. With CAI it is also possible to feed into the computer details of the learner's past history, his previous learning, intelligence, personality characteristics, and so on, and this information can be used to determine which of a number of programs of instruction is chosen, or to determine the manner of progress through a given instructional sequence. Hence more ways of presenting information become available, and it is possible to make better use of the information provided by the learner. In theory at least, CAI has enormous potential, and there is a wide range of ways by which teaching by computer can be flexible and adaptive to the particular needs of the learner.

However, there are difficulties related to cost and to various practical problems, so that although it is true that computer-assisted instruction has exciting potentialities, it has a long way to go before they are realized. Large sums of money have been made available, but up to the present most uses of CAI have not differed very much from what can be done without expensive computer facilities. Baker (1971) considers that computers may one day have profound effects both upon instruction and upon the management of instruction, but his review of facilities is concluded with the suggestion that systems in use at present provide the teacher very little assistance. This will change in the future, and it is likely that the cost of using CAI, enormous at present, will be reduced as development proceeds. An advantage of CAI that may lead to eventual reductions in cost is that information can be communicated instantaneously over long distances. A central terminal can handle the needs of a large number of students situated in a variety of geographical locations.

Machines and Speed-Reading

It has been claimed that mechanical devices are valuable in courses aimed at increasing reading rate. There are two basic kinds of devices. The first are designed to display symbols such as words or numbers for a brief period, typically between 1/100 and 1/10 of a second. It has been suggested that instruments of this type can enable the reader to improve skills such as scanning which are used in reading. The second kind of device has the function of controlling the pace of reading and generally involves a shutter which descends at various rates, exposing successive segments of reading material as it does so. In some instances, the shutter also moves from left to right across each printed line, or a beam of light moves across each line and down the page (Berger, 1969). The findings of research on the effects of such devices on rate of reading have been generally negative, in that they have not been found to produce marked gains in reading, when comprehension is taken into account. Berger (1969) points out that students who used the devices did achieve gains in reading flexibility, the latter being defined as the ability of students to read some passages rapidly and others slowly. Whether these gains justify the expense of the mechanical devices is open to question.

There is some controversy about the value of speed-reading courses, irrespective of whether they use mechanical devices or not. It is reasonably clear that students who take such courses find that they are able to read faster than before. However, this may be largely due to readers simply becoming aware that it is possible to read at faster than their normal rate, and getting practice at reading faster. Hence it is possible that most people may be able to increase their reading rate, but it is highly questionable whether one needs to invest the several hundred dollars sometimes paid for speed-reading courses in order to produce such an increase. Most probably, a student who is willing to read a short book on reading habits and spend some time practicing will achieve an equivalent increase.

The Learner's Perspective

There is little doubt that programmed learning methods and computer-assisted instruction can have a useful role in education and, at least in the case of the latter, its use is likely to increase. However, even if it does become technologically feasible to use CAI for a majority of the educational school experiences of any child, to do so would imply a misunderstanding of the nature of human abilities and human learning. The main objection to indiscriminate use of CAI is that both in CAI and in programmed learning generally, the learner himself is "programmed" in the sense that he is carefully guided, shaped, given feedback and cues to help him attend, and so on. The learner himself has little part in determining the outcome of learning; rather he is molded and "fed" in ways which lead him to acquiring knowledge or skills that others have deemed useful for him to acquire. However, as we have shown in earlier chapters, such constant guidance in learning is not only unnecessary but educationally damaging, in that it is likely to interfere with a student's obtaining skills required for autonomy and independence as a learner. Human learners can become good at guiding their own learning if they have the opportunity to acquire some necessary skills, and if they perceive value in the learning process.

In short, given a learning task that is worthwhile to the individual, the human learner is extremely well equipped to carry out for himself most of the functions that are so carefully done for him when CAI is used. This is not to deny that such a medium can have uses, such as for the presentation of a number of media simultaneously, which requires complex electronic devices. In addition, there certainly are *some* situations where careful structuring is necessary, and in which the guidance and feedback functions, provided to some extent with conventional programmed learning methods and to a greater extent with CAI, are particularly valuable. One should remember that structure is not entirely absent with other instructional formats, such as books.

It has been suggested that the careful sequencing of instruction found in programmed instruction may sometimes hinder the growth of independence in the learner. On some occasions it may have a very different effect; for instance, it may help to "wean" a young and immature learner from overdependence on the teacher. In addition, the student whose personal relationships with teachers are poor may welcome the impersonal interaction with programmed materials, and a person entering on what is to him a completely new area of knowledge may have a strong need for the initial support and guidance that is provided in programmed learning and computer-assisted instruction.

Modern technology has opened up exciting new ways of

communicating information, and it is possible that by concentrating their energies on computer-assisted instruction and computer-based instructional management systems, educational researchers have been prevented from looking at other possibilities involving the use of advanced technology in education. For instance, it would be technically feasible to devise a system by means of which any visual or auditory materials that can be recorded on tape could be provided on demand for a child in school. The child would need a television with some sort of dialing mechanism. Dialing a catalogue number for the material required would result in selection of the appropriate tape at a central terminal (which might serve thousands of schools), on which the content of the tape would be transmitted by cable to the child's television set. Since one cable can accommodate thousands of TV channels, the total system would have vast capacity for simultaneous communication of numerous different types of materials. A system such as this would be expensive, but there would be enormous savings in the costs of duplicating and transporting films, videotapes, and even books and other written materials. The use of such a system would also tend to encourage, rather than restrict, initiative and independence in students, and, for that matter, in teachers.

Mathemagenics

It has been suggested that some advantages of programmed learning are due to the provision for active responses, small-frame presentation, and feedback having the function of helping the learner pay attention to the material to be learned. Some disadvantages lie in its lack of flexibility, even with branching programs or when computer-assisted instruction is used, compared with media such as books. The learner reading a book can look things up in the index, can refer forwards or backwards, can read a chapter at a time or a page at a time, can look up a single sentence, and in general can use the book in a wide number of different sorts of ways depending upon his particular needs at the time. With programmed learning this type of flexibility is simply not available. It would be useful to find out if some of the advantages of programmed learning, in facilitating attentiveness, for instance, could be built into modes of instruction which retain in the flexible and less rigid form of conventional books and written materials. How can we retain a flexible form of instruction which incorporates the attention-holding functions that accompany programmed learning?

The development of what is called "mathemagenics" by E. Rothkopf seems to go some way to providing an answer. Mathemagenic behaviors are described by Rothkopf (1968) as activities which give birth to learning. They include reading, asking questions, inspecting objects, attending to the teacher, and mentally reviewing learned materials. They refer to activities carried out by the student which influence the possibility of him learning from materials which are objectively presented. The study of mathemagenic activities is "the study of actions on the part of the students that are relevant to the achievement of specified instructional objectives" (Rothkopf, 1970). Rothkopf makes a distinction between "nominal" and "effective" stimuli in learning. A nominal stimulus is whatever is presented by the teacher, whereas an effective stimulus is that which the learner perceives, and these two may not be identical. Discrepancies between the two types of stimuli result from the learner's activities. The effective stimuli are determined by learners' set and attention, which are not directly under the control of the teacher or the instructional medium. We have already made the point that learning is largely determined by what the individual student does with the material available so that without activity on the learner's part instructional objectives cannot be achieved. Hence, as Rothkopf observes,

> A serious interest in the effective management of the
> instructional process requires a serious attempt to describe
> and understand those actions on the part of the student
> that are relevant to the attainment of instructional objec-

tives. That is the chief purpose of the study of mathema-genic behaviors.

(Rothkopf, 1970, page 326.)

In previous chapters we have noted that learning depends largely on what the individual learner brings to the learning situation, processing and coding by the learner being important in determining the learning output. Rothkopf has provided some practical suggestions about procedures to encourage such activities. One such suggestion, which has been examined and validated in a number of experimental research studies, is to use questions at appropriate places in a prose text. Rothkopf found that when two questions were inserted every third page in a 36-page prose passage, retention of the passage was considerably more effective than when no such questions were used. It could be argued that the reason for this result was not that the questions helped the learner to pay attention to relevant aspects of the material, as Rothkopf supposed, but that they simply provided a practice test for items which were required in the test of learning. Rothkopf looked into this possibility by using two different kinds of questions. Some of the questions contained material which was directly relevant to, and presumably may have facilitated performance in, the subsequent test of retention of the whole passage, but other questions did not contain any material that would directly facilitate performance in the later test. It was found that questions which were relevant to the later test did indeed facilitate performance, but questions which had no direct relationship to the items of the retention test also had a positive effect on performance of the later test. So it does appear that some mathemagenic effect, such as helping learners pay attention to the material, was gained from the questions.

Rothkopf (1970) also compared the effectiveness of different kinds of questions. Some of the questions referred to materials in the pages immediately succeeding the question, and others concerned materials on the previous pages. He found that only questions that referred to previous materials were effective in improving retention. In other words, having questions every few pages does improve the performance, even if the content of the questions does not relate directly to what will be tested later, but only when the questions are on materials which the learner has just read, and not on content that he has yet to read. By way of explanation, it is possible that questions referring to succeeding material have the effect of restricting learners' attention to the content covered in those questions, hence narrowing what is learned.

There is a limit to the value of research on the importance of the spacing and the type of questions used in prose learning; it is not likely to produce a revolutionary breakthrough in knowledge about learning. What does seem to be more important in this kind of research, and in Rothkopf's development of the concept of mathemagenics, is that it provides opportunities to look directly at what learners themselves do in learning situations, and to see how the individual activities of the learners affect the outcome. This research clearly focuses on the learner's role, and at the same time uses quantifiable, experimental methods in investigating school learning. The shift in emphasis away from the characteristics of the materials used in instruction, and towards "promoting these activities in the student that will allow him to achieve instructional goals with available materials" (Rothkopf, 1970) may have good results.

Chapter 12
Teachers in the Classroom

Teachers, being human, are sensitive to criticism which they sometimes receive in large doses. Teachers have been reviled, caricatured, and stereotyped. Thus, one witty but uncharitable account reads:

> For example, there is the type of teacher who believes that he is in the lighting business. We may call him the lamp-lighter. When he is asked what he is trying to do with his students, his reply is something like this: "I want to illuminate their minds, to allow some light to penetrate the darkness." Then there is the gardener. He says, "I want to cultivate their minds, to fertilize them, so that the seeds I plant will flourish." There is also the personnel manager, who wants nothing more than to keep his student's minds busy, to make them efficient and industrious. The muscle builder wants to strengthen flabby minds, and the bucket filler wants to fill them up.*

There is also the characterization of the teacher as the feeble, inadequate person who chooses teaching because he can do nothing else. The old adage, "If you can't do anything,

---

* From *Teaching as a Subversive Activity* by Neil Postman and Charles Weingartner. Copyright © 1969 by Neil Postman and Charles Weingartner. Reprinted by permission of the publisher, Delacorte Press. P. 82.

teach," is a good illustration of an ignorant but not uncommon point of view.

Teaching Skills

Most teachers these days probably have enough confidence in their own training and ability not to be put out by hostile attitudes and criticisms of their work. One comforting thought is that people usually criticize the things they regard as most important in their lives. More threatening is the view sometimes expressed that schooling has little or no effect on the intelligence and abilities of children. Research into the influence on children of different types of schooling, length of schooling, various teacher attributes, and educational methods has produced few clear answers. Certainly, as the research evidence in Chapter 5 and 6 demonstrated, acquisition of intellectual abilities and growth in intelligence is closely dependent on the quality of the environment in which a child learns, but schools are not the only learning environment. There is no doubt at all that achievement by a child at school is influenced by variables outside the school, such as socio-economic class, interests of parents, and the attitudes of the parents towards the school.

One educator (Stephens, 1967) goes so far as to suggest that one school is likely to be as good as another, and that the specific abilities and training of particular teachers are relatively unimportant. He admits that teachers are essential, but he feels that there is no particular body of skills or knowledge that is required in a person to teach:

> . . . *the mechanisms actually responsible for academic growth reside in humble, spontaneous tendencies which are always in operation when an adult consorts with maturing children . . . teachers need not be the paragons of virtue and skills so often suggested in inspirational commencement addresses. In filling the thousands of classroom positions, we need no longer restrict ourselves to these model creatures.*
>
> (Stephens, 1967, pages 10–12.)

The present author strongly disagrees with this point of view. It is difficult, of course, to determine the precise role and importance of schooling in the development of abilities in children. There are difficulties in interpreting research on this problem area, because covarying with education in the school are numerous other factors related to wealth and family background. These factors sometimes interact in complex ways. For instance, compared with the child of articulate, middle-class parents, the child from a "deprived," poor environment is not only likely to be intellectually handicapped, but may also suffer from the fact that the school environment is strange to him and therefore uncomfortable. We shall pass over the confusing findings of research in this area and examine one study showing clearly that the effects of schooling *can* be extremely powerful in some instances.

The Importance of Schooling

Schmidt (1966) has described the situation in South Africa among an East Indian community where education is not compulsory, but is highly valued. The adult Indian population is predominantly poor and uneducated, the parents often being semiliterate or illiterate. Nevertheless, almost all the parents in the community perceive education as being highly valuable, and they make considerable efforts to get their children to school. The number of school places for children is far less than is necessary for those who want them, and hence among the children of parents who value education equally highly, some children go to school, and some are unable to go because of lack of space. For the same reason, among the children of parents who place equal value on education, there are differences in the numbers of years for which school has been attended.

Thus particular economic and social conditions make possible a research comparison that would not be possible in studies carried out in Europe or North America where the type and length of education is rarely unrelated to other factors, such as social class, that are also likely to influence academic and intellectual achievement. In the study described by Schmidt, the investigator measured the effects of schooling on the performance of pupils at tests of intelligence and scholastic attainment, holding age and socioeconomic status constant, with the reasonable certainty that factors, such as parental attitudes, were also constant. A strong indication that the parents of those pupils who did not receive proper schooling were at least as positively motivated towards education for their childen as the parents of children at school is given by the fact that the majority of the former parents sent their children to so-called private schools, not officially recognized, where ignorant teachers taught large masses of children under abominable conditions in return for fees which the parents could ill afford to pay.

The results of Schmidt's study show that schooling can greatly influence intelligence test scores. With age held constant, and socioeconomic status partialled out, the correlation between number of years at school and verbal intelligence (New South African Group Test) was + .68, indicating a strong relationship. The correlation between number of years of schooling and nonverbal intelligence was + .49, and the correlation between years of schooling and score on another reliable and frequently used test of intelligence, Raven's Progressive Matrices, was + .51. These findings leave no doubt that in a situation where there is little or no interaction between number of years of schooling and other variables that would influence achievement schooling per se is an extremely important factor. Schmidt also found that by the time the children have been at school for several years, those who had started early had significantly higher intelligence scores than those whose entry to school had been delayed (owing to lack of places). Again, this result is independent of socioeconomic status, which was carefully controlled in the research design. The correlations between number of years at school and various other indices of school achievement, such as vocabulary and arithmetical skills, are no larger than those between number of years at school and verbal intelligence.

This shows that schooling affected scores of intelligence tests just as much as it influenced those scores of achievement which one might assume are more directly determined by schooling. Hence, the belief that intelligence test scores are less affected by schooling than are scores of academic achievement was not true for the non-Western student sample examined in this study. It is interesting to note that within the Indian group, there were no statistically significant relationships between socioeconomic status and scores on intelligence tests.

These findings cannot be directly applied to schooling in Western societies, but they do show that schooling *can* have extremely large effects on the abilities measured in tests of intelligence.

Quite apart from the influence of school in general, there is no doubt that particular teachers are very important in determining children's learning. Much crucial learning occurs through imitation and modeling, especially in younger children, as we showed in Chapter 7. The present book has placed emphasis on those types of learning which are specifically academic and intellectual, involving cognitive factors and complex forms of behavior rather than on types of learning that probably occur as much in the home as in the school, but it is worth repeating that the teacher also serves as an important model for social learning, especially in relatively young children.

Teaching and Cognitive Style

Various teacher attributes related to training, achievement, personality, and attitudes are important for children's learning. The research findings indicate that relationships exist between pupils' success and factors, such as teacher's intelligence, training, and knowledge, although the correlations are generally rather low. From studies of teacher personality characteristics, there is some evidence that achievement of students is related to what has been called "teacher warmth," the latter being a measure of warm, understanding, and friendly and emotionally supporting behavior toward pupils. An interesting series of investigations has examined the implications of "cognitive complexity" (Harvey, Hunt, and Schroder, 1961) in teachers. High scores in the cognitive complexity scale indicate the tendency to think abstractly rather than concretely, in relatives rather than absolutes, and to show independence and originality in thought. Cognitively complex teachers are likely to be more resourceful than those low in cognitive complexity and to have greater empathic understanding of children, as measured by their capacity to perceive the learners' frame of reference, and to encourage inquiry in learning. There is some evidence (Harvey, Prather, White, and Hoffmeister, 1968) that the students of abstract teachers achieve more highly than students taught by concrete teachers, and are more involved and more cooperative in the classroom.

Some of the most important capacities in teachers are difficult to define and measure, and it is correspondingly difficult to specify how they can be acquired. From the perspective of a "traditional" definition of the teacher's role, with emphasis on transmission of information by the teacher under somewhat authoritarian conditions, it can be said that the skills required include subject matter knowledge and ability for clear expression. However, when the conception of the teacher's role is altered to place greater emphasis on helping children gain the habits and skills necessary for acquiring independence in learning and thinking, the additional teacher abilities required are much harder to define. In general, the teacher needs to have empathy to understand children and communicate with them at deeper levels than those required for simple acquisition of knowledge, and needs to understand how the school situation appears from a learner's perspective. "Friendliness" alone is not enough; abilities for human communication on emotional as well as purely cognitive planes are necessary. Also, unusual powers of empathy become more necessary when there are large cultural and class differences between the teacher and the students.

It is difficult to specify in a precise manner the skills and abilities required in a teacher, and especially difficult to state them sufficiently precisely to devise appropriate programs of training. It does not seem possible to prescribe the exact skills that have to be learned by the teacher in order to acquire empathy and human understanding, but one thing is certain. However conservative or traditional the preferred classroom approach, it is nonsensical to conceive of teaching in the absence of learning. If the word "teaching" is to be meaningful at all, it must imply some sort of communication. Thus, we cannot agree with the statement that, "even if teaching is manifestly competent, it does not necessarily lead to learning if the pupils concerned are inattentive, unmotivated, or cognitively unprepared" (Ausubel, 1969, pages 14–15). Surely, a definition of teaching that does not take learning into account has little value or meaning. The point is made again by Postman and Weingartner (1969), who say:

> It is not uncommon, for example, to hear "teachers" make statements such as, "Oh, I'd taught them that, but they didn't learn it." There is no utterance made in the teacher's room more extraordinary than this. From our point of view, it is on the same level as a salesman remarking, "I sold it to him, but he didn't buy it"—which is to say, it makes no sense.*

A Modest Proposal

Leonard (1968) has made a suggestion which, if followed, might do much to increase empathy and understanding in would-be teachers. Writing for parents (but his suggestions are equally valid for teachers), he suggests that the parent arranges a visit to his child's school on an ordinary weekday. Leonard recommends that the parent arrives at the same time as his child, and after being introduced to the class takes a

---

* From *Teaching as a Subversive Activity* by Neil Postman and Charles Weingartner. Copyright 1969 by Neil Postman and Charles Weingartner. Reprinted by permission of the publisher, Delacorte Press. P. 37.

chair near the back of the room where the child can be seen.
Leonard asks the parent to try and focus in on the child, to
assume his viewpoint, to feel what he feels and to learn what
he learns. The parent is told to be sensitive to positions of the
body, to see when the child sits straight and when he hunches
over, when he squirms, and when he languishes.

> Balance the weight of the teachers words against the
> pressure on your seat. Try not to daydream. Remember
> that time goes more slowly for a child than an adult.

> Now are you ready for a little walk? A cup of coffee?
> A visit to the rest room? A cigarette? Forget it. Stay with
> your child, stand only when he stands. Leave the room
> only when he leaves the room. Concentrate on him. Become
> your child.

> Bored beyond experience? Let us hope not.
>   (Leonard, 1968, page 107.)

Leonard tells the parent to take out his watch and mark
the lines of a sheet of paper with hatches, each representing
ten seconds. Selecting a typical period, a parent marks each
ten-second interval during which the child is really *learning*
something. The other intervals are left blank. The parent
should bear in mind that true learning involves change, and
this does not include needless repetition of something already
known. Real learning has to do with the child's own response,
not with what the teacher is doing. Leonard points out that
this exercise will take sensitivity since it involves the parent
being, in a sense, inside his child's mind. Leonard suggests
the results of the exercise will be a discouraging revelation;
however generous the marking, it will be rarely possible to
fill in more than a third of the intervals with marks to indicate that learning is occurring.

Leonard continues:

> When you have had enough of this exercise, stay where
> you are. No coffee, no cigarettes, no moving around to
> relax your body and stimulate your thoughts.
>   (Leonard, 1968, page 108.)

The parent is then asked to go out with the children in the play interval and sit down among them.

> *But are you observing play? Probably not, unfortunately. The children are likely to be merely letting off steam, with shrill yells and fanatic running about. It has been my experience, whenever the classroom situation is repressive and antithetical to learning, the playground situation, in direct ratio, is hyperactive, and equally antithetical to learning. In true play, the child is intent, responsive, completely involved.*
>
> (*Leonard, 1968, page 109.*)

After the interval the parent is required then to go back into class with the children, and then to lunch. The experience drags on into the afternoon. "Does the classroom seem stuffy?" asks Leonard. The parent is told to watch the eyes of his child and all the others and to observe whether they are becoming heavy with incipient sleep. "And how about your own eyes? Do you find yourself stifling yawns? Let us hope not. Let us hope the day has been an exhilarating one," Leonard adds, somewhat ironically.

It is not unlikely that any parent, teacher , or other adult who submits himself to this experience will find himself strongly agreeing with Leonard's suggestion that to bore children is far more cruel than to beat them.

Teachers, being human, have human needs. Some of these needs, for good training, decent salaries, and adequate status, for instance, are common to many occupations. Other needs are manifest more specifically in the context of the particular job. We have already suggested that just as children need the attention of the teacher, the teacher has needs which the children can meet. All but the most self-confident of people need some external evidence that they are communicating successfully, having an impact, and succeeding in their roles. Hence, teachers are pleased when children give the right answer, put their hands up, show that they are attending, and in other ways demonstrate to the teacher that she is effective at her job. However, what is done to meet a teacher's needs may have destructive results on the children, particularly when teachers give praise for neatness, conformity, and "good behavior" at the expense of behaviors that are equally important for learning, but which do not happen to provide the teacher such obvious indications of her success. Holt's (1964) convincing demonstration of the relationship between overemphasis by the teacher on right answers and on producing rather than thinking, on conformity rather than individual initiative, is a useful warning. Although it is relatively easy for most teachers to understand this intellectually, it may be more difficult to change one's behavior in the necessary ways.

Changes in Role

Particularly for older teachers, some of the changes in the classroom shown to be necessary by the growing knowledge about learning processes in children may be disturbing and even threatening. What we know now about human learning processes makes it clear that to be an adequate teacher requires a high degree of intellectual competence, great flexibility, and highly developed powers of empathy and understanding. Putting into practice what is known about helping children to learn is extremely difficult, and requires abilities far in excess of those once seen as necessary for the teacher's role as traditionally defined. A person can very easily be given adequate subject matter knowledge and instruction about clarity of presentation to be competent in a job whose requirements are based largely on these functions. The same teacher, however, may be unable to undertake a different type of role. It is as if one constructed a factory for making nails, training craftsmen in the nail-making process. Later, it is decided to switch from nail-making to the manufacture of complex machinery, and the craftsmen are reluctant and unable to carry out the new jobs. This is not surprising; people who have been trained for one job are now being asked to do something entirely different for which they are quite untrained, and since they are manifestly incompetent, they feel threatened and attempt to reject the changes. This illustration exaggerates the situation in teaching, but there are important similarities. If people are trained to do one job and the nature of the job is later changed, one has to be very careful to ensure that the necessary training and support is available for people to change roles, especially when the second job is both intellectually and emotionally more demanding than the first.

Learning to do something new and difficult is not just a matter of memorizing appropriate instruction. Practice is required under conditions which are not threatening, and where failure is not important. Adequate informal discussion situations where teachers can talk about their fears and difficulties are essential in any program of training for change which is to have any chance of success. If it was a universal practice for every teacher to spend two months of each year in full-time training, we might be making a good start towards more effective schools for our children.

Group Experiences

Apart from intellectual competence, the qualities desirable in a teacher are, we have suggested, hard to specify with any precision. A list of necessary qualities might include related terms such as warmth, "being human," empathy, perceptiveness, sympathy, ability to change, understanding, and adaptiveness. Clearly, these are not the kinds of abilities that can be acquired through formal instruction, and it has been claimed by a number of psychologists, among whom the most distinguished is Carl Rogers (1969), that a type of learning environment in which such qualities are most likely to develop is the relatively unstructured small group setting. Various group experiences, known to some extent interchangeably as "T groups," "encounter groups," "sensitivity training," and "human relations laboratories," have in common an emphasis on close and "deep" interaction in a group setting, uninhibited communication, and an awareness of emotions. It is claimed that such experiences help participants to communicate honestly with others and to gain self-awareness. There is no doubt that many people, including teachers, have found such experiences valuable, although clear empirical evidence of resulting changes has not yet become available.

Unfortunately, there has been a certain amount of polarization in attitudes to group experiences, their most extreme supporters regarding them as something of a cure-all for what is wrong with the world, while detractors see the activities as little more than a cult or fad with no lasting value. On balance, the present writer considers that group interaction can be valuable in helping to develop some of the capacities that are desirable in teachers (and in all humans), but elevation of the methods and techniques into a kind of total philosophy of life or life-style, as sometimes happens among enthusiasts, is not justified.

Self-fulfilling Prophesies

It has often been noticed that some teachers have rather definite expectancies about the achievement and ability of different children, based on little or no evidence or on evidence which the teacher incorrectly thinks to be valid for predicting individual achievement, such as progress of siblings or skin color. If a teacher decides that Johnny is unlikely to learn much, she may transmit this expectancy to Johnny in ways which do in fact limit his achievement. Thus, it is claimed, the teacher's expectancy may fulfill itself, and on the basis of such self-fulfilling prophecies, a teacher might more confidently make them about other children in the future. There is no doubt that some teachers do have very definite expectancies about their students, and these expectancies are not always based on factors that have genuine predictive value for individual children. In Jonathan Kozol's book *Death at an Early Age* (1967), for instance, there are a number of incidents that show some of the white teachers at the Boston school he describes had expectancies which they communicated in their behavior, whereby black children were seen as having limited potential for achievement, compared with the white children.

In Chapter 2, we referred to another way in which self-fulfilling prophecies might operate in the classroom. It is often thought that children in middle-class schools tend to be better behaved than children in poor, inner-city areas, and this is usually attributed entirely to differences in family upbringing, or in social class and cultural values. As we pointed out, a teacher in a ghetto school who is told that the children in his class are likely to be disruptive may react by using a "firm" approach, giving more punishment and disapproval than encouragement and praise. Partly as a result of this strategy, the children may behave badly, strengthening the teacher's belief in the necessity of the negative methods of control. Hence a vicious circle results in which the teacher, on the basis of his expectancies, acts in ways which lead to those expectancies being fulfilled.

Yet another form of self-fulfilling prophecy may occur if there are differences in teacher interactions with boy and girl pupils. The findings of research in this area are somewhat contradictory, and comprehensive studies by Davis and Slobodian (1967) and Good and Brophy (1971), attempting to explain the superior performance of girls over boys in the early grades at learning to read, failed to produce evidence of differences between boys and girls in pupil-teacher interaction. Palardy (1969) found that if first grade teachers believed that boys would achieve as well as girls in reading, the boys did in fact perform better than boys with teachers who believed them to be less successful in reading than girls.

The Pygmalion Study

Considerable publicity has been given to the findings of an empirical study of self-fulfilling prophecies in a school setting, published in the form of a book *Pygmalion in the Classroom: Teacher Expectation and Pupils' Intellectual Development* by R. Rosenthal and L. Jacobson. Rosenthal and Jacobson (1968) carried out their investigation in an ele-

mentary school in the San Francisco area. At the beginning
of the study, the teachers were told that research was being
carried out on a new kind of test, designed to predict intellectual gains or academic "blooming" in children. The children were given the test (in fact a standard but unfamiliar
intelligence test) and on a later occasion each teacher received
a list containing the names of about 20 percent of the children
in the class. They were told that on the basis of the test these
children were predicted to be potential academic bloomers,
and their performance was likely to improve in the near
future. The teachers were given the designated names at the
beginning of a term, and the children were given three later
tests, after four months, nine months and eighteen months.
According to Rosenthal and Jacobson, the results of their
study strongly indicated that children from whom teachers
expected greater intellectual gains (on the basis of these predictions) showed such gains in objective tests of intelligence
and achievement compared to the other children. Children in
the first and second grades showed the largest gains at the
end of the first year, and at the end of the second year the
biggests gains were made by the children who at the start of
the experiment had been in the fifth grade. Rosenthal and
Jacobson reported that the children for whom intellectual improvement was predicted were described later as having a
better chance at being successful in life, and as being happier,
more curious, and more interesting than the other children.
The authors report that the designated students were perceived by their teachers as being more alive and autonomous
intellectually, and that this was especially true of the children
in the first grade. Rosenthal and Jacobson conclude that the
change in the teacher's expectations regarding the intellectual
performance of the predicted "bloomers" produced an actual
change in their intellectual performance.

In fact, the original names on the lists given to teachers
had been selected purely on a random basis, and not on the
results of any test. Hence, the improvement in achievements
of the designated "bloomers" compared to the others appears

to be due to the teachers' new expectancies, which presumably influenced their behavior towards the selected students.

So we seem to have very clear evidence that self-fulfilling prophesies can influence classroom learning, and Rosenthal and Jacobson state:

> As teacher-training institutions begin to teach the possibility that teachers' expectations of their pupils' performance may serve as self-fulfilling prophesies, there will be a new expectancy created. The new expectancy may be that children can learn more than has been believed possible, an expectation held by many educational theorists . . . the new expectancy, at the very least, will make it more difficult when they encounter the educationally disadvantaged for teachers to think "well—after all, what can you expect?" . . . The teacher in the school room may need to learn that the same prophecies within her may be fulfilled; she is no casual passerby. Perhaps Pygmalion in the classroom is more her role.
>
> (Rosenthal and Jacobson, 1968, pages 181–182.)

However, there have been a number of important criticisms of the Rosenthal and Jacobson study indicating that there are deficiencies which lead to serious doubts about the validity of the results. The first source of doubt resides in the fact that a number of attempts to replicate the experiment have not produced the same results. Self-fulfilling prophesies have not been observed in the majority of these experiments. Generally, when an experiment is reported but further studies fail to reproduce the original results, their validity appears somewhat doubtful. Secondly, and more serious for the Rosenthal and Jacobson study, there have been a number of criticisms of the data. It has been suggested that the methods of gathering test scores, the techniques of analysis, and the data presentation are so seriously deficient as to question the validity of the conclusions made. Thus, Snow (1969) states that some of the reported IQ scores suggest that the children must have been functioning at imbecile and low moron levels, if the tests were being correctly used, that assumptions necessary for the statistical analyses used were violated, and that graphs and tables in the report are misleading. He considers that teacher expectancy may well be a powerful phenomenon, but that the study by Rosenthal and Jacobson has not come close to providing adequate demonstration of it, or any understanding of the process, and that the inadequate and premature reporting of the results has done a disservice to educational research. Similarly, Thorndike (1968), who also points to the unlikely test scores which, he feels, "show that the testing was utterly worthless and meaningless," concludes that the basic data are so untrustworthy that any conclusions based on them must be suspect. He admits that the conclusions *may* be correct, but if so, he says, it must be considered a fortunate coincidence. Although Rosenthal has made some attempts to reply to the critics, the replies have not removed all the doubts about measurement and data analysis, and these doubts, coupled with failures to replicate their results in further experiments (for example, Clairborn, 1969), seem to indicate that the experimental method of Rosenthal and Jacobson has not convincingly proved that arbitrary predictions in education act as self-fulfilling prophesies.

Further Research on Self-fulfilling Prophesies

Despite the failure of the widely quoted study by Rosenthal and Jacobson (1968) to provide entirely convincing evidence, the findings of some other research investigations indicate it is very likely that self-fulfilling prophesies do occur. The mechanisms by which they influence performance are probably more complex and subtle than those reproduced in Rosenthal and Jacobson's study, and detecting such mechanisms requires correspondingly subtle methods of measuring interactions between teachers and individual children. Traditional methods of interaction analysis (see, for example, Amidon and Flanders, 1963) can be useful, but since they measure interaction between the teacher and the class as a whole, they are probably too crude to detect all of the teacher-pupil interactions that might lead to self-fulfilling prophesies.

Studies in which there has been careful analysis of interactions between teachers and individual pupils have provided a number of findings supporting the belief that self-fulfilling prophesies occur. For instance, Brophy and Good (1970) found that in one school high-achieving, first-grade students received more praise and support from the teacher, the boys had more interactions with the teachers than girls, the teachers directed more evaluative comments towards boys, and the teachers not only demanded better performance from those children for whom they had high expectations, but were more likely to praise such performance when it occurred. In short, the teachers did communicate differential performance expectations to different children in ways that might have encouraged the children to respond in ways which would confirm teacher expectancies.

A number of investigators have obtained similar findings. Thus, Rubovits and Maehr (1971) observed that trainee-teachers provided different patterns of attention and praise to two groups in grades six and seven arbitrarily designated as "gifted" and "nongifted." Mendoza et al. (1971), found that low-achievement high school pupils received much less teacher contact than high achievers. Rothbart et al. (1971), observed teachers to be more attentive to high school students who had been randomly designated as having high expectations. Consequently, these students talked more and were ranked by the teachers as being more intelligent than the students (arbitrarily) designated as "lacking in intellectual potential."

A nightmarish account is provided by Rist (1970) who describes a situation in which children were ranked by a teacher on the basis of her guesses at their potential ability at the beginning of their lives at school, in the complete absence of measures of their capacity. From this point, the children received differential treatment in ways that all too certainly led to differences in performance. For instance, the individuals who the teacher had decided would not perform well at school were placed around the table in the classroom furthest from the teacher where it was difficult to hear her, and received considerably less attention than the closer groups. Rist describes how the process was perpetuated as the children advanced from grade to grade.

An interesting variation on the research about self-fulfilling prophesies in education is a study by Tuckman and Bierman (1971). Instead of simply providing the teachers with information about the students' (real or imaginary) ability, they also gave similar information to the students, moving randomly chosen junior high and high school students into higher ability groups. Students moved into higher groups performed better on standardized tests than students who were not moved, and it was also found that 54 percent of the students moved into higher groups were later recommended by their teachers to be retained in the high groups, while only 1 percent of the other students received recommendations for this promotion. The authors suggest that the tendency for students who were moved up to stay in the new group may be partly a function of inertia in the grouping process. If so, suggest Tuckman and Bierman, this indicates that current grouping procedures tend to "lock students in and out" causing frustration and disillusionment, and are something less than educationally sound.

In summary, despite Rosenthal and Jacobson's failure to provide a convincing demonstration, there is considerable alternative evidence of destructive self-fulfilling prophesy effects on school learning. The effects are likely to be subtle, and ones which are most likely to be detected by precise analysis of interactions between teachers and individual children. Brophy and Good (1970) suggest that expectation effects follow a sequence, making a chain of behaviors, as follows:

A. *The teacher forms differential expectations for student performance.*

B. *He then begins to treat children differently in accordance with his differential expectations.*

C. *The children respond differentially to the teacher because they are being treated differently by him.*

D. *In responding to the teacher, each child tends to exhibit behavior which complements and reinforces the teacher's particular expectations for him.*

E. *As a result, the general academic performance of some children will be enhanced while that of others will be depressed, with changes being in the direction of teacher expectations.*

F. *These effects will show up in the achievement tests given at the end of the year, providing support for the "self-fulfilling prophesy" notion.*

(Brophy and Good, 1970, pages 365–366.)

Teachers are likely to be unaware of the small differences in their behavior with different pupils that produce self-fulfilling prophesies, if they do occur, and hence their prevention, may be correspondingly difficult. However, as Brophy and Good (1970) make clear, teacher behavior, however subtle, is observable and measurable, and therefore it is potentially subject to modification and control.

Chapter 13

Research and Human Learning

The Need for Research

Research on human learning is needed to provide a basis of knowledge that can be used in making decisions to help produce environments in which people can learn. Most of the statements and suggestions in this book are based on knowledge gained, directly or indirectly, from research. It is an essential ingredient for amassing a body of practical knowledge.

In education, teachers have managed without research for many hundreds of years, and some would argue that they have done quite well without it. They might add that, up to now at least, research does not seem to have added greatly to the effectiveness of school learning. Ten years ago it would have been hard to argue with this view, but just recently educational research has been starting to have an exciting impact which is rapidly growing. Even if that negative opinion were correct, it would be no argument against research as such. Existing research may be inadequate or insufficient in relation to the complexities of the problems. Without knowledge about the factors that contribute to learning, we have to rely on our own experiences and those of others, handed down as folklore, and the judgments of so-called authorities, carrying "the weight of tradition."

The limitations of tradition as a source of directives are well known. Personal experience is certainly valuable, and in

its way experience is as much based on evidence as is empirical research, but research as a source of knowledge has
certain advantages. Evidence is obtained from systematic observations under conditions where procedures are tightly
controlled, and measurement is generally more objective than
is the case with observation in daily experience. Personal
experience alone is clearly inadequate as a basis for prescrib-
ing the behavior of others. In education, as in all spheres of
human life, there are countless examples of wrong thinking
based on so-called "experience." These are often expressed
in statements beginning "I've been teaching for 30 years
(more or less) and I *know* . . ." followed by "they won't
respect you if you smile during the first six months," "these
black kids are only capable of learning half as fast as the
white children we used to have here," "keep the desk between
you and them, or you'll never be able to keep control," "he'll
never learn anything because his brother didn't," "progressive ideas may work in some schools, but not with these children," and so on, *ad nauseum*. The awful thing about these
statements is that they may have a measure of truth (as self-
fulfilling prophesies) for the people who utter them, given
their underlying feelings and attitudes. As prescriptions for
the behavior of other teachers, given as they are in the form
of advice for the young, such "experience-based" statements
can be useless and even harmful.

Not everyone would agree with the 30-year-old upstart
who wrote:

> No way of thinking or doing, however ancient, can be
> trusted without proof . . . what old people say you cannot
> do, you try to find that you can. Old deeds for old people,
> and new deeds for new. . . . I have yet to hear the first
> syllable of valuable or even earnest advice from my seniors.
> They have told me nothing, and probably cannot tell me
> anything to the purpose. Here is life, an experiment to a
> great extent untried by me; but it does not avail me that
> they have tried it. If I have any experience which I think

valuable, I am sure to reflect that this my Mentors said nothing about.

(Thoreau, 1854, 1962 ed., page 19.)

These words are from Henry David Thoreau's *Walden*. Some may find the emphasis extreme, but Thoreau's point that experience is no guarantee of wisdom is well taken.

Even those who agree that research into human learning is essential are occasionally impatient because it has been slow to provide breakthroughs that suddenly revolutionize our understanding of learning or multiply the efficiency of learners. In fact, it is unrealistic to look to scientific research to provide sudden, dramatic discoveries. Such discoveries have occurred on occasions in some sciences, but they are always the exception rather than the rule. More often, the effect of scientific research has been to bring about steady progress by gradually developing a body of knowledge and concepts that extend understanding. It is through such growth of knowledge and related changes in the understanding of phenomena that research will most likely produce increased awareness of processes in human learning. Travers (1970) draws attention to John Dewey's remark that a major contribution of research is to enable the practitioner to think more intelligently about problems that he encounters. Travers states:

Half a century ago the teacher confronted with a child who was not learning was able to suggest little except perhaps that the child did not have the moral fortitude required to pursue his studies effectively. The teacher today immediately has a number of reasonable hypotheses about why a child is not learning. The modern teacher will question whether the child is a victim of brain damage at birth. Or whether the child comes from an environment where no value is placed on academic learning, or whether the child has a hearing loss. . . . This kind of search is vastly more intelligent than that of the teacher near the turn of the century who might have lectured or punished the child. . . . Note that the modern teacher does not have a rule of thumb procedure to follow when confronted with a child who does not learn. Scientific knowledge, rarely, if ever, produces a simple rule for handling practical problems.

(Travers, 1970, page 3.)

Dewey (1929) points out that this state of affairs is characteristic of situations where understanding has been influenced by science in the more "traditional" scientific areas. By way of an example, Travers notes that Isaac Newton's development of principles relevant to an understanding of stresses had no immediate impact on the design of bridges. However, after Newton, although the bridges continued to look very much like earlier ones, new understanding opened up fresh approaches for bridge builders. It now became possible to calculate the stresses that would occur in parts of the bridge, and thus to determine how strong the various elements would have to be in order to stand up to their loads. Thus, gradual application of Newtonian physics provided the builder with tools for intelligent bridge design. The improvements did not come from any sudden discovery, nor did Newton's theories supply simple rules of thumb, but increased understanding made it possible to think more effectively than before about the various problems and hence to build more functional bridges.

Dewey points out that command of scientific methods and systematized subject matter "liberates" individuals, enabling them to see new problems and to devise new procedures. He concludes,

Science signifies, I take it, the existence of systematic methods of enquiry, which when they are brought to bear on a range of facts, enable us to understand them better and to control them more intelligently, less hazardly and with less routine.

(Dewey, 1929, pages 8–9.)

Some Important Limitations

To conclude that research is invaluable is not to deny that there are limitations in the extent to which what is gained from research into learning can form a basis for strategies of teaching. William James' famous statement that teaching is an art rather than a science is reformulated by Becker (1970), who emphasizes that not all the problems that teachers have are ones which can be solved by scientific knowledge. He refers to the opinion of James that the teacher and the psychologist approach the child from different directions; the teacher's attitude being concrete and ethical, while that of the psychologist is abstract and analytic. Certainly, the psychologist can do much to help the teacher, but Becker suggests that educational psychologists tend to "diminish those aspects of teaching that depend upon talents that do not lend themselves to the conceptual structure of their science" (Becker, 1970, page 5). To insist that science ought to be the final arbiter of all things educational is to close our minds to the fact that educational thinkers have had important ideas about education that cannot be examined by scientific approaches. We may be attempting the impossible if we try to deal with qualitative problems in quantitive terms. The assumption that scientific research is the only guide to wisdom is quite wrong.

Jackson (1969) expresses a related concern which is shared by the present author.

> *Another suspicion that kept creeping into my mind was that educational psychologists, as a group, seem to honour research more than thought. It seems strange, I admit, to conceive of research and thinking as separable activities for, ideally, they are both natural manifestations of an inquiring mind. But, unfortunately, research may be done thoughtlessly, just as thinking may soar free of empirical moorings. Among educational psychologists, it seems that*

nonempirical thinking is a far more grievous fault than thoughtless empirical research.

(Jackson, 1969, page 67.)

The conflict implicit in the remarks of Becker and Jackson between the activities of those who do research on learning and the needs of those whose job it is to help individuals learn, needs some explaining. One important point, which was discussed in Chapter 1, is that not all basic research into human learning, however well conceived, is likely to lead in the near future to usable knowledge about the types of learning that are important in, for instance, school situations. Because of this, we argued, it is important that research is carried out that *does* directly investigate the complex types of human learning essential in education. Yet the remarks of Becker and Jackson indicate an additional problem; some of the contributions of researchers who inquire into learning may not be valuable to teachers because they are made in a frame of reference from which nonempirical and extra-scientific considerations are excluded. The researcher thinks within a "system" (Bertalanffy, 1968) that is only part of the larger system in which human learners and teachers have to operate. A specific example will clarify this point. The researcher might seek to know which of two methods of instruction will be most effective for a particular learning task, using a predetermined measure of learning. For the practitioner, on the other hand, the factors that are "givens" to the researcher are important variables in the total system wherein he operates. While the researcher assumes a learning task, the teacher has to ask what is worth learning; while the researcher uses a given instrument for measuring learning, the teacher has to think about which of many aspects of learning he is going to measure and whether the chosen instrument will really measure it. We might say that the domain of the researcher into learning is only part of the broader system constituting human learning situations in life.

As a scientist, the researcher typically takes an "analytic" approach, studying in relative isolation some of the elements of learning that are present in educational situations. However, as Bertalanffy (1968) points out, application of the analytic procedure requires certain conditions to be met, and one of these is that the interactions between parts of a system be nonexistent or relatively weak. If this requirement is met, the parts can be examined separately and the findings assembled later. Insofar as the relationship between "learning in school" and "laboratory learning" is not unlike that between systems and their parts in the physical sciences, the same principles apply. For learning, the interactions between the "parts" are generally by no means nonexistent, and the practical utility of much research on learning suffers to the extent to which such interactions are important.

The relationships between analytical research and its application in the human sciences are more complicated than in the physical sciences. Knowledge about the effects of temperature changes on steel, for example, can be applied in a relatively straightforward manner to engineering practice. However, while physical scientists can normally pursue their research without having to pay much attention to issues in society which are outside their jurisdiction, the researcher in school learning is in a very different position. There are some political, philosophical, moral, and socioeconomic issues that affect his work rather directly. One cannot pursue research into school learning without thinking seriously about certain questions, such as "What is worth learning?"; "What are the purposes of school learning?"; and "To what extent should individuality and independence or the ability to adjust to existing society predominate as attributes of the educated person?" The author has discussed this issue elsewhere (Howe, 1971).

Deep-rooted attitudes, values, and beliefs are important in determining the criteria which any individual chooses as indicating the effectiveness for learning of educational practices. People differ very much in their judgments about what is important in education. The difference in outlook between a teacher who believes, with Max Rafferty, that "the child should be taught first to love his country so that later on in his schooling he will have a motive strong enough to spur him on to understand her," and the person who believes that no one can *teach* another person to love anything or anyone, is not a difference that is going to be resolved on the basis of research results. In short, research cannot do much to alter the differences between people in what they believe to be the aims or goals of education. It can only be useful if we have some agreement about the goals to be set.

Practical Considerations in Educational Research

A problem in research on learning is that some *criteria* of learning are more easily measured than others. A researcher who has to choose what criterion to use as a basis for comparing two methods of instruction may be tempted to choose one which is easily measurable. Researchers, after all, are human, and being sometimes contaminated by what, after Holt, we might call "the producer syndrome," like to get clear results. The criteria of learning achievements that are most readily quantified and measured include number of facts retained, accuracy of spelling, and number of correct responses. It could well be argued that some of the most important criteira are less tangible factors, such as attitudes to further learning, willingness to think, and ability to apply learning in a wide variety of situations. However, these things are hard enough to define, let alone measure. It is a small wonder that the more quantifiable and easily measurable criteria are the ones that are most often measured. There is no reason why a researcher has to decide on just one criterion by which to assess learning. He might decide to use a number of relevant criteria, such as immediate retention of information, speed of learning, number of errors, transfer to other situations, retention after one year, and attitudes to the learning experience. However, practical considerations impose severe limitations on the number of criteria that can be used, and those quantities that can be most easily measured, and which do not require too much time to be spent in waiting for results (as do long-term measures of retention, transfer, and long-term attitudes, for example) are the ones which receive the most attention, at the expense of other criteria which many would judge to be of greater real importance.

Similar practical considerations may affect decisions about the particular experimental variables (the independent variables) that are chosen to be examined. Some of the factors that would seem especially important in learning, such as interest and relevance to the learner, and comprehensibility, have received rather little attention in experimental research, whereas other variables that might appear to be less critical —mode and rate of presentation, and spacing of materials, for example—have been studied in large numbers of experimental investigations (Howe, 1971). There are a number of reasons for this state of affairs, but it seems likely that a major influence in the choice of variables to study—just as with the choice of criteria—is a practical consideration, the ease with which phenomena can be quantified. In the case of a variable, such as rate of presentation, it is relatively easy to choose different values (fast, medium, slow), but for a variable like comprehensibility, it is more difficult to set up experiments in which its values are systematically varied. One reason is that comprehensibility is not a simple one-dimensional concept in the sense that presentation rate is, and a more important difference is that while presentation rate can be measured and defined by the experimenter, he can hardly assign values of comprehensibility without also taking the *learner* into account. So again, we have a situation in which practical considerations make it more awkward and difficult to carry out research on the effects of some of the variables which may be most crucial in real learning situations than to examine the effects of factors that may be less important, at least in the long run.

What types of research on human learning are the most useful? Attempts to answer this question would fill a number of lengthy books. At this juncture three considerations can be raised. First, an issue which was raised in Chapter 1, not all research on learning is likely to lead in the reasonably near future to increased understanding of learning processes that are important in school. There are many different kinds and varieties of learning, and much basic psychological research into learning processes has quite justifiably examined the simplest forms of learning. To attempt to extrapolate knowledge gained from situations involving very simple learning to those in which learning is much more complex, is, we argued, roughly analogous to attempting to design brick buildings on the basis of knowledge of characteristics of single bricks. In designing a brick building we need know something about the properties of the bricks being used, but knowledge of single bricks can only make a relatively small contribution to the architectural understanding required. Similarly, in learning, although it is necessary to know about the characteristics of simple elements, what we gain from such study will not take us all the way to understanding complex learning situations.

The second consideration that requires attention when one is deciding on the types of research to attempt is that sometimes it is necessary to choose between precise, well-controlled studies in which circumstances are somewhat different from those of "real-life" classroom situations, and field studies which are imperfect in experimental design or in which the experimenter cannot have tight control over all the variables influencing learning. In field studies, such as those carried out in classrooms, there is normally little doubt about the relevance and applicability of the findings for school learning. When precisely controlled laboratory studies are used, it is relatively easy to ensure that the factors determining performance can be known and measured by the investigator. It is often possible to incorporate the advantages of both these types of research in an experimental investigation, but practical considerations of time and expense sometimes make a conflict inevitable.

These two points, relating to (1) the form of learning and (2) the circumstances in which learning is observed, have sometimes been confused. It has been argued, for example, that the main reason why much psychological research on learning has not been applicable to the classroom is the artificiality of the learning situation in the research, especially when it was conducted in laboratories. This is important, but probably more important than differences in learning settings are differences in the *types of learning* involved.

Finally, there is the wider problem of the relationship between basic and applied research. It is sometimes argued that solving real problems is only possible when there is a considerable body of knowledge built up from basic or "pure" research. In psychology, it is claimed, there needs to be considerably more experimental research and theoretical advances before we can begin to think about how it can be applied. In fact, as Ausubel (1968) implies and Arthur (1971) states more directly, this is a completely mistaken view. The opinion that applied science is always closely dependent on and tied to advances in basic science is by no means supported by the evidence of history in other areas, such as the medical sciences. Certainly, basic research is necessary, but to improve the quality of human learning we also require, to use Arthur's (1971) words, "an independent, or additional, if you will, scientific approach to the everyday problems of human behavior, which has as its aim not the understanding or the explanation of behavior, but the engineering of behavior itself and understanding of the technology of such engineering" (Arthur, 1971, page 33.)

Interactions

Research into any important aspect of human behavior is bound to be difficult, if only because humans are so complex. One problem is implicit in the earlier remarks about the value of analytic science being limited to the extent by which a total system is determined by interactions between its parts, rather than simply their summative action. Since human actions are determined by the interactions between a large number of factors, much of the research we undertake will be correspondingly complicated if it is to be effective. It has to be in order to take into account a reasonable number of the many factors that determine human learning. In experimental research, the presence of interactions indicates that the effects of one of the factors depends on the values of other factors. An example of interaction in everyday life is the observation that the time it takes to drive across town depends on the route that is taken, but the route that takes the least time when traffic is light may be the slowest route in heavy traffic. Thus route and time of day are factors, but the effect of the first (route) depends on the value of the second (time of day).

In many instances, knowledge obtained from scientific experiments will be of limited practical value unless the interactions between different variables are examined. For instance, a scientist might decide to plan an experimental program to discover which of a number of species of wheat produces the largest grain output. He decides to carry out a simple experiment, planting a number of seeds of each type in a small plot of land. Application of the results would be restricted to situations approximating the particular conditions of the experiment. It might turn out, for instance, that the relative output of the different types of wheat depended on the type of soil in which the seeds were planted, the amount of rainfall that occurred during growth, and the temperature during growth. Seed A might prosper best in a warm damp climate and sandy ground, whereas Seed B might grow well in soil high in lime content, and in cool dry weather conditions. The different variables interact with one another so that one cannot make a simple statement about which seed is most successful. The *combination* of the variables is important; the information about their effects could not be obtained from simple experiments varying one factor at a time, and it is necessary to vary the different factors jointly to discover the most effective combinations.

If it is important to look at interactions in trying to predict plant growth, it is even more important to examine interactions in attempts to understand human behavior. By way of illustration, imagine that we wish to compare students' attitudes to three different teaching methods, A, B, and C. We start by carrying out a study simply comparing attitudes of a large group of students to the three methods, and find no difference between them. However, before concluding that there are no differences, it might be wise to find out if different subgroups of students vary in their reactions. Accordingly, a more elaborate experiment is designed in which not only are the methods of instruction compared, but the students are subdivided by sex, age, and by scores on an intelligence test. It is then found that despite the lack of *overall* differences in attitude, the various subgroups differ considerably. The girls who score high on the intelligence test favor method A, while older boys who get low scores on the intelligence test favor B, and all the younger children, irrespective of sex and test scores, react most favorably to the third method. So in answer to a question about which method students like best, we must answer that it depends on age, sex, and measured intelligence.

Interactions are probably important in most situations where human learning is involved. Naturally, the complexity of experimental research is increased when we examine the interactions between variables, and this complicates the researchers' job. If we also take the advice given earlier, to consider more than one criteria of learning, experiments become even more complex. For instance, to compare the effectiveness of learning under three different conditions, for boys and girls of different ages and levels of ability, taking three separate indices of learning into account, such as number of errors, immediate retention, and retention three months after initial learning—and we might have a good reason to expect all these factors to be important—we might need a research design that was very expensive in the amount of time and financial resources required. Some compromise may be necessary towards greater simplicity and less cost.

Thus, even when problems are ones to which research can

legitimately be applied, practical considerations may limit what can be done. Only recently has educational research begun to add a great deal to our understanding of school learning, and there is some truth in Jackson's (1969, page 70) remark that, if all our solid knowledge in the field was suddenly lost, "I doubt that we would have lost much ground as humans or that the state of teaching would suffer terribly in the wake of ignorance that followed." It is also true, however, that we have not been involved in educational research for long, and that the sheer quantity of time, money, and talent invested in research will have to be much greater in the future if it is to help solve the problems that exist in school learning.

Questions of Research Validity

Anyone who intends to *use* the results of research on learning must have some understanding of the processes by which it is produced if only to judge its validity and applicability to particular situations. This necessitates (in addition to an understanding of simple statistical analysis) some knowledge of how controlled experments are designed. By a "controlled" experiment is meant one in which variables other than the ones deliberately manipulated are held constant.

Imagine that as a school superintendent you have to decide whether or not to adopt a new method of reading instruction. Its supporters insist that "research has proved" the new method to be superior to existing ones, but, having heard such a claim on previous occasions you decide to look rather carefully at the research on the new reading method. Basically, the questions that need answering concern validity. First, there are matters of "internal validity," relating to the question, "Were the results caused by those factors manipulated by the experimenter (that is, the experimental variables), or could they have been caused by extraneous causes not adequately controlled in the design of the study?" Secondly, there are questions of "external validity." These ask whether the results obtained would occur outside the particular circumstances of the research experiment, and, more specifically, whether they are applicable to the circumstances in which you might use the new method. An instance where we might question external validity is in applying to a high-school some of the behavior modification research on methods of elementary classroom control. One might be quite satisfied about the internal validity, that is, that the findings resulted from differences between methods and no other factors, but question whether the research results would apply in a high school classroom.

Deciding whether particular research findings have external validity for a given situation requires experience and good judgment. For internal validity, it is possible to list specific points that can be checked. Campbell and Stanley (1963) have provided such a list of "factors jeopardizing internal validity," and the most common ones are summarized in the succeeding paragraphs. These are, to recapitulate, factors other than those deliberately manipulated by experimenters that might influence research findings. Educational research has internal validity only if such factors are either absent or adequately controlled. Listed by Campbell and Stanley (1963) are the following:

Maturation. This refers to extraexperimental events occurring between measurements. Imagine an enterprising teacher sets up a training course in running for 2-year-old children. Before the course he measures the running speed and finds that the average child takes 40 seconds to run 50 yards. The course lasts for 3 months, and afterwards children who have been through it take only 30 seconds, on average, to run the distance. On the basis of this, the teacher concludes that the course in running skills has been effective in increasing speed. Such an assumption would be invalid, since various factors associated with growth might have contributed to the improvement. Considerations of this type need especially close attention in research on the role of learning in human development, as discussed in Chapter 5.

History. This second form of threat toward internal validity is similar to maturation, but refers to more specific events. An example of a study in which this factor was probably important is one carried out in France in 1940. The investigators were measuring the effects on people's attitudes of Nazi propaganda materials. During the duration of the study, France fell to the German armies. Accordingly, it is likely that any changes in attitude occurred largely as a result of the latter factor, compared to which any effects of propaganda as such were probably insignificant.

Testing. This is a more common effect. If you take a test today, and tomorrow take a different form of the same test, your performance tomorrow is likely to be different to what it would have been had you not taken the earlier test. Among other reasons for this is the fact that when one takes a test, he may become "test-wise." The findings described in Chapter 6 show that practice effects in intelligence testing can very strongly influence scores. It is not usually possible to eliminate testing effects, but they can be controlled by making sure that subjects in all experimental conditions have the same testing experiences.

Instrumentation. This refers to changes in the calibration of measuring instruments. In educational research this type of effect is likely when human observers are used for judging performance. It is sometimes difficult for observers to avoid small changes in the way they measure things: if papers are being graded, for instance, the grading standards may subtly shift. Most studies in behavior modification (Chapter Two) for example, use human observers, and in such studies it is necessary to make careful precautions to prevent changes in measurement, particularly when a study is conducted over a lengthy period of time. Such factors can lead to differences in experimental results that reflect changes in measurement and not changes in the quantities being measured.

Experimental Mortality. This can occur if the sample of subjects measured in one experimental condition is drawn from only part of the population used in the other condition. For instance, we might compare the average weight of third-year unmarried female graduate students with that of the first-year graduate students, and discover that the first-year students weigh less. Before leaping to the conclusion that being in graduate school causes girls to gain weight, it would be worth considering the alternative explanation that by the fourth year more of the slimmer girls have married so that those remaining single are not a random sample of the students who entered originally.

Hawthorne Effects. Various other effects can jeopardize the internal validity of experimental research. Of these, the best known, and probably the most frequently occurring, are called "Hawthorne effects." Generally speaking, Hawthorne effects can be described as products of subjects' awareness that they are in a special situation. Let us imagine that Dr. X has devised a new method of teaching children to read, and he firmly believes that it is much more effective than all other existing methods. He is extremely enthusiastic about the new method and arouses great enthusiasm among the teachers who are trying it out in their classrooms. In a study comparing the new methods which the one used previously, the children become aware of their teachers' enthusiasm, and they know that they are being taught in a way which is novel and different from the "old" way. They are also aware that their performance is being carefully observed and that considerable interest and attention are being focused upon them. As a result, the whole experience, the social situation, and the types of interaction with their teachers become very different from the previous classroom circumstances which still exist among the comparison "control" group who are using the old method, as a basis for comparison. In short, there are a number of differences between the experimental and comparison groups in addition to the objective differences between the methods. Consequently, if the children in the experimental condition perform differently to those in the other condition, one cannot be certain that the specific differences between methods of instruction caused the differences in results. It is not always possible to eliminate Hawthorne effects, but it is usually possible to minimize them by ensuring that comparison groups receive, so far as is possible, exactly the same treatment in all ways other than the precise experimental method.

Finally, there are "regression effects." For various reasons, if a large group of subjects are tested and then retested, the subjects whose scores were at the extreme ends of the total distribution of scores on the first test are likely to have scores nearer the mean average of the total on the second test. There are occasions when it is possible to mistake regression effects for genuine experimental effects. For instance, a teacher might test 100 second-grade students on a measure of reading achievement, and make arrangements for the 10 students scoring lowest to be given a short remedial reading course. After the course, all students are again tested, and it is found that the performance of those who received the course has improved in relation to the average. It is tempting to assume that this finding demonstrates the effectiveness of the course, but in fact the effect might be partly or wholly due to statistical regression. Without attempting to explain the causes of regression effects, their nature may be clearer if it is noticed that when one examines the subjects whose scores were at the extremes on the *second* test, their scores on the first tests are found to be closer to the average.

It should be apparent that research, to be valid, needs careful planning. Otherwise, the findings will have no value. Before making use of research findings one has to be satisfied about the internal validity of the experimental design, and the user needs to give close consideration to questions of external validity.

A Concluding Remark

The tone of this chapter has been cautious, stressing limitations to the role of research on school learning, and the difficulty of some problems and the pitfalls to be avoided. Nonetheless, the impact of scientific research in this area is beginning to be extremely powerful, and in this book I have attempted to illustrate this impact, indicating ways in which research can contribute to progress in education. In Chapter 1, it was suggested that education, like medicine, is a profession which was practiced for many centuries without the support of scientific research. As research begins to make its presence felt, it is likely that there will be tensions, and there may be unreasonable claims about the extent of the educational problems for which research can provide solutions. However, the modern engineer or medical practitioner is highly dependent on scientific research, and a similar state of affairs is beginning to exist for those whose professional responsibility is in human learning.

References

Allport, G. W., and Postman, L. *The psychology of rumor.* New York: Holt, Rinehart and Winston, 1947.

Amidon, E. J., and Flanders, N. A. *The role of the teacher in the classroom.* Minneapolis: Amidon, 1963.

Arthur, A. Z. Psychology as engineering and technology of behavior. *Canadian Psychologist,* 1971, *12,* 30–36.

Ash, P., and Carlton, B. J. The value of note-taking during film learning. *British Journal of Educational Psychology,* 1953, *23,* 121–125.

Ausubel, D. P., Robbins, L. C., and Blake, E. Retroactive inhibition and facilitation in the learning of school materials. *Journal of Educational Psychology,* 1957, *48,* 334–343.

Ausubel, D. P., and Youssef, M. The role of discriminability in meaningful learning. *Journal of Educational Psychology,* 1963, *54,* 331–336.

Ausubel, D. P. *Educational psychology: a cognitive view.* New York: Holt, Rinehart and Winston, 1968.

Ausubel, D. P., Stager, M., and Gaite, A. J. H. Retroactive facilitation in meaningful verbal learning. *Journal of Educational Psychology,* 1968, *59,* 250–255.

Ausubel, D. P., and Robinson, F. G. *School learning: an introduction to educational psychology.* New York: Holt, Rinehart and Winston, 1969.

Baker, F. B. Computer-based instructional management systems: a first look. *Review of Education Research,* 1971, *41,* 51–70.

Bandura, A., and Walters, R. H. *Social learning and personality development.* New York: Holt, Rinehart and Winston, 1963.

Bandura, A. Influence of models' reinforcement contingencies on the acquisition of imitative responses. *Journal of Personality and Social Psychology,* 1965, *1,* 589–595.

Bandura, A. *Principles of behavior modification.* New York: Holt, Rinehart and Winston, 1969.

Baratz, J. C. A bi-dialectical task for determining language proficiency in economically disadvantaged Negro children. *Child Development*, 1969, *40*, 889–901.

Bartlett, F. C. *Remembering*. London: Cambridge University Press, 1932.

Becker, W. C., Madsen, C. H., Jr., Arnold, R., and Thomas, D. R. The contingent use of teacher attention and praise in reducing classroom behavior problems. *Journal of Special Education*, 1967, *1*, 287–307.

Becker, N. The psychology of educational psychology. *Educational Psychologist*, 1970, *7*, 5–6.

Benjamin, H. *The sabre-tooth curriculum*. New York: McGraw-Hill, 1939.

Bereiter, C., and Engleman, S. *Teaching disadvantaged children in the preschool*. Englewood Cliffs, N.J.: Prentice-Hall, 1966.

Berger, A. Are machines needed to increase reading rate? *Educational Technology*, 1969, *9*, No. 8, 59–60.

Berger, A. Questions asked about speed reading. *The Clearing House*, 1970, *45*, 272–278.

Bernstein, B. A public language: Some sociological implications of a linguistic form. *British Journal of Sociology*, 1959, *10*, 311–336.

Bertalanffy, L. von. *General system theory*. New York: Brazilier, 1968.

Biggs, J. B. Towards a psychology of educative learning. *International Review of Education*, 1965, *11*, 77–93.

Biggs, J. B. *Information and human learning*. North Melbourne, Australia: Cassell Australia, Ltd., 1968.

Bloom, B. S., ed. *Taxonomy of Educational Objectives. Handbook One: Cognitive Domain*. New York: David McKay, 1956.

Bloom, B. S. *Stability and change in human characteristics*. New York: Wiley, 1964.

Brophy, J. E., and Good, T. L. Teachers' communication of differential expectations for children's classroom performance: some behavioral data. *Journal of Educational Psychology*, 1970, *61*, 365–374.

Bruner, J. S. On going beyond the information given. In Bruner, J. S., Brunswick, E., Festinger, L., Heider, F., Muenzinger, K., Osgood, C. E., and Rapaport, D. *Contemporary Approaches to Cognition*. Cambridge, Mass.: Harvard University Press, 1957.

Bruner, J. S. Learning and thinking. *Harvard Educational Review*, 1959, *29*, 186–190.

Bruner, J. S. *The process of education*. Cambridge, Mass.: Harvard University Press, 1960.

Bruner, J. S. The growth of mind. *American Psychologist*, 1965, *20*, 1007–1017.

Bruner, J. S. Some elements of discovery. In Shulman, L. S., and Keislar, E. R., eds. *Learning by discovery: a critical appraisal*. Chicago: Rand McNally, 1966*a*. Pp. 101–103.

Bruner, J. S. *Toward a theory of instruction*. Cambridge, Mass.: Harvard University Press, 1966*b*.

Bruner, J. S. The skill of relevance or the relevance of skills. *Saturday Review*, April 18, 1971, *53*, 66.

Bruner, J. S., Oliver, R. R., Greenfield, P. M., and others. *Studies in cognitive growth*. New York: Wiley, 1966.

Bugelski, B. R. Words and things and images. *American Psychologist*, 1970, *25*, 1002–1012.

Campbell, D. T., and Stanley, J. C. Experimental and quasi-experimental designs for research. *In Handbook on research on teaching*, edited by N. L. Gage. Skokie, Ill.: Rand McNally, 1963.

Church, J. *Language and the discovery of reality*. New York: Random House, 1961.

Clairborn, W. Expectancy effects in the classroom: a failure to replicate. *Journal of Educational Psychology*, 1969, *60*, 377–383.

Cohen, S. The development of aggression. *Review of Educational Research*, 1971, *41*, 71–85.

Cook, J. O. "Superstition" in the Skinnerian. *American Psychologist*, 1963, *18*, 516–518.

Corman, B. R. The effect of varying amounts and kinds of information as guidance in problem solving. *Psychology Monographs*, 1957, *71*, Number 2 (Whole No. 431).

Cloward, R. D. Studies in tutoring. *Journal of Experimental Education*, 1967, *36*, 14–25.

Crouse, J. H. Retroactive interference in reading prose materials. *Journal of Educational Psychology*, 1971, *62*, 39–44.

Davis, O. L., and Slobodian, J. J. Teacher behavior toward boys and girls during first grade reading instruction. *American Educational Research Journal*, 1967, *4*, 261–270.

DeCecco, J. P. *The psychology of learning and instruction: educational psychology*. Englewood Cliffs, N.J.: Prentice-Hall, 1968.

De Mille, R. *Put your mother on the ceiling: children's imaginative games*. New York: Walker, 1967.

Deutsch, M. Happenings on the way back to the forum: Social science, IQ, and race differences revisited. *Harvard Educational Review*, 1969, *39*, 523–557.

Dewey, J. *Interest and effort in education*. Boston: Houghton Mifflin, 1913.

Dewey, J. *The sources of a science of education*. New York: Liveright, 1929.

Durkin, D. *Children who read early*. New York: Teachers College Press, 1966.

Eisner, S., and Rohde, K. Note-taking during or after the lecture. *Journal of Educational Psychology*, 1950, *50*, 301–304.

Engelman, S., and Engelman, T. *Give your child a superior mind*. New York: Simon & Schuster, 1966.

Flavell, J. *The developmental psychology of Jean Piaget*. Princeton, N.J.: Van Nostrand, 1963.

Fowler, W. The effect of early stimulation in the emergence of cognitive processes. In Hess, R. D., and Bear, R. M., *Early education: current theory, research and action*. Chicago: Aldine Publishing Co., 1969. Pp. 9–36.

Gagné, R. M. *The conditions of learning* (1st ed.). New York: Holt, Rinehart and Winston, 1965.

Gagné, R. M. Contributions of learning to human development. *Psychological Review*, 1968, *75*, 177–191.

Gagné, R. M. Context, isolation and interference effects on the retention of facts. *Journal of Educational Psychology*, 1969, *60*, 408–414.

Gagné, R. M. *The conditions of learning* (2nd ed.). New York: Holt, Rinehart and Winston, 1970.

Gagné, R. M., and Brown, L. T. Some factors in the programming of conceptual learning. *Journal of Experimental Psychology*, 1961, *62*, 313–321.

Gagné, R. M., and Wiegand, V. K. Effects of a subordinate context on learning and retention of facts. *Journal of Educational Psychology*, 1970, *61*, 406–409.

Gardner, R. A., and Gardner, B. T. Teaching sign language to a chimpanzee. *Science*, 1969, *165*, 664–672.

Gardner, R. C., and Lambert, W. E. Motivational variables in second language acquisition. *Canadian Journal of Psychology*, 1959, *13*, 262–272.

Gesell, A., and Ilg, F. *Infant and child in the culture of today*. New York: Harper & Row, 1943.

Gesell, A., and Thompson, H. Learning and growth in identical twin infants. *Genetic Psychology Monographs*, 1929, *6*, 1–124.

Glaser, R. Variables in discovery learning. In Shulman, L. S., and Keislar, E. R. (eds.) *Learning by discovery: a critical appraisal*. Chicago: Rand McNally, 1966.

Glasser, W. *Schools without failure*. New York: Harper & Row, 1969.

Good, T. L., and Brophy, J. Analyzing classroom interaction: a more powerful alternative. *Educational Technology*, 1971, in press.

Guinagh, B. J. An examination of Jensen's view of intelligence. Paper read at conference of American Educational Research Association, New York, February, 1971.

Harlow, H. F. The formation of learning sets. *Psychological Review*, 1949, *56*, 51–65.

Hartley, J., and Cameron, A. Some observations on the efficiency of lecturing. *Education Review*, 1967, *20*, 30–37.

Harvey, O. H., Hunt, D. E., and Schroder, H. M. *Conceptual systems and personality organization*. New York: Wiley, 1961.

Harvey, O. J., Prather, M., White B. J., and Hoffmeister, J. K. Teacher's beliefs, classroom atmosphere and student behavior. *American Educational Research Journal*, 1968, *5*, 151–166.

Hill, W. F. *Learning: a survey of psychological interpretations*. (Revised ed.) San Francisco: Chandler, 1971.

Hoffmann, B. *The tyranny of testing*. New York: Collier, 1964.

Holland, J. G., and Kemp, F. D. A measure of programming in teaching-machine material. *Journal of Educational Psychology*, 1965, *56*, 264–269.

Holt, J. *How children fail*. New York: Pitman, 1964.

Howe, M. J. A. Intra-list differences in short-term memory. *Quarterly Journal of Experimental Psychology*, 1965, *17*, 338–342.

Howe, M. J. A. Consolidation of word sequences as a function of rehearsal time and contextual constraint. *Psychonomic Science*, 1966, *4*, 363–364.

Howe, M. J. A. An analysis of recall effects in short-term memory. *Journal of Verbal Learning and Verbal Behavior*, 1969, *8*, 161–165.

Howe, M. J. A. *Introduction to human memory: a psychological approach*. New York: Harper & Row, 1970*a*.

Howe, M. J. A. Note taking strategy, review, and long-term retention of verbal information. *Journal of Educational Research*, 1970*b*, *63*, 100.

Howe, M. J. A. Positive reinforcement: a humanizing approach to teacher control in the classroom. *The National Elementary Principal*, 1970*c*, *49*, 31–34.

Howe, M. J. A. Repeated presentation and recall of meaningful prose. *Journal of Educational Psychology*, 1970*d*, *61*, 214–219.

Howe, M. J. A. The psychology of human memory: recent progress. *The Science Teacher*, 1970*e*, *37*, 15–18.

Howe, M. J. A. Using students' notes to examine the role of the individual learner in acquiring meaningful subject matter. *Journal of Educational Research*, 1970*f*, *64*, 61–63.

Howe, M. J. A. Some comments on research into school learning. *Journal of School Psychology*, 1971, *9*, 51–54.

Howe, M. J. A. What is the value of taking notes? *Improving College and University Teaching*, in press.

Howe, M. J. A., and Cavicchio, P. M. The possibility of retroactive interference in a meaningful learning task. *Alberta Journal of Educational Research*, 1971, *17*, 49–53.

Howe, M. J. A., Gordon, R., and Wilman, L. S. Motivational factors in learning a foreign language. *Peabody Journal of Education*, 1969, *47*, 26–31.

Hunter, I. M. L. *Memory* (2nd ed.). Harmondsworth, England: Penguin Books, 1964.

Jackson, P. W. *Life in classrooms*. New York: Holt, Rinehart and Winston, 1968.

Jackson, P. W. Stalking beasts and swatting flies: comments on educational psychology and teacher training. In Herbert, J., and Ausubel, D. P., eds. *Psychology in teacher preparation*. Toronto: Ontario Institute for Studies in Education, 1969.

James, W. *The principles of psychology*. New York: Holt, Rinehart and Winston, 1890.

Jensen, A. R. How much can we boost I.Q.'s and scholastic achievement? *Harvard Educational Review*, 1969, *39*, 1–123.

Jensen, A. R., and Rohwer, W. D. Verbal mediation in paired-associate and serial learning. *Journal of Verbal Learning and Verbal Behavior*, 1963, *1*, 346–352.

Jensen, L., and Anderson, D. C. Retroactive inhibition of difficult and unfamiliar prose. *Journal of Educational Psychology*, 1970, *61*, 305–309.

Jones, R. M. *Fantasy and feeling in education*. New York: New York University Press, 1968.

Kay, H. Learning and retaining verbal material. *British Journal of Psychology*, 1955, 44, 81–100.

Kay, H., Dodd, B., and Sime, M. *Teaching machines and programed instruction*. Harmondsworth, England: Penguin Books, 1968.

Kellogg, G. S., and Howe, M. J. A. Using words and pictures in foreign language learning by children. *Alberta Journal of Educational Research*, 1971, 17, 89–94.

Kelly, E. L. Transfer of training: an analytic study. In Komisar, B. P., and Macmillan, C. J. B., ed. *Psychological concepts in education.* Chicago: Rand McNally, 1967, pp. 30–50.

Kemp, F. D., and Holland, J. G. Blackout ratio and overt responses in programmed instruction: resolution of disparate results. *Journal of Educational Psychology*, 1966, 57, 109–114.

Klinchy, B., and Rosenthal, L. Analysis of children's errors. In Lesser, G. S. (Ed.) *Psychology and educational practice.* Glenview, Illinois: Scott, Foresman, 1971.

Koestler, A. *The ghost in the machine.* London: Hutchinson, 1967.

Kohl, H. *36 children.* New York: New American Library, 1967.

Kozol, J. *Death at an early age.* Boston: Houghton Mifflin, 1967.

Leacock, E. B. *Teaching and learning in city schools.* New York: Basic Books, 1969.

Leask, J., Haber, R. N., and Haber, R. B. Eidetic imagery in children: II. Longitudinal and experimental results. 1968. University of Rochester. Mimeographed paper.

Lenneberg, E. H. A biological perspective of language. In Lenneberg, E. H. (Ed.), *New directions in the study of language.* Cambridge, Mass.: M.I.T. Press, 1966. Pp. 65–88.

Lenneberg, E. *Biological foundations of language.* New York: Wiley, 1967.

Leonard, G. B. *Education and ecstasy.* New York: Delacorte Press, 1968.

Levi-Strauss, C. *The savage mind.* Chicago: University of Chicago Press, 1967.

McClendon, P. An experimental study of the relationship between the note-taking practices and listening comprehension of college freshmen during expository lectures. *Speech Monographs*, 1958, 25, 222–228.

McDonald, F. J. *Educational Psychology* (2nd ed). Belmont, Calif.: Wadsworth, 1965.

McGraw, M. B. Neural maturation as exemplified in achievement of bladder control. *Journal of Pediatrics*, 1940, 16, 580–590.

McLeish, J. *The lecture method.* Cambridge Monographs on Teaching Methods, Number One. Cambridge, England: Cambridge Institute of Education, 1968.

McNeill, D. *The acquisition of language: the study of developmental psycholinguistics.* New York: Harper & Row, 1970.

Madsen, C. H., Jr., Becker, W. C., and Thomas, D. R. Rules, praise and ignoring: elements of elementary classroom control. *Journal of Applied Behavior Analysis*, 1968, 1, 139–150.

Mager, R. F. *Preparing instructional objectives.* Palo Alto, California: Fearon Publishers, Inc., 1962.

Marshall, S. *An experiment in education.* Cambridge, England: Cambridge University Press, 1963.

Maslow, A. H. A theory of human motivation. *Psychological Review,* 1943, *50,* 370–396.

Mendoza, S. M., Good, T. L., and Brophy, J. E. The communication of teacher expectancies in a junior high school. Paper read at the conference of the American Educational Research Association, New York, 1971.

Miller, G. A., Galanter, E., and Pribram, K. H. *Plans and the structure of behavior.* New York: Holt, Rinehart and Winston, 1960.

Miller, G. W. Factors in school achievement and social class. *Journal of Educational Psychology,* 1970, *61,* 260–269.

Montagu, A. *The human revolution.* Cleveland, Ohio: World Publishing Company, 1965.

Neisser, U. *Cognitive psychology.* New York: Appleton-Century-Crofts, 1967.

Norman, D. A. *Memory and attention: an introduction to human information processing.* New York: Wiley, 1969.

O'Leary, K. D., and Becker, W. C. The effects of the intensity of a teacher's reprimands on children's behavior. *Journal of School Psychology,* 1968, *7,* 8–11.

Orme, M. E. J., and Purnell, R. F. Behavior modification and transfer in an out-of-control classroom. Paper delivered at American Educational Research Association Convention, Chicago, February, 1968.

Paivio, A. Mental imagery in associative learning and memory. *Psychological Review,* 1969, *76,* 241–263.

Palardy, J. M. What teachers believe—what children achieve. *Elementary School Journal,* 1969, *69,* 370–374.

Poppleton, P. K., and Austwick, K. A. A comparison of programmed learning and note-taking at two age levels. *British Journal of Educational Psychology,* 1964, *34,* 43–50.

Postman, N., and Weingartner, C. *Linguistics: a revolution in teaching.* New York: Dell, 1967.

Postman, N., and Weingartner, C. *Teaching as a subversive activity.* New York: Delacorte Press, 1969.

Premack, D. The education of S*A*R*A*H. *Psychology Today,* September, 1970, *4,* 54–58.

Pressey, S. L., and Kinzer, J. R. Auto-elucidation without programming. *Psychology in the Schools,* 1964, *1,* 359–365.

Pribram, K. H. The four R's of remembering. In Pribram, K. H. (Ed.) *On the biology of learning.* New York: Harcourt, Brace and World, 1969. Pp. 191–225.

Razran, G. The observable unconscious and the inferable conscious in current conditioning, semantic conditioning, and the orienting reflex. *Psychological Review,* 1961, *68,* 109–119.

Richardson, E. S. *In the early world.* Wellington, New Zealand: New Zealand Council for Educational Research, 1964.

Rist, R. C. Student social class and teacher expectations: the self-fulfilling prophesy in ghetto education. *Harvard Educational Review*, 1970, *40*, 411–451.

Roderick, M., and Anderson, R. C. A programmed introduction to psychology versus a textbook-style summary of the same lesson. *Journal of Educational Psychology*, 1968, *59*, 381–387.

Rogers, C. R. Actualizing tendency in relation to "motives" and to consciousness. In M. R. Jones (Ed.), *Nebraska Symposium on Motivation*, Lincoln, Nebraska: University of Nebraska Press, 1963. Pp. 1–24.

Rogers, C. R. *Freedom to learn.* Columbus, Ohio: Merrill, 1969.

Rosenthal, R., and Jacobson, L. *Pygmalion in the classroom: teacher expectation and pupils' intellectual development.* New York: Holt, Rinehart and Winston, 1968.

Rothbart, M., Dalfen, S., and Barrett, R. Effects of teacher's expectancy on student-teacher interaction. *Journal of Educational Psychology*, 1971, *62*, 49–54.

Rothkopf, E. Z. The concept of mathamagenic activities. *Review of Educational Research*, 1970, *40*, 325–336.

Rothkopf, E. Z. Two scientific approaches to the management of instruction. In R. M. Gagné, and W. J. Gephart (Eds.) *Learning research and school subjects.* Itasca, Illinois: Peacock, 1968. Pp. 107–132.

Rubovits, P. C., and Maehr, M. L. Pygmalion analyzed: toward an explanation of the Rosenthal-Jacobson findings. Paper read at the conference of the American Educational Research Association, New York, 1971.

Sanders, N. M. *Classroom questions: what kinds?* New York: Harper & Row, 1966.

Sarason, S. B., Davidson, K. S., Lightall, F. F., Waite, R. R., and Ruebush, B. K. *Anxiety in elementary school children.* New York: Wiley, 1960.

Scandura, J. M. Expository teaching of hierarchical subject matter. *Journal of Structured Learning*, 1969, *2*, 17–25.

Schmidt, W. H. O. Socio-economic status, schooling, intelligence, and scholastic progress in a community in which education is not yet compulsory. *Paedogogica Europa*, 1966, *2*, 275–286.

Simon, H. A., and Newell, A. Human problem solving: the state of the theory in 1970. *American Psychologist*, 1971, *26*, 145–159.

Skinner, B. F. The behavior of organisms. New York: Appleton-Century-Crofts, 1938.

Skinner, B. F. The science of learning and the art of teaching. *Harvard Educational Review*, 1954, *24*, 86–97.

Snow, G. *The public school in the new age.* London: Geoffrey Bles, 1959.

Snow, R. E. Unfinished business: review of "Pygmalion in the Classroom." *Contemporary Psychology*, 1969, *14*, 197–199.

Staats, A. W. *Language, learning and cognition.* New York: Holt, Rinehart and Winston, 1968.

Staats, A. W. *Child learning, intelligence, and personality.* New York: Harper & Row, 1971.

Staats, A. W., and Butterfield, W. H. Treatment of non-reading in a culturally deprived juvenile delinquent: an application of reinforcement principles. *Child Development*, 1965, *4*, 925–942.

Stephens, J. M. *The process of schooling: a psychological examination.* New York: Holt, Rinehart and Winston, 1967.

Stone, L. J., and Church, J. *Childhood and adolescence* (2nd ed.). New York: Random House, 1968.

Taylor, C. W. *Learning and creativity: with emphasis on science.* Washington, D.C.: National Science Teachers Association, 1967.

Thibaut, J. W., and Kelley, H. H. *The social psychology of groups.* New York: Wiley, 1959.

Thomas, D. R., Becker, W. C., and Armstrong, M. Production and elimination of disruptive classroom behavior by systematically varying teacher's behavior. *Journal of Applied Behavior Analysis*, 1968, *1*, 35–45.

Thoreau, H. D. *Walden: or life in the woods and on the duty of civil disobedience* (First published 1854). New York: Collier Books, 1962.

Thorndike, R. L. Review of "Pygmalion in the Classroom." *American Educational Research Journal*, 1968, *5*, 708–711.

Tinbergen, N. *The study of instinct.* Oxford, England: Oxford University Press, 1951.

Travers, R. M. W. *Man's information system.* Scranton, Pa.: Chandler, 1970.

Tuckman, B. W., and Bierman, M. L. Beyond Pygmalion: Galatea in the schools. Paper read at the conference of the American Educational Research Association, New York, 1971.

Vernon, P. E. *Intelligence and cultural endowment.* London: Methuen, 1969.

Vygotskii, L. S. *Thought and language.* Cambridge, Mass.: M.I.T. Press, 1962.

Wallach, M. A., and Kogan, M. *Modes of thinking in young children.* New York: Holt, Rinehart and Winston, 1965.

White, B. L. *Human infants: experience and psychological development.* Englewood-Cliffs, N.J.: Prentice-Hall, 1971.

White, R. W. Motivation reconsidered: the concept of competence. *Psychological Review*, 1959, *66*, 297–333.

White, S. H. Evidence for a hierarchical arrangement of learning processes. In Lipsitt, L. P., and Spiker, C. C. (Eds.) *Advances in child development and behavior.* Volume 2. New York: Academic Press, 1965. Pp. 187–220.

Wiegand, V. A study of subordinate skills in science problem solving. Paper presented to American Educational Research Association Convention, March 1970.

Wong, M. R. Retroactive inhibition in meaningful verbal learning. *Journal of Educational Psychology*, 1970, *61*, 410–415.

Index of Names

Index of Subjects